Attachment-Based
Psychotherapy

Attachment-Based
Psychotherapy
Helping Patients Develop Adaptive Capacities

Peter C. Costello

American Psychological Association • Washington, DC

Published by
American Psychological Association
750 First Street, NE
Washington, DC 20002
www.apa.org

To order
APA Order Department
P.O. Box 92984
Washington, DC 20090-2984
Tel: (800) 374-2721; Direct: (202) 336-5510
Fax: (202) 336-5502; TDD/TTY: (202) 336-6123
Online: www.apa.org/pubs/books
E-mail: order@apa.org

In the U.K., Europe, Africa, and the Middle East, copies may be ordered from
American Psychological Association
3 Henrietta Street
Covent Garden, London
WC2E 8LU England

Typeset in Goudy by Circle Graphics, Inc., Columbia, MD

Printer: United Book Press, Inc., Baltimore, MD
Cover Designer: Mercury Publishing Services, Rockville, MD

The opinions and statements published are the responsibility of the authors, and such opinions and statements do not necessarily represent the policies of the American Psychological Association.

Library of Congress Cataloging-in-Publication Data

Costello, Peter C.
  Attachment-based psychotherapy : helping patients develop adaptive capacities / Peter C. Costello. — First edition.
    pages cm
  Includes bibliographical references and index.
  ISBN 978-1-4338-1302-3 — ISBN 1-4338-1302-5 1. Attachment behavior. 2. Psychotherapy. I. Title.
  RC455.4.A84C67 2013
  616.89'14—dc23
                                    2012044760

British Library Cataloguing-in-Publication Data

A CIP record is available from the British Library.

Printed in the United States of America
First Edition

http://dx.doi.org/10.1037/14185-000

For Rosemary, Andrew, and Jonathan

CONTENTS

ACKNOWLEDGMENTS

There is a line from a short story by G. K. Chesterton that John Bowlby especially liked and that captures the human truth at the heart of attachment theory: "Throughout all this ordeal his root horror had been isolation, and there are no words to express the abyss between isolation and having one ally" (see Bowlby, 1973, p. 201). While writing a book is perhaps not quite an ordeal in the sense that Chesterton meant it, I have been blessed and supported by the allies I have had in my work and in life. My friends and colleagues and my discussions with them over the years have been the deep background to this work, and I choose here to acknowledge and to thank them collectively. I think you all know who you are. I am very grateful to my patients, who have permitted me to know them in a way that has been a gift and that has very much deepened my own experience of life. I also thank the remarkable editors at APA Books, who guided this project from its inception until the last ellipsis was dotted. I particularly thank Susan Reynolds, whose steadfast interest in and encouragement for this book weathered it through difficulties and interruptions, and Beth Hatch, whose fine judgment and incisive (but tactful!) editing of the initial manuscript turned that manuscript into a much better book than it could ever have been without her. I also thank Ron Teeter and Cooky Bysura, who created a cover that I love; Robin Easson, who found and righted errors with insight and precision; and Margaret Sullivan, whose skills and confidence played a key role at an early point in the writing. Finally, I want to thank my wife, Rosemary, and my sons, Andrew and Jonathan, whose encompassing presence and love is the sustaining context for all that I do.

Attachment-Based
Psychotherapy

1

ATTACHMENT, COMMUNICATION, AND AFFECT: AN INTRODUCTION

Those who are given to us as our caretakers or attachment figures are always imperfect. Some are better caregivers than others. Some are cheerful and resilient, and some are depressed, weary, and preoccupied. All are different in their moods and emotional states and in the stresses to which they are vulnerable, better at some times and in some types of situations and worse in others. For example, some are easily wounded by anger. Others tolerate expressions of need poorly or not at all. All are complex individuals with personal histories and relationships of their own that long predate our arrival. All have lives and minds and urgent needs of their own. And so, when we are infants, we find ourselves in the arms of those who may wish us well but who may also have limitations that arise from their own upbringing or have other things to think and feel about that make it difficult for them to notice and respond to what we need and want.

Evolutionary biologists remind us that a mother's interests are not perfectly identified with the interests of any particular child. Other children,

http://dx.doi.org/10.1037/14185-001
Attachment-Based Psychotherapy: Helping Patients Develop Adaptive Capacities, by Peter C. Costello

the needs of an adult partner, the demands of work and resource provision, and the requirements of her own body all make demands on our caretaker that compete with our own. This competition of conflicting interests extends even to the process of pregnancy itself, wherein fetus and mother biologically negotiate the allocation of the body's resources and the most desirable set points of physiological processes like blood pressure (e.g., a higher blood pressure is optimal for the fetus but may be dangerous to the long-term health of the mother). So, the economic, physical, and interpersonal situations of our attachment figure also affect how she might respond to us.

It is also true that some of us are more difficult to take care of than others might be. We may have more than the usual difficulties in reaching a state of physiological ease, and so we may require more active soothing and very gentle, attentive handling. We may have had a greater inborn tendency for the rapid escalation of our emotional state, been readier to become angry or more brittle in our experience of distress. We may have felt fear or anxiety more quickly and more painfully than others might, startling more easily and calming more slowly.

The question then that each of us has faced from the first moments and during the first years of our life is this: How can we get our primary caregiver to respond to us and take care of us in the way that we need? What must we do and be in order to maximize the caretaking that we get from our attachment figure? Our ability to answer this question determines whether we will flourish or diminish in our development. This is also a key clinical and psychotherapeutic question because attachment theory makes clear that each of us is shaped in our self and in our relationships to others throughout our life by how this question is answered—by how we have shaped ourself to fit our attachment figure.

As infants and children, we become experts in having an attachment relationship with the very particular person who is our caregiver, the single, unique person, out of the entire world, from whom it is most important that we receive a helpful, life-supporting response. We learn to recognize and to respond differentially to the varying states of our caregiver and even to the different types of situations and interpersonal signals that are associated with these states. We learn the patterns of emotions, communications, responses, and situations that characterize life with our caregiver. How should we cry, where should we look, what should we notice? What should we not "see" and never say? What will happen at bedtime, at feeding time, when we are carried or when we are scared? What will happen when our caregiver is angry or happy or sad or anxious? What will happen when we are lonely or afraid? Should we cry out more loudly or stifle our sobbing? Does the person we want to tell want to listen to us? What should we do with our own anger or sadness or fear? Communicate it? Hide it? Communicate it how? Suppress it how?

What will work in terms of getting a response from our caregiver? What will keep her close when we need her? What, dangerously, will drive her away? As a result of these experiences and motivated by the profound biological imperative to maintain an attachment, we learn to suppress or to heighten our own degree of arousal; to emphasize some communications, emotional experiences, and forms of interpersonal relationships and to avoid others; to direct our attention toward some events in our environment and within our own minds and bodies and away from others. We thereby become a particular person.

This book explores in detail how our early attachment experiences with a primary caregiver affect our development into adulthood. In particular, it explores how suboptimal attachment experiences can lead to psychopathology (especially depression, anxiety, and maladaptive anger) and difficulties in interpersonal relationships. Finally, it describes how psychotherapy can mitigate the detrimental effects of negative early attachment experiences.

Psychotherapists of various theoretical orientations will benefit from this book because it will help them understand the origins of common patient problems, as well as offer an approach for addressing these problems in therapy. Attachment theory offers a framework for conceptualizing and treating a wide range of problems because many interpersonal problems and mood disorders are related to our early attachment experiences. The theory is interdisciplinary, with empirical and theoretical support from developmental and social psychology, evolutionary biology, and ethology. Thus, this book presents research and theories from diverse disciplines to explain the physiological, psychological, and behavioral mechanisms by which our early experiences influence our development. Additionally, the book provides clinical cases to illustrate concepts. The first such illustration is the following, which shows how one person's early experiences led to problems with depression, anxiety, and interpersonal relationships later in life.

NATALIE

Natalie is a single woman in her early 40s. One of Natalie's earliest and most resonant memories—hazy, indistinct, perhaps partially imagined, partially real—is of waking in her crib and calling for her mother. Her mother doesn't come. Natalie begins to cry, and she continues to cry, louder and more and more forcefully. Finally, at last, her mother does come, but her mother has been very slow. Natalie, who has learned that her mother will finally respond if she cries loudly enough and long enough, is now very distressed—red-faced, nose running, heaving with deep breaths, sobbing, and very, very angry. She has gotten her mother to come and to respond to her but only after a period of intensely calling out and amplifying her protests, during which time Natalie became progressively more upset and dysregulated. Her distress has now become very difficult to bring back down to a tolerable level, to modulate and resolve. So, she is now difficult to soothe, angry at her mother for the absence, but also very much in need of her mother's continued presence—both angry and needful. Natalie's mother is soon exasperated by her angry and difficult-to-soothe child and feels exhausted, but Natalie continues to press her needs. Her mother continues to respond as best she can.

Although I have described here only a single hazy memory of a single incident in Natalie's early life, assume for the moment that this incident stands accurately for an important pattern in Natalie's relationship with her mother. It is in moments such as these that the shaping of Natalie's self takes place. It is in moments and interactions such as these with her mother that Natalie is acquiring a particular form and pattern of response to distress, specific expectations about the trustworthiness and responsiveness of other people, an expertise in a particular way of understanding others, a particular way of communicating with others, and a particular form of affect regulation within herself and between herself and other people. She is learning how long it takes to get someone to respond to her, how distressed she has to become, what strategies of communication are ultimately rewarded by a response, and how she must manage the feelings of distress within herself. To the extent that these elements are confirmed and remain unaltered by subsequent experience, these shapings will give specific form to who Natalie is and to how she interacts with others in other relationships, not only when she is a child but also in her adult life.

Shift now to 40 years later. Natalie is an attorney on a business trip to a ski area in Vermont. At the end of the day, she returns alone to her room in a beautiful resort hotel. The day has gone well enough, but as always there were some problems, some moments when it seemed to Natalie that people judged her or disapproved of her in a way that made her feel tense and bad. She worries that there is something wrong about her and about how she has been with these clients. She's not quite sure what it could be—that she has gained some weight, said the wrong thing, misunderstood them, or not been what they wanted her to be. She is tired. She wants to go to sleep, but she also wishes she had someone to talk to first. She feels lonely. She begins to feel anxious. Though she has had a significant number of romantic involvements over the years, few have evolved into extended relationships; none have reached a stage of permanence. There is no spouse or lover or partner in Natalie's life at the moment.

Natalie finally climbs into a large bed in what feels to her to be an enormously empty room. The feelings of loneliness and of big, empty spaces around her are familiar to Natalie, part of a background feeling that she always carries with her, a hovering sense of impending rejection and abandonment and of other people being at distance from her. She finally falls asleep. A few hours later, at one in the morning, Natalie wakens. She is in the dark in a strange bed in a strange room in a strange city, and she is alone. Her very first sensations as she just begins to become conscious are a rising fear and a strong sense of being completely alone—no one is near her, she has no one, and she is connected to no one. The feelings are sharp and intense, even nightmarish. The feeling of being alone is overwhelming. She feels she is about to cry. There is a fullness in her throat and a tension, a pain growing in her abdomen. The feelings make her desperate. She needs to talk to someone, to be with someone, to not be alone. She begins to think to herself, "Who can I call?" At the same moment that she begins to think about whom she can call, she begins to become angry at those she thinks of and at their unavailability, feeling the anger even as she remains frightened and lonely and determined to find someone to talk to. It is the middle of the night; she feels angry that her friends are asleep in another city. She thinks of each of them and how each might react if she called in distress over "nothing" in the middle of the night. She thinks they would not understand. She feels angry at the man she last dated for not being more involved with her. The sense of aloneness and of personal defectiveness deepens—why wasn't he more involved with her? But Natalie is determined, and she finally thinks of friends she might call in the place she grew up, a continent away, where it is still evening. She makes the calls. At last, after several attempts, she finds someone to talk to. Natalie's friend is glad to hear from her, though a bit confused about the purpose of the call. Although the friend is responsive, Natalie is most attuned to the moments of confusion or disengagement on the friend's part; she notices these acutely, and she responds with suppressed anger, a sense that the friend does not really care. The first call ends, and Natalie makes another call, again finding someone to talk to. Natalie's needs are so pressing and urgent that she puts aside her thoughts of how her friends might view her phone calls to them in the middle of her night after a long period of little contact. She presses her distress on them without much attuning to their own states of mind, except for her constant vigilance for any signals of rejection. After three long-distance phone conversations, she finally goes back to sleep, crying but somewhat quieted. In the morning, she is exhausted and emotionally raw, and in this exhausted state she gets ready for her first meeting.

As with Natalie's hazy early memory of her mother, this is only a single incident in Natalie's life. But assume for the moment, as with the earlier memory, that the incident is part of a familiar pattern in her adult life and notice the stark similarity between the early memory and the night in Vermont 40 years later. There is the actuality of being alone, the intensified feeling of aloneness, the heightened anxiety and distress, the rising anger at the responses—either real or imagined—of others, and the very determined efforts to find someone to connect to. There is also the sense that the responses that are available will not be good enough.

This book is about the causal relationship between the two patterns in Natalie's life—the way she related to and communicated with her mother as a child and how she now relates to other adults in intimate relationships. This book is also about how psychotherapy can be used to alter or to reshape the adult pattern in Natalie's life. It is about how the emotions, communications, strategies for affect regulation, behaviors, perceptions, and cognitions that were cultivated in Natalie's earliest attachment relationships came to shape who she is and the way she approaches and experiences the relationships and events in her adult life. Especially, it is about the specific interpersonal and intrapersonal components (the interpersonal nuts and bolts, so to speak) of early attachment relationships and later adult relationships and about the specific interpersonal and intrapersonal components (again, the nuts and bolts) of change through psychotherapy. How, specifically (through what means, by what psychological processes), does the earlier pattern of a relationship with a primary caregiver remain alive and present in adult relationships and behaviors many years later? And how, specifically (through what techniques and therapeutic strategies), can psychotherapy change the adult pattern in a way that is realized in the patient's actual relationships and life in the world?

In one sense, the child's understanding of relationships that each of us carries within ourself is written in our neurons and neural networks (Cacioppo et al., 2002), and ultimately it is this neural scribing that must be changed. In another, more behavioral and experiential sense, one more directly relevant to the clinical process, our child's understanding is coded in the automatic behaviors and communications, the unconscious beliefs about ourself and others, and in the interpersonal and intrapersonal competencies and practices that we have acquired through our attachment relationships. It is coded in our competencies and practices in the detailed and textured processes of interpersonal communication, in the intrapersonal processes of affect regulation, in the processes of perception and cognition, in the behaviors that have become automatic and unthinking, in the situations that we are primed to recognize and to respond to with anxiety, security, or avoidance. The history of our attachment relationships is written in how we control ourself, how we heighten or suppress or accurately express our emotions and thoughts and perceptions to others; they are written in the messages, thoughts, feelings, perceptions, and situations that we are primed to respond to with engagement, avoidance, understanding, or imperviousness.

These are exactly the ways in which Natalie's early experiences with her mother, as represented by her memory of crying for so long alone in her crib, are related to her later life as a struggling and unhappy adult. My purpose in this book is to trace this relatedness of early attachment experience with later life in specific detail, to provide the theoretical context for understanding the patterns of influence, and to describe how the effects of early attachment experiences can be altered through the therapeutic process.

SECURE, INSECURE, AND DISORGANIZED ATTACHMENT

In Natalie's case, her attachment experiences led her to be anxious about relationships and hypersensitive to any signs of rejection from others, to feel perpetually uncertain that anyone would really be there for her. A broad way of describing Natalie's difficulties would be to say that she was high in attachment anxiety. Another type of attachment style involves avoiding intimacy and dismissing any initiation of intimacy from others. A person with these characteristics might be broadly described as high in attachment avoidance. In attachment theory, both of these styles are considered *insecure* because they prevent the individual from experiencing specific feelings or engaging in the relationships, situations, and events that may evoke those feelings. A third broad category of attachment involves individuals who are high in both attachment anxiety and attachment avoidance and who may fluctuate between desperately pursuing attachments and avoiding them or who may unhappily and fearfully withdraw from contact with others. Because their attachment behaviors are often contradictory and changeable and these individuals lack a consistent strategy for being with others, this attachment type is referred to as *disorganized*.

Insecure and disorganized individuals cannot effectively communicate with others in a sufficiently open and accurate way to permit close alliance and intimacy. They cannot negotiate conflict and disagreement in relationships. In short, they cannot experience the emotions necessary to respond adaptively to their environment. In contrast, people with *secure* attachment styles communicate openly and accurately with others and do not unrealistically fear being abandoned. They experience in an appropriately modulated way a full range of realistic emotions and are therefore able to respond adaptively to their environment. Individuals with insecure or disorganized attachment styles tend to develop problems in the form of dysregulated emotions—especially anxiety, depression, and excessive or displaced anger—and in the form of compromised, misdirected thinking about their experiences. They may become unhappy in their relationships and ineffective at achieving life goals. And they may come to therapy.

ATTACHMENT-BASED THERAPY

Attachment-based therapy is an approach to therapy that specifically targets those thoughts, feelings, communications, behaviors, and interpersonal exchanges that patients have learned either to suppress and avoid or to amplify and overemphasize because of early attachment experiences. Two central processes run throughout an attachment approach to therapy. The first is no surprise to any working therapist and is one of the most robustly supported findings of all psychotherapy research: It is the creation of a progressively more open and more secure relationship between the therapist and the patient. The quality of the therapeutic relationship is the single most powerful element that has been identified by psychotherapy research for producing a good therapeutic outcome. Attachment theory has a particular understanding of the characteristics of a security-engendering relationship that is based on research with security-engendering mothers. The construction of a secure, responsive, and open relationship around precisely the issues that are difficult and troublesome for the patient is a major component of the therapy. It is itself an effective technique because of the progressive developmental processes that it unleashes in the patient. The second central process in attachment-based psychotherapy depends on the first: It is the facilitation and strengthening of adaptive capacities by addressing the emotions and the communications that the patient has learned to suppress or to overemphasize in early attachment relationships. These two processes—the creation of a secure-base relationship and the reclaiming of lost capacities—are central to attachment-based therapy. Our ability as therapists to reshape these capacities depends on our understanding exactly what the patient cannot safely think, feel, perceive, communicate, or do. There are many different approaches to psychotherapy, and one of the striking things about this diversity of approaches is that, in one way or another and for one reason or another, most of them seem to work (Luborsky et al., 2002, 2004; Wampold, 2001). In other words, psychotherapy works. Given the abundance of workable approaches, what is the special value of basing an approach to psychotherapy on attachment theory? There are three reasons to embrace this approach.

First, attachment theory arises from a strong scientific and empirical foundation. It is now the major theoretical and research paradigm within the study of human development and adult relationships. To an unprecedented extent in the history of psychotherapy, attachment theory has developed in close conjunction with literally thousands of empirically based research studies. Although it addresses exactly those emotional and relational nuances in which therapists are particularly interested (e.g., John Bowlby compared the process of forming a secure attachment to the experience of falling in love), it is primarily a biologically based theory whose conceptual foundations are the scientific work for which Konrad Lorenz and Nikolaas Tinbergen were awarded the Nobel Prize in Medicine or Physiology. It is a perspective based in human evolutionary theory, and its fundamental views of how humans have come to have the characteristics that they do are widely accepted by evolutionary scientists. Its intellectual ancestor is perhaps more Charles Darwin than Sigmund Freud.

In the last 20 years, attachment researchers and theorists have focused on the connections between early attachment experiences and adult emotional life, intimate relationships, and behavior—precisely the areas of interest to psychotherapists. In many ways, attachment theory is to the contemporary period what Freud's ideas were to the early and middle decades of the 20th century—a compelling view of our development as psychological persons and of the consequences of our early experiences for the lives that we live as adults. Although Freud was frustrated by the limited scientific knowledge of the brain and of the physiology of behavior and emotion that was available to him during his lifetime and therefore had to theorize in what he himself described as a series of metaphors, attachment theory has been based in biological science and a strong research tradition from its inception. Psychotherapy has never before rested on a foundation of such intellectual breadth and rigor.

Attachment theory is thus unique as a basis for psychotherapy. It began with Bowlby's understanding of the profound process by which a newborn infant becomes connected to and then progressively more integrated with the company and care of its mother. The initial understanding of this profound process in humans gave rise to a research tradition, first in the hands of Mary Ainsworth and then by thousands of researchers around the world. This research identified specific factors in the process of attachment—how favorable and pathological variations of attachment are related to the behavior and characteristics of the mother and the ways in which these influence the characteristics of the child. More pathological versions of attachment (e.g., disorganized attachment, which is discussed at length later in the book) were recognized and clarified. Researchers documented the connection of early attachment experiences to later difficulties and strengths in older children, adolescents, and adults. In recent years, attachment theory has especially addressed the connection between variations in early attachment experiences and the vicissitudes of adult romantic relationships. Freud spoke of mental health as the ability to love and to work, and attachment theory and research have grown to address both of these concepts in compelling and satisfying ways.

Attachment theory and research have thus created a causal theory of how early and continuing attachment experiences are related to a broad array of strengths and difficulties in psychological and emotional states, in functioning in the world, and in the capacity for romantic and intimate relationships. Both the theory and research speak to how these difficulties may be addressed and remedied by therapists. Attachment theory and research speak to the issues that most concern psychotherapists in their work with patients—the same issues that concern all of us in living our lives—on the basis of deep and detailed knowledge.

A second reason to base a psychotherapy on attachment theory is that attachment theory is remarkably open in its ability to embrace and incorporate the many approaches to psychotherapy that have established their efficacy in helping patients. It is in effect a highly integrative theory that encourages eclecticism and flexibility and that prompts therapists to add to their technical and theoretical capacities rather than to limit themselves by hewing to a single perspective or set of techniques. Moreover, attachment theory provides a potential explanation for why so many different types of psychotherapy—with so many different theoretical rationales and sets of technique—can all be as effective as research suggests they are. The ability of diverse psychotherapies to work for patients is well established; attachment theory is virtually unique in being able to provide a compelling theoretical explanation for why this should be so.

John Bowlby was explicit about the broad integrative capacity of attachment theory, and in his own work he explicitly embraced the metapsychological insights of psychodynamic, cognitive, and behavioral theorists (Bowlby, 1980, 1988). He was able to do this because attachment theory is a broadly based developmental theory of the way in which we each form relationships; use communication; think of ourself and others; regulate our emotions; and explore, learn, and work in the world.

Attachment theory was not originally a clinical theory—though Bowlby was always focused on its clinical implications—and thus it did not arise with a privileged set of special technical practices already formed, as did, for example, psychoanalysis or cognitive-behavioral therapies. Attachment theory is quite comfortable taking understandings either from cognitive-behavioral theories or from psychodynamic approaches. Although attachment-based therapy is unlike either of them (see below), it is not opposed or hostile to their insights and understandings.

The power and appeal of attachment theory are apparent in the current theoretical and research literature of the various schools of clinical thought, wherein attachment theory is referenced and incorporated by writers from all schools of psychotherapy—psychoanalytic, cognitive-behavioral, experiential, somatic, family systems, trauma focused, and even psychopharmacological (Alston, 2001; Brockman, 2007; Curtis & Winarick, 2008; Erdman & Caffery, 2003; Fonagy, 2001; Fosha, Paivio, Gleiser, & Ford, 2009;

Gleiser, Ford, & Fosha, 2008; Holmes & Newman, 2006; Luyten, Blatt, & Corveleyn, 2005; Marvin, 2003; Moore, 1997; Ng & Smith, 2006; Rendon, 2008; Vetere & Dallos, 2008; Weems & Carrion, 2003). In fact, an inability to convincingly tie a particular therapeutic theory or approach to attachment theory may be counted as a mark against the theory that cannot be so connected.

The important point here is that a therapist need not abandon her present ideas in order to take an attachment approach to psychotherapy—rather, she adds a perspective and ideas to what she already knows and practices. Although what she knows and practices may change and be used in different ways, it will not be abandoned or rejected by an embrace of attachment theory.

There is a third reason that an attachment-based approach to psychotherapy is worth undertaking. As Christopher Peterson and Nansook Park (2007a, 2007b) have written in their reflections on attachment theory, it sometimes seems that all of our psychological knowledge about what makes life worth living can be reduced to three words: *Other people matter.* People who have experienced the right kind of relationship at a formative moment in their lives are happier and function better as human beings. Childhood is one such moment, and psychotherapy can be another.

Attachment theory is explicitly relational in a way that behavioral and cognitive approaches really are not and that psychoanalytic approaches have struggled for decades to clarify and accommodate (Bornstein, 1985; J. Greenberg & Mitchell, 1983; Mitchell, 1998; Mitchell & Aron, 1999; Zamanian, 2011). Attachment theory begins with the enduring influence of relationships as its first principle. It speaks to our personal knowledge that our relationships are central to the people we have become and to the sense of safety or of insecurity with which we live our lives. Our early relationships have mattered most of all, and the person we have become includes the key relationships we have had with those we have needed most and upon whom we have most depended. These relationships have formed us, and we each continue to live with these others within ourself.

Attachment theory emphasizes and seeks to understand the central role of a special type of security-engendering relationship in the fostering of a wide array of positive human qualities. Among these qualities are our sense of personal safety, security, and optimism; our capacity for positive, empathic, and stable relationships; how lonely we feel or how connected we feel to others; the resiliency of our self-acceptance and confidence in the face of stress; strength regarding mortality and fear of death; our sense of self-efficacy in undertaking tasks; lower levels of anxiety and fear; openness in communication; a greater capacity for emotional self-regulation under difficult circumstances; the fluency and coherence of our emotional communication; enhanced cognitive functioning; and lively engagement in learning, work, and exploration (Mikulincer & Shaver, 2007).

In its emphasis on the generative role of a special type of relationship, attachment theory also emphasizes the relationship between therapist and patient in psychotherapy. It deepens our understanding of one of the most useful findings of psychotherapy research—that the qualities of the relationship between patient and therapist are by far the most important determinants of the effectiveness of the treatment (Ackerman et al., 2001; Baldwin, Wampold, & Imel, 2007; Botella et al., 2008; Lambert & Barley, 2002; Messer & Wampold, 2002; Norcross, 2002a, 2002b; Orlinsky, Grawe, & Parks, 1994; Wampold, 2001, 2007; Wampold & Bolt, 2007; Wampold, Goodheart, & Levant, 2007; Wampold, Ollendick, & King, 2006).

But attachment theory, despite its emphasis on the importance of relationships, does not require that a therapist choose an allegiance either to the relationship or to a specific set of techniques. This is because the type of relationship that is emphasized as security engendering and growth promoting by attachment theory is specifically a relationship that is "sensitively responsive to the signals and communications" of the other person (Ainsworth, Blehar, Waters, & Wall, 1978, p. 152) and that offers help to the other in regard to his or her states, needs, wishes, and goals. Effective techniques are ideally suited to provide such helpful assistance—but only if they are a part of a relationship that is sensitively and responsively allied with the person who is being helped.

Bowlby described the attachment figure in such a relationship as a "trusted companion," and it is not difficult to see how this could be an apt description for the optimal relationship of psychotherapist to patient in therapy. It is good if our companions come with useful tools and ideas and a willingness to help. The techniques the therapist brings can work only in the context of a good relationship, but the techniques can add to the helpfulness and supportiveness of the relationship, provided they are used in response to the patient and the patient's states, needs, wishes, and goals.

OVERVIEW OF THIS BOOK

The remainder of this book is divided into two parts. Part I presents an attachment-informed view of development. I begin by describing the evolutionary function of attachment (Chapter 2) and the neurophysiological processes by which attachment is formed (Chapter 3). These two chapters provide critical background for understanding attachment theory, which is next presented in depth (Chapter 4). The motivation to form an attachment underlies our development of communication patterns (Chapter 5) and affect patterns (Chapter 6).

In Part II, I relate the concepts from Part I to psychopathology and psychotherapy. I discuss defensive exclusion as the root of psychopathology and the focus of attachment-based therapy (Chapter 7). Next, I conceptualize anxiety, depression, and maladaptive anger from an attachment perspective (Chapter 8). Finally, I discuss the two components of attachment-based therapy in depth: the security-engendering therapeutic relationship (Chapter 9) and the therapeutic task of helping patients access and communicate that part of themselves that they have learned to suppress—a process I call *deconstructing aloneness* (Chapter 10).

I

AN ATTACHMENT-BASED
VIEW OF DEVELOPMENT

2

WHY MOTHERS MATTER: THE EVOLUTION OF MATERNAL CARE

This chapter discusses the importance of mothers—especially the idea that our relationships with our mothers shape us in regard to emotional communication and interpersonal relationships in ways that endure throughout our lives. It describes the formation of this first and most important relationship, starting even before birth, and begins to explain what can happen if this relationship goes wrong. Several key ideas from attachment theory are introduced, including how attachment theory was influenced by Nobel Prize research about the process of maternal imprinting in other animals.

AN ANCIENT BEHAVIOR

Maternal care is a truly ancient type of behavior, evolved over millions of years. From an evolutionary point of view, maternal care—or, as we often think of it, a mother's love—is a strategy to improve the survival of the young.

http://dx.doi.org/10.1037/14185-002
Attachment-Based Psychotherapy: Helping Patients Develop Adaptive Capacities, by Peter C. Costello

In the natural history of life, the ministrations of a mother have been so power-ful a means for promoting survival that maternal care has evolved repeatedly and independently in different classes of animals in different epochs of geo-logical time (Leckman et al., 2005). Maternal care is also what evolution-ary biologists call a *highly conserved strategy* within each class of animals that exhibits it, meaning that it has been so successful for so long that it has come to be present in many, many species that share an ancestor only in the very distant past. This is evolution's tribute to a mother's love—that it has been discovered by many different species of animal and that once found it is never abandoned as a strategy for survival. Mothers are one of the greatest success stories of natural selection and of evolution, and the effects of a mother's care on her young are an old and powerful story. It is the tribute of a ruthless, competitive, and often brutal natural world to the strength of alliances and connections to others.

The experiences of maternal care are especially intense among animals such as ourselves, for whom the mother's body becomes the source of food for the young. In species where a mother nurses her young, communication and contact between the mother and her infant are the most fully developed and most elaborated, and the mother's own physiology and behavior are most affected by her interactions with her newborn. No other mammal has so intense a form of maternal care, extended over such a long period of time during which so many critical developmental shapings occur, as do humans.

We are built out of the relationships that we have with our mothers. Because maternal care developed so long ago in the evolutionary history of our species and because it is so effective at promoting the survival of the young, many of the other behaviors and characteristics of our species have evolved and are built on the foundation of the behaviors and biology that are necessary to the phenomenon of a mother interacting with her young. Behaviors or characteristics that evolved to enable maternal care often have been coopted by natural selection for the creation of other behaviors and characteristics that are extremely important to us because they serve major purposes in our lives.

This is a key point for understanding why our early attachments echo throughout our lives, long after we are no longer children. Maternal care is the evolutionary foundation of our relationships with other people and there-fore for much of what humans are as a species (Eibl-Eibesfeldt, 1989). This foundational, generative aspect of maternal care is one of the reasons that our attachment experiences are so profoundly influential in the rest of our lives and across multiple domains of social and cognitive functioning.

To give one very basic example, maternal care requires the ability to reliably distinguish one individual from another—to know that this infant (or this mother) is mine and that other one is not. Not all species can do this, but ours can. As evolution wended its way, this ability to distinguish and encode different individuals ultimately became the basis for individuated social relationships in which we recognize and treat each other as separate individuals with whom we have a specific history and relationship. Similarly, maternal care requires an enhanced ability to communicate so that a mother may respond to her infant's signals of need. In our species, this became the basis for complex communication and for caring, helpful responses to all those with whom we have affectionate bonds. In other words, the development of the abilities to recognize individuals and to responsively communicate with them became the basis for further evolutionary developments that took advantage of these abilities—changes such as the enhanced social memories and the enduring individualized relationships that so characterize human beings, as well as our enormously elaborated capacity for complex and subtle communication and strong emotional ties to each other (Eibl-Eibesfeldt, 1989).

This is the biological and evolutionary reason that our experiences with our mothers can be so influential: because so many of our mature behaviors and capabilities—such as language, intimacy, affectionate social relationships, reproduction, the care of our own young—evolved and are built on the foundation of the behaviors and neurophysiology that first operate between a mother and her child. Our adult relationships are based on the same neural networks and hormonal and neurophysiological responses that were active and were shaped in our relationships with our mothers (Balbernie, 2001; Broad, Curley, & Keverne, 2006; Champagne & Curley, 2005; Curley & Keverne, 2005; Polan & Hofer, 2008). Our "mother tongue"—the language that we first learned with our mothers and that forevermore throughout our adult lives is "native" to us—is coded in our neurons and the morphology of our brain and is the easiest, most natural form of our verbal communications with others. The same is true of the approach to intimacy that we learned with our mothers—from our mother's arms to our lover's arms, as Theodore Waters (2004) put it. The musical and dance-like rhythms, responses, and sounds of our early vocal but nonverbal protoconversations with our mothers are not only the basis for learning language, they also become the emotional valences and the forms of relatedness that we find most natural and possible as adults (Malloch & Trevarthen, 2009a). Our attachment experiences with our mothers are so important to our development because these early experiences are rudimentary templates that become woven throughout our behavioral repertoire. Even our lovemaking in our adult lives is influenced by patterned oxytocin responses resulting from varying intensities and distributions of oxytocin receptors that were laid down in early experiences with our mothers (Marazziti, 2005; Marazziti et al., 2008; Neumann, 2008; Snowdon & Ziegler, 2000; Uvnäs-Moberg, 1994; Wismer Fries, Ziegler, Kurian, Jacoris, & Pollak, 2005).

In every case, the prototype of an adult social and relational behavior is a process, with biological and neurohormonal underpinnings, that is also necessary to the possibility of maternal care and that has then evolved into a more elaborated form. The biological linkage remains intact through time. Mother–child relationships are the foundation of human social behavior because human social life is built out of what happens between a mother and her child.

MOTHER GOOSE, IMPRINTING, AND SHAPING

The concepts of a behavioral system and a set-goal, two of the scientific concepts that undergird attachment theory, were introduced to Bowlby when a neighbor of his on the island of Skye, the leading evolutionary biologist Julian Huxley, gave him a copy of Konrad Lorenz's *King Solomon's Ring* (Holmes, 1993). Bowlby, who had already for some years been focused on the effects on children of maternal separation, was taken with Lorenz's account of imprinting, resistance to separation, and following behavior in baby geese. Bowlby saw in this an animal analogue of the human infant's driven connection to and need for his mother. "He suddenly saw the possibility of bringing together object relations theory and these neo-Darwinian ideas. Attachment theory was born" (Holmes, 1993, p. 431). Lorenz and Nikolaas Tinbergen eventually received a Nobel Prize for the work that so influenced Bowlby.

Bowlby had been struggling to find a new way of thinking about and theorizing the mother–infant relationship. For some time, he had been dissatisfied with traditional psychoanalytic approaches. In his subsequent adoption of Lorenz's work, Bowlby made a conceptual leap out of the frame of psychoanalysis. Although he brought important aspects of psychodynamic theory with him, he joined them in a thoroughly transformed way to the modern biology and psychology of animal behavior and evolutionary theory.

The central idea that Bowlby adopted from Lorenz was the concept of *imprinting*. Imprinting is the process by which the young of a species form a bond or a focus on another individual of their species. The characteristics and responses of this focused-upon individual then stimulate and shape developmental processes in the young. Optimally, at birth, the individual upon whom the young animal becomes imprinted is the mother. The young individual becomes connected (or attached) to the mother in a way that rapidly becomes physiologically wired and determinative, virtually fixed. In a broader sense, imprinting is the process by which an animal, including a human, becomes sensitized to some relevant feature of its physical or social environment (e.g., the phonetic sounds that make up language, the patterns of social interactions that make up a relationship; Bolhuis, 1999). The animal is thereafter especially attuned and responsive to this specific stimulus in its environment (e.g., the kinds of communicative sounds and movements made by its mother) and then reacts to these stimuli in an especially sensitized way. In humans, this is the process by which we become sensitized to particular ways of relating and communicating through our interactions with our mother. We become imprinted on her way of communicating, managing affect, and relating to us.

Lorenz famously illustrated this process with his demonstration of imprinting among baby geese. Lorenz found that newly hatched greylag geese would respond to the first moving object they saw by becoming socially bonded to it, following it, seeking it out, and eventually even becoming sexually focused on similar objects to the relative exclusion of members of their own species.

In usual circumstances, the first moving object that a newly hatching baby goose would see would be its mother, who might well assist it in cracking through its shell and entering the world. And so, in the expectable environment for hatching goslings, the triggers for imprinting would be appropriate and useful, leading the goslings to stay close to their mother, to enter and leave environments as she did, and to become reproductively focused on other geese.

In nature, the imprinting served the survival of the goslings by attaching them firmly to their mother and thus providing a basis for her maternal care. But the goslings were capable of becoming imprinted on and sensitized to a range of phenomena. Their connection to their mother was not determined by a genetically determined fixed focus on the specific individual who was in fact their mother. Rather, what was genetically available to the goslings was a predisposition to respond to certain characteristics in their environment by forming a particular relationship to the first encountered object that had these characteristics.

Lorenz found that the "relationships" formed by goslings were variable. By so arranging things that his own wading boots were the first moving objects seen by a group of hatchlings, he was able to create an attachment between the goslings and the boots that led to his being followed everywhere by the baby geese as long as he was wearing those particular boots. (And he had then to arrange, as the goslings were not following their biological mother, for the regular feeding of his hungry brood.) He found that he could elicit similar responses from the goslings to a red wagon and to a white rubber ball, as long as he arranged things so that these were the first moving objects the hatchlings saw. The goslings resisted separation: If he wore his red boots into his home, closing the goslings out, they would cluster by his door waiting for the boots to return.

The key idea here is that we, like many other animals who depend on maternal care, become tuned to respond in important ways to particular aspects of our early social environment. Once we are so tuned, we lose much of our capacity to respond to other stimuli.

A profound biological process such as imprinting is not wasted on trivial behaviors. The behavioral responses that become sensitized and tuned to the imprinted stimuli are always very powerful behaviors that are key to the animal's way of living and survival—behaviors like seeking one's mother and communicating with her, finding a mate and producing children, and raising those children to maturity. These are all activities that are centrally a focus of attachment theory.

Imprinting is the essence of the process described here as *shaping*—the increased sensitivity to some stimuli that are important aspects of our environment (e.g., emotional expressions, tones of voice, interpersonal interactions, internal emotional experiences) and a corresponding loss of sensitivity to others. Shaping is the process that joins our attachment (or imprinting) experiences with our mothers to our capacities for interactions and relationships as adults. It necessarily includes the idea that we lose our sensitivity and responsiveness to other stimuli on which we have not become imprinted (e.g., we do not respond to the appearance of other persons in the way we do to the appearance of our mothers; each of us is sensitive to our mother's facial characteristics, the sound of her voice, her smell, in a way that we are not sensitive to the characteristics of other women; we become more attuned to her emotional expressions than to those of others).

There were three characteristics of the process of imprinting as described by Lorenz that were taken by Bowlby as directly relevant to an understanding of human attachment. One of these is the idea that imprinting or attachment takes place most readily and strongly during a specific *sensitive period* in the individual's life. These early imprinting or attachment experiences change the individual in a way that leaves permanent effects that are unlikely to be eradicated—although they may be modified and added to by subsequent experiences such as psychotherapy or other types of new relationships. In humans, this attachment-sensitive period appears to be especially the first 2 years of life, followed by the remainder of childhood and early adolescence. The formation of the imprinting or attachment relationship during this period unleashes and shapes within the developing infant, child, and adolescent a complex set of behaviors that will be critical to his or her relationships throughout life. Bowlby, following ethological usage, referred to these complex sets of behaviors as *behavioral systems*. Bowlby called the imprinting system in the child the *attachment behavioral system*. He called a corresponding and complementary system in the mother the *caregiving behavioral system*. The child's attachment behavioral system was directed at the mother. The mother's caregiving behavioral system was directed toward the child. These behavioral systems were designed by evolution to make it possible for the mother and the child to be together in the intense relationship that is characteristic of mothers and infants. These behavioral systems are the basis of the experiences of maternal love and of filial love and dependency. They give rise to these relationships and generate the feelings that go with them.

The second key idea adopted by Bowlby, implicit in what already has been said, is that the process of imprinting or attachment is essentially a dyadic process—that the infant is responding to signals provided by its mother and is responding to them in a way that then further influences the mother. In other words, the infant develops within an intense relationship. Attachment was not something that unfolded in a predetermined way; rather, it depended on the relationship that the developing infant found in his new world. In this sense, the mother and her infant constitute a single dyadic entity—two individuals who have been designed by natural selection to join together in a strong and specific relationship. In this relationship, each is changed by the other. Attachment is about our transformation by another person into someone whose qualities and characteristics are molded by the qualities and characteristics of the other individual. This happens with our mothers, with our lovers, and also with our psychotherapists. Attachment is a dyadic process that becomes a characteristic of the individual. We become who we are through the presence of other people in our lives. The individual in all of his or her varying potentials achieves actuality—becomes a specific person— only through a specific relationship. That relationship becomes a part of the person. For the developing child, the attachment relationship is constitutive of the self. A thoroughgoing emphasis on the dyadic quality of individual experience is characteristic of attachment theory in a way that distinguishes it from many other approaches to psychotherapy.

Finally, a third idea from the biologist Lorenz that fell quite naturally into the hand of the psychoanalyst Bowlby was that the actual operation of these behavioral systems in the real world is shaped by nature and nurture in interaction with each other—that there is a biological substrate in the behavioral systems of both mother and child that responded to and was shaped by experience and learning (Lamm & Jablonka, 2008). Our genes work in interaction with our environment in an especially powerful way during periods of development (Carroll, 2005; Caspi & Moffitt, 2006; Jablonka, 2007; Leckman & March, 2011), yielding a range of possible outcomes for each set of genetic potentials. Which of our genes are expressed, how they are expressed, and how they interact with others of our genes depend on what we are doing, feeling, thinking; who we are with; and even what we are eating (Cicchetti, 2007; Dudley, Li, Kobor, Kippin, & Bredy, 2011; McGowan, Meaney, & Szyf, 2008; McGowan et al., 2009; McGowan & Szyf, 2010; Robinson, Fernald, & Clayton, 2008; Roth, Lubin, Funk, & Sweatt, 2009;

Weaver, 2011). The greater the animal's capacity for learning and flexible responding, the greater the environment's influence on behavior and the underlying physiology of that behavior is likely to be.

In humans, the expression of socially relevant genes is shaped by the infant's experiences with his or her mother, and, in turn, the biological capacities of the mother to give care to her infant are shaped not only by her genes but also by the effect on the expression of her genes by her own experiences of being cared for by others during her own development (Franklin et al., 2010; Weaver, 2009, 2011). Mother and child are each shaped by social experiences within an envelope of biologically based innate potentials to become a unique and specific dyadic entity. The influences on the shaping of each child are intergenerational (Masterpasqua, 2009). The shaping of individual variations is persistent through time and across generations, constituting a kind of family and relational culture that becomes encoded in biological form.

Attachment is the process by which we become closely interwoven with those who are physically closest and most responsive to us, particularly the person who is our primary caretaker. Our self and our personality, with the accompanying biological variations on which these are based, take form in relationship to this person. This interweaving of self and other that takes place between a mother and her child is a deep and fundamental human process that actively alters both partners in the relationship. For the child, this relationship establishes the capacity and the conditions for the interpersonal connections and relatedness that lie at the core of the nature of human beings. It establishes the basis for selfhood, the slowly and gradually strengthening of self-awareness and internal organization that will continue within the child as long as he or she lives. Our first and earliest interweavings with our attachment figures shape us in fateful ways that are often difficult to change, marking us almost indelibly with our first experiences of contact and dependence on another person. We begin this interweaving even before we are born.

LOOKING FOR HER

When a baby is born, he comes into the world with extremely limited physical abilities. He is able to do almost none of the things that he will eventually need to do to live in the world. He cannot crawl or walk, sit up or hold his head erect, or do much apart from rooting reflexively to find food. He has almost no control over the movements of his arms and legs. He can't pick anything up. He cannot control the distance at which his eyes focus, and he can barely see anything beyond the length of his mother's arm—his vision is dimmed and indistinct. His capacity to engage with the world of physical objects is almost nonexistent. He cannot even regulate his own body temperature or sleep cycles very well but instead requires the active assistance of another person to stay warm or to cool off and to find a pattern of sleeping and waking. But there is one thing that the newborn is able to do from his very first hours of life outside his mother's body: He can begin to look for his attachment figure, find her, communicate with her, and develop an intense relationship with her.

The baby enters the world with a ready-made ability to recognize and differentiate particular individuals, to begin to know who is whom and what relationship each of these other people has to the baby's self. Babies are particularly able to identify their primary caregivers, to distinguish them from others, and to begin to form a specific and very individualized connection to them. They don't yet do this with the explicit consciousness that they will develop over the first few years of life. But they nonetheless are able to distinguish one person from another by the way in which they seek and become entrained to the voices, sounds, scents, appearances, and rhythms of particular people.

From their first moments of postnatal life, and even before, babies are possessed by a desire to communicate with these others, to join with them, find companionship with them, and to integrate themselves—changing and forming themselves as they do so—into the complex matrix of communication that human beings use in making relationships and sharing activities (Murray & Trevarthen, 1986; Trevarthen, 1988, 1993; Trevarthen & Aitken, 2001; Trevarthen & Logotheti, 1989). Acquiring this communicative matrix is a form of both cultural learning and personal development (Liszkowski & Tomasello, 2011; Tomasello, 2008, 2009; Trevarthen, 1992, 2002), and the matrix itself—the ways in which communication occurs—is highly specific to cultures, families, and individuals (Tomasello, Carpenter, Call, Behne, & Moll, 2005; Tomasello, Dweck, Silk, Skyrms, & Spelke, 2009; Tomasello & Rakoczy, 2007). So, the infant is not just expanding his capacity to communicate. He is learning to communicate in a highly specific way that shapes who he is.

When one considers how limited the newborn's physical abilities are, his readiness and strong desire to begin engaging in communicative interaction with individually identifiable others is quite remarkable and meaningful. It is a signpost about human nature and about the way that communication, social relationships, and cultural learning are so much more important for humans than for any other species. We are the animals who talk with each other.

In an extensive comparison of the intelligence of humans with the intelligence of our closest primate relatives (chimpanzees and orangutans), Herrmann, Call, Hernàndez-Lloreda, Hare, and Tomasello (2007) found that 2½-year-old humans were essentially indistinguishable from chimps and orangutans in their capacity for thinking about the physical world—for understanding things such as object permanence and the physical rotation of an object, judging and discriminating numerical quantities, using a tool to retrieve an object, or understanding sources of noise or changes in the shapes of physical objects. But the human children were very different and far advanced from both ape species in their social intelligence for understanding and solving problems in the social domain—their ability to communicate, to cooperate, to judge what others were thinking or trying to do, and to learn from a social interaction. This difference indicates that communication, learning from others, and social collaboration are distinctive and special-ized skills for humans that characterize our species and that mark the special adaptations that make us who we are (Tomasello & Herrmann, 2010). These abilities arise quite early in ontogeny, developing well ahead of our physical abilities, because they are the foundation of how we live in the world.

There is a twofold process at work here: The baby comes with a very strong desire to find companions and to communicate with them. The strength of this desire to communicate, the complex means we develop for doing so, and the ways that we are changed by our communication with others are defining hallmarks of our species. The baby also comes with a powerful desire to form connections to individualized others, to form rela-tionships with particular people. Our neurophysiological responses shape us toward those we know and with whom we have communicated trustfully in the past. The process that Lorenz called imprinting obliges our physiology and commits it to specific others. So the baby's developing attachment system focuses his communication and relating and his learning how to communi-cate more fully, like a magnifying lens focusing sunlight, on the progressively more defined person of his attachment figure to be. This individualized rec-ognizing, communicating, and relating is the very beginning of the process of attachment. It starts even before birth.

During the third trimester of development, while still in his mother's uterus, a fetus begins to learn about what will be—in fact, already is—his social environment, and he begins to shape himself in response to it. One of the ways in which this prenatal socialization is possible is because dur-ing the third trimester, fetuses not only can hear but also are influenced in an ongoing, long-term way by sounds from the external world transmitted to them through their mother's amniotic fluid. Their later responding, both as fetuses and then later as newborns, is influenced by their earlier experi-ence of hearing particular sounds, especially the sounds of voices (DeCasper, Lecanuet, Busnel, & Granier-Deferre, 1994; Krueger, Holditch-Davis, Quint, & DeCasper, 2004; Lecanuet, Granier-Deferre, & DeCasper, 2005; Lecanuet, Graniere-Deferre, Jacquet, & DeCasper, 2000; Sandman, Wadhwa, Hetrick, Porto, & Peeke, 1997).

In addition to responding to the sounds of voices, the fetus is influenced by other forms of external stimuli, such as someone's touching their mother's abdomen, or by different styles of rocking, walking, and body motion (Brazelton, 1995; Diego et al., 2002; Lecanuet & Jacquet, 2002). Fetuses acquire a familiarity with and preference for the sound of their mother's heartbeat, and as newborns they will alter the pattern of their sucking to match and imitate the sound of a heartbeat (DeCasper & Sigafoos, 1983). The infant thus attunes his own behavior to the rhythm of signals coming from his social environment (DeCasper & Carstens, 1981).

Fetuses learn the sound of their mother's voice while still in the uterus, and this affects their preferences for voices and people immediately after birth. In this sense, each infant is born with an already present means of identifying his mother—the infant recognizes the voice of his mother, the person who has been with him and whose voice and vocal qualities he has been exposed to for the preceding months. The infant then begins to orient himself and to respond to this particular person in preference to all others. What is happening here is that fetuses, late in their development, begin to form a relationship with their likely caregivers. The learning that fetuses do while still in the uterus focuses very specifically on socially and communicatively relevant aspects of their environment. It is not that they are practicing reach-and-grasp movements or learning how to walk while swimming in the amniotic fluid. But they are acquiring social and communicational information about those with whom they will begin to live their lives when they are born. This speaks to the preeminence of communicative and relational capacities for the newborn and for humans generally.

The specificity with which fetuses are acquiring the ability to distinguish their mother from other people is similar to the process described by Lorenz's concept of imprinting. The specificity of this connection makes these very early distinctions between people a part of the process of attachment. Processes such as these, whether in goslings or in human babies, make it possible for the newborn to begin to connect himself socially to an other. It is the foundation and the beginning of attachment (Gandelman, 1992).

Babies shape their own preferences and behaviors in order to connect more fully to their mother and to elicit more reliable responses from her. In one study, newborns could produce either their mother's voice or the voice of another female by the way in which they sucked on a plastic nipple. On the basis of their exposure to the mother's voice prior to birth (DeCasper & Fifer, 1987), the newborns quickly shaped and adjusted their way of sucking in order to produce the voice of their mother. While still in the uterus, fetuses are quieted (as measured by a decrease in fetal heart rate) by hearing a recording of a nursery rhyme that their pregnant mother had previously read aloud for several weeks; they are not quieted by a recording of another, not previously heard rhyme (DeCasper et al., 1994). If mothers sing "Mary Had a Little Lamb" regularly during the 2 weeks prior to birth, their newborn children will show a clear recognition and preference for this song over other children's songs in the days following their birth (Panneton, 1987). The fetus develops the rudiments of a relationship before birth. As its nervous system tends toward completion, it forms specific communicative connections to others.

Fetuses and newborns also appear to become shaped in their responses to smells, both before and immediately after birth (Durand, Baudon, Freydefont, & Schaal, 2008; Schaal, Soussignan, & Marlier, 2002), and they demonstrate a clear preference for the smells associated with their own mother (Schaal, Doucet, Sagot, Hertling, & Soussignan, 2006). For example, newborns are more likely to turn toward the smell of their own mother's amniotic fluid than they are toward the smell of another woman's amniotic fluid (Marlier, Schaal, & Soussignan, 1998a, 1998b). Newborns just a few hours old show a clear preference for the smell of their own mother's milk rather than the milk of another mother who has also just delivered a newborn—they can distinguish the scent of her milk from another mother's. And nursing mothers whose breasts contain a larger number of scent-bearing areolar skin glands (something that varies from one mother to another) had infants who latched onto the breast more firmly, nursed more energetically, and gained weight more quickly—suggesting that infants respond to a stronger scent and recognition of their own mother by nursing more vigorously and effectively (Schaal et al., 2006).

In fact, babies not only recognize and prefer the scent of their own mother's breasts and milk, they also prefer the scents of the foods that she has eaten regularly during their fetal development (Schaal, Marlier, & Soussignan, 2000). Each baby learns the smells of his pregnant mother's diet and show stable preferences for what she has eaten, thus influencing his tastes in food via a process of chemosensory communication that has taken place before birth. If she has eaten anise-flavored foods and drinks, her baby likes the smell of anise!

Remarkably, there is also evidence that newborns come into the world having learned to distinguish, in a physiologically based way, emotional cues and patterns of their mother as expressed by her speech. That is, immediately after birth an infant can distinguish his mother's emotional state via the qualities of her vocalizations based on what he has experienced prenatally. The infant's ability to differentiate emotional communications seems to be based on two aspects of prenatal experience: hearing and learning the patterns of maternal speech and then pairing these speech patterns with his experience of the distinctive physiological and intrauterine changes that have accompanied changes in his mother's emotional state (Mastropieri & Turkewitz, 1999). In other words, the fetus experiences changes in the intrauterine environment that are paired with cues and changes in the mother's speech patterns. These changes, in tandem with vocal cues and intrauterine physiological cues, are driven by the mother's emotional state. Mastropieri and Turkewitz (1999) found that newborns as young as 12 days respond differentially to different emotion cues as expressed in speech in a way that suggests they learned an emotional meaning of the qualities of that speech while still in the uterus. For example, neonates open their eyes more in response to happy speech (something that perhaps many mothers already knew). But the newborns do this only when the emotional speech is in the language that is spoken by their mother and that the newborns were exposed to during late fetal development. The newborns show no differential responding to the same emotion cues when spoken in a language they have not heard previously. This suggests that infants, rather than responding to universal cues, have learned to associate their mother's specific speech and vocal patterns with her particular physiological and emotional states and that they have begun to do this prior to birth (Mastropieri & Turkewitz, 1999, p. 204). To do this, they have had to learn and become responsive to their mother's habitual speech patterns and her typical physiological responses to her own emotional experience that accompany those speech patterns. In this process, one can see the infant shaping himself for communication and social interaction with his mother by literally learning the relationship between the mother's vocal communication and her internal physiological state, a state to which the fetus has unique and privileged access.

All of this means that infants come into the world looking for someone with whom to form an intimate and intricate relationship, and they have begun to tune and shape themselves in order to become the infant of that particular someone. Even before birth, they have acquired a preference for her voice, the way she sings, the foods she prefers, the kinds of language sounds she makes, the rhythm of her heartbeat, the way she moves, and the distinctive smell of her body. They also have acquired the ability to distinguish emotional cues in her way of speaking, as these vocal cues have corresponded to changes in their intrauterine environment. The developing fetus is acquiring the ability to enter into a highly nuanced communicative exchange with the specific person who is most likely, in the typically expectable environment, to be his caretaker—like the goslings that follow the mother who pecks open their shells. These abilities are the foundation of the attachment of a particular child to a particular mother.

MAKING OUR NERVOUS SYSTEM FIT OUR MOTHER'S NERVOUS SYSTEM

The mother's intense relationship with the child is not only about the two of them. For the mother, her relationship to the child reflects elements of all of her intimate relationships, from her own childhood onward.

And correspondingly, for the child the relationship with his mother is the template of the intimate relationships that will follow, including those with his own children. The relationship between mother and child is the center of the interpersonal and social universe. In the specificity with which the child is learning about his mother and about the way she interacts and communicates, one can see the beginnings of what Bowlby called the *internal working model of self and other in relationship*—an internal model and representation of what we are like, of what other people are like, of how they respond to us, and of what we can and cannot do to get them to respond to us.

The internal working model of social relationships begins to take form in these early interactions, as the brain takes form in response to our experiences and interaction with others. In significant part, this form is created by the synaptic connections among neurons in the brain. Neurons that have 2,500 synaptic connections at birth will have 15,000 connections to other neurons by 3 years of age (Gopnik, Meltzoff, & Kuhl, 2000). It is the formation of these new synaptic connections that accounts for much of the doubling of the brain in size and weight that occurs during the first years of life.

The formation of these new synaptic connections is based on experience. Neuronal connections that are used frequently—for example, those that fire in response to the mother's face or voice or smell—grow stronger, while those that are not used wither and disappear. So the wiring of the brain, over time, becomes a map of the infant and child's experiences. The more frequently a particular experience occurs, the more deeply is the brain's structure formed and changed by the experience. This process of synapse formation occurs across many physical modalities and realms of experience— vision, hearing, motor movements, and so on. But many of the experiences that occur most often to us during our first years, and to which we are designed to be most attuned and responsive, are the interactions we have with others. Above all, we respond to the experiences we have with our primary caregiver. This is the key to how attachment experiences shape our capacities for and styles of personal relationships.

The neurophysiological states that we experience while with others— especially with others, like our mothers, with whom our experiences are especially intense and strongly motivated—become traits, neurophysiologically based, that we possess and that we experience while in relationships with others (Perry, Pollard, Blakley, Baker, & Vigilante, 1995). Our relationships with our mothers shape our brains in regard to emotional communication and interpersonal relationships in ways that are more or less permanent. I say more about this in Chapter 5.

FINDING HER

In optimal circumstances, the fitting of baby and mother to each other that begins prenatally will continue and accelerate in the weeks and months after birth as the two together move toward an attachment relationship that will be firmly in place by 6 or 7 months. Although the communication between mother and baby is still very limited in comparison with what will soon come, from birth the baby wants to communicate with his mother, and he is able to do so. As we have seen, the baby has prenatally learned the sound and rhythms of his mother's voice, and he has developed a preference for her voice. Now, he turns toward her, seeks her face, relaxes in the aura of her smell (Varendi, Christensson, Porter, & Winberg, 1998). If placed on her abdomen in the first minutes of postnatal life, he will clumsily and slowly crawl toward and find her breast (Varendi & Porter, 2001). Although his visual acuity is so limited in the first postnatal weeks that he can only discern shapes and outlines, he scans and learns to recognize the outline of her head and face like an adult scanning and recognizing a city skyline. He quickly learns to distinguish her face from the faces of other women, and he is more interested in looking at her face than at the faces of others. As his vision gradually becomes more acute, the baby increasingly seeks out the eyes of his mother and looks at them longer than he looks at other parts of her face, making eye contact and entering into moments of mutual gaze. These moments of mutual gaze are intensely meaningful and affecting for both mother and child. Mutual gaze often occurs during breast feeding, when the distance of the baby's face from the mother's face optimizes the child's limited visual focus and acuity. The baby's nursing and touching of his mother's breast produces a release of oxytocin in the mother that stimulates feelings of closeness and warmth in her. During such nursing gazes, mother and infant are seeing each other closely and communicating their awareness of the other just at the moment that their biological systems are directly interlocked and interacting with each other's. Intense, intimate communication and profound biological experience are synchronized.

The baby's orientation to his mother is expressed in ways that are visible and felt by her. She is engaged by him. Exhausted though she may be, she wants to look at him, see him, hold him; examine his face, his body, and his movements; touch his head, his face, his hands and feet. The baby feels his mother's touch and is affected by it, stimulated both to nurse and to interact, and is able to sense the emotions conveyed by the way he is touched (Carlson et al., 1999; Field, 2001a, 2001b, 2002; Hertenstein, 2002; Hertenstein, Holmes, McCullough, & Keltner, 2009). Mother and child are beginning their postnatal and lifelong conversation and involvement with each other.

The formation of attachment emerges from this developing and enlarging communicative matrix that mother and baby have been weaving from the beginning of the third trimester of development—from their increasing ability to understand each other through their co-creation of an individuated and dyadic communication system.

Two very powerful motivations are operating here. One is the baby's intense desire to enter into a communicative relationship with those around him. The second is the baby's motivation to enter into a close communicative relationship with a particular and individually identified caregiver—usually his mother—who will become his attachment figure. The baby wants his mother's companionship, to interlace himself with her through a continually unfolding process of communication between them. Thus, attachment and communication are closely intertwined at the beginning of the infant's social experience. The mother becomes very adept at reading the signals her baby sends, and for his part the baby begins to shape the way he communicates to fit the contingencies of his mother's responding. In other words, he tends to communicate what she tends to attune to (Stern, 1985).

NOT FINDING HER

The formation of a closely interwoven, highly interactive communication system between mother and baby is a central component of human development. Babies are disposed and designed to look for communication and companionship with their mothers, and their mothers are disposed and designed to provide it (Trevarthen, 1998). They go looking for each other. In optimal circumstances, they find each other.

But what happens if circumstances are not optimal and a baby does not find a mother who responds to him in an at least adequate way? How important are the relational and communicative aspects of the mother–infant relationship? What would happen if a baby were cared for in terms of his strictly physical needs—fed, kept warm, given a place to sleep, and so on—but was otherwise not communicated and played with, not engaged in that rich communicative matrix that creates a normal, healthy, densely constituted human relationship? We know the terrible answer to this question: The baby will die or will fail to develop in catastrophic ways.

One example of this is the cruel experiment reportedly conducted by the Holy Roman Emperor Frederick II (A.D. 1170–1250). Frederick was reported by contemporaneous sources to have separated four children from regular human company at birth, bidding foster-mothers and nurses to suckle and bathe and wash the children, but in no wise to prattle or speak with them; for he would have learnt whether they would speak the Hebrew language (which had been the first), or Greek, or Latin, or Arabic, or perchance the tongue of their parents of whom they had been born. But he labored in vain, for the children could not live without clappings of the hands, and gestures, and gladness of countenance, and blandishments. (Salimbene, quoted in Coulton, 1906, pp. 242–243)

Similar forms of severe deprivation, occurring for different reasons, have occurred many times in history. In our own era, these circumstances have been occasioned by economic and political circumstances, by the social devaluation of orphans, or, usually less drastically, by ignorance of what now seems to us obvious—that infants and children need much more than physical care.

In the first half of the 20th century in America, prominent pediatricians such as L. Emmett Holt, the author of an influential baby guide, were concerned about calming babies in the face of the frenetic modern world (Hulbert, 2003). They thought this could be done by not overstimulating the child with too much play or interaction and by providing a routine controlled by external factors rather than by the child's requests. Holt advised parents to keep their children calm by avoiding too much holding or touching, by not playing with them, and by maintaining an exact schedule of feeding, sleeping, and waking by the clock. Further, according to Holt, a baby's crying was a natural form of developmental exercise that developed the lungs, and it required no intervention if it did not go beyond 30 minutes. Toilet training, Holt recommended, should occur by 3 months (Hulbert, 2003).

In mid-20th-century America, Rene Spitz (1945) found orphanages influenced by ideas such as Holt's. They were filled with infants whose physical care was impeccable but who were offered very little opportunity for human company. The threat of infectious diseases in these institutions was real. In an attempt to prevent the spread of infections, cribs were kept separated. The sides were draped with sheeting that blocked the children's view, creating for each child a kind of white isolation chamber, and physical contact was discouraged. The children were picked up by their nurses for feeding on a schedule but otherwise spent most of their time alone in their cribs in a world of blank white walls.

These children fell further and further behind in their intellectual, emotional, and physical development and died more frequently than family-reared children despite adequate physical care. At 4 years, many of these children barely used language, were unable to feed themselves, were markedly lethargic, and were well below normal height and weight.

Perhaps the saddest and most distressing instance of the modern era's neglect of children is the Romanian orphans, whose plight was discovered following the fall of the communist government in Romania in 1989. These unwanted children were born as a result of a government drive to increase population by forbidding birth control, and the resulting unwanted children were abandoned in large numbers to an impoverished system that, having forced their existence, could not care for them. The institutions for orphans could not cope with the influx of abandoned children. The sudden increase in the numbers and the dire financial circumstances of the Romanian government combined to create circumstances that treated the children like warehoused merchandise.

These children suffered extended periods of very limited social interaction and consequent severe developmental delays in their cognitive and social functioning (Morison, Ames, & Chisholm, 1995; Rutter, Beckett, et al., 2007; Spira et al., 2000; Wilson, 2003). Among other difficulties, they showed evidence of posttraumatic stress disorder (Hoksbergen et al., 2003), an unusual form of inattention/overactivity syndrome that was distinct from the usual pattern of this disorder (Hoksbergen et al., 2003; Sonuga-Barke & Rubia, 2008; Stevens et al., 2008), and a high rate of a quasi-autistic pattern of interaction that included an inability to make or maintain eye contact and patterns of stereotypical physical movements such as continuous hand lapping (Hoksbergen et al., 2005; Rutter et al., 1999). When some of these children were subsequently placed in international adoptions, they had long-standing difficulties and disorders of attachment that usually were not fully repaired even after years with the adoptive family (Chisholm, Carter, Ames, & Morison, 1995; Colvert et al., 2008; L. Fisher, Ames, Chisholm, & Savoie, 1997; Rutter, Colvert, et al., 2007a, 2007b).

Not being able to find a mother is a catastrophe for a child.

FINDING A DEPRESSED MOTHER

What happens if a mother is relatively unavailable or unresponsive in more ordinary ways—if the child is less drastically deprived than the Romanian orphans but still underresponded to in terms of what we would consider to be optimal, underresponded to in the ways that Ainsworth and Bowlby thought would produce insecure attachment?

Infants have an intense need to engage themselves deeply and actively in communication with their mothers and others to whom they are regularly close. Disturbances in this communication are distressing to the infant. One of the ways in which the infant's communication with the mother has been studied is by artificially creating such disturbances in a controlled setting.

(Most famous of these studies are the Strange Situation studies conducted by Ainsworth in the 1970s, discussed in later chapters, are the empirical basis for much of what we know about attachment and child development.)

In one study of disturbed communication, a 2-month-old infant interacts with his mother through a specially designed glass screen (Malloch & Trevarthen, 2009b). When the angle of the screen is altered slightly by the experimenter, the mother continues to face the infant. She no longer sees his face but rather the reflected face of the experimenter, with whom she then proceeds to interact. The infant, however, continues to see his mother "normally," but now her responses and facial expressions are no longer related in a synchronized and contingent way to what the infant is expressing and communicating. The infant notices immediately and becomes distressed.

If one watches a film of one of these sessions, what one sees is at first the mother and the infant interacting normally, usually with a degree of delight and pleasure. There is a close interactivity and mutual smiling and a joining of each other in rhythmic movements, actions, and sounds that have many of the aspects of a musical dance (Malloch & Trevarthen, 2009b). Even more striking are the infant's attempts to reengage his mother when the change in the angle of the glass screen disrupts their interaction. When the mother moves out of close expressive and rhythmic synchrony with the infant, all the while continuing to face toward him as though engaging with him, the infant experiences a rupture and a loss that he tries to remedy. He amplifies his facial expressions, widens his eyes, kicks his feet, twists his body, moves his head within the limited range he can control, and begins to wave his hands to catch his mother's attention. The infant throws his whole physical and emotional being into the effort to recapture the communicative engagement with his mother. But she can no longer see him through the angled screen and so does not respond. As one watches, the infant's efforts gradually subside: His arms fall to his side, his body slackens, his eyes turn downcast, and a sad expression appears on his face. In the interpretation of the researcher, John Tatam (1974, cited in Trevarthen, 1998), the infant becomes depressed.

In this type of experiment, the mother's loss of communicative engagement and responsiveness was artificially created. But such nonresponsiveness can occur naturally for many reasons. Approximately one in seven new mothers experience depression severe enough to impair their ability to interact with and care for their infants (Wisner, Chambers, & Sit, 2006). What does the infant of a depressed mother find when he seeks to interact with her?

In optimal situations, a mother interacting with her infant is engaged, responsive, mutual, and synchronous, both joining the child when the child welcomes it and permitting disengagement and separateness as the child signals a desire for it (Tronick, 1989). Depressed mothers may have difficulties accomplishing both types of interactions. They may, in depressive withdrawal and passivity, have difficulty being responsive and engaged with their child, but they also may become intrusive, angry, overly stimulating, and controlling of the child in a way that is unattuned to the child's needs, interests, and communicative signals (Field, Hernandez-Reif, & Diego, 2006; Malphurs, Raag, Field, Pickens, & Pelaez-Nogueras, 1996).

In general (reviewed in Field, 2010), depressed mothers are less attuned to their infants in a variety of ways. They engage in less vocalizing and make less mutual eye contact with their infants. They smile less often. They touch their infants less often, and when they do touch them it is often in a rougher and more controlling manner. A depressed mother uses less infant-directed motherese (i.e., baby talk) when speaking to her infant, she employs longer and more complex sentences, and she does not vary the complexity of her speech as a function of the infant's age and development. She provides less stimulation and fewer enrichment activities—fewer songs, stories, shown objects, games, and playful engagements. When she does engage in turn-taking speech with her infant, her timing is off and unpredictable in a way that disturbs the synchrony of the interaction.

The infants of depressed mothers show a range of effects that involve taking themselves out of communicative engagement with other people. These babies touch themselves more often, perhaps providing self-stimulation in place of the missing maternal stimulation (Herrera, Reissland, & Shepherd, 2004). They become accustomed to and show a habituation to the nonresponsiveness and misattunement of their mothers, show less physiological reaction to a nonresponsive face, and become less responsive in general to the faces and voices of other people (Field, Diego, & Hernandez-Reif, 2009).

Infants of depressed mothers live within a world of negative emotion and impoverished, noncontingent communication that engenders negative affective states within them and shapes their future interactional styles and capacities with others. The way in which the infants are affected may depend on whether their mothers are withdrawn and nonresponsive or angry and intrusive (Tronick & Reck, 2009). Infants of the withdrawn mothers find themselves alone in the world, reaching out for an other who does not respond, and responsible for a degree of emotional self-regulation that is beyond their capacity to accomplish. They are lonely, sad, and desirous of establishing contact with others. The infants of angry, intrusive mothers, on the other hand, experience a mother who is misattuned but actively present, engaged, and controlling. Their struggle is to push the other away, prevent interference, and maintain a degree of autonomy—but not so far away that she disappears. They often lead with anger and engage with others through their own anger, dissatisfactions, and complaints.

In either case, what is happening is that the child's ways of experiencing himself and of interacting with the world are shaped and structured by his early interactions with his mother.

FINDING THE MOTHER WE HAVE

The central point of this chapter is that each of us spent the earliest months and years of our life looking for a relationship with our mother and trying to find a way to fit with her as well as might be possible. We do this because humans have been designed by natural selection to seek a close alliance with our mothers and then to neurophysiologically change in response to them, and our mothers have been designed by natural selection to respond to our seeking. This is an extremely powerful process that on the one hand reaches back toward the emergence in fetal development of the primordial biological substrate of which we are made and that simultaneously reaches outward toward the family group, society, and culture of which we will become a part. This process is one of the most powerful and successful of human evolutionary adaptations, and in its particularities it underlies much of what makes us distinctive as a species.

We each create a relationship with our mother through the process of communication with her, and in creating this relationship we learn her particular ways of communicating. Her ways of communicating, in all regards, become our mother tongue. We recognize the language she speaks, the way she moves, the emotions in her voice, and the expressions on her face. Because we are so strongly motivated to communicate with her and through our communication to form a continually deepening attachment to her, and because we are neurophysiologically changed by this communication and attachment, we adopt a language and a way of relating to others that we have learned as we have formed our relationship with her. These become imprinted on us in a profound way, as a part of the tissue of our being. In this process, we become a particular person, and the pattern of our relationships with others and to the world around us begins to assume form. The form it takes is written in our own biological and neurophysiological characteristics.

WHAT ABOUT FATHERS?

Attachment theory and attachment research have focused primarily on the relationships between mothers and children, and fathers have generally been considered as a possible secondary attachment for children. In writings about attachment, fathers are usually included under the rubric of attachment to parents or as the second term in the expression *mothers and fathers*. But there is only a scant literature that focuses primarily on the attachment of children to fathers or on the developmental consequences of this relationship.

To a great extent, this is a function of two factors. First is the concept of *monotropy* (Bowlby, 1958), which is the idea that attachments are formed in a way that emphasizes a strong connection to one specific individual (Bowlby, 1969/1982, Chapter 15). This pattern is the norm among mammals and especially primates (Eibl-Eibesfeldt, 1989), and it may be seen even in the way a child singles out a particular teacher or caregiver in day care. Second is the predominant role of mothers in child care, especially of infants and the very young, both among the animal species that were the model for attachment theory and among humans themselves. This latter factor, for humans, is of course a moving target, perhaps variable over historical time and from one sociocultural context and from one family to another. But mothers still provide the major portion of care for young children. Even with the rapid rise in work outside the home by mothers of young children, the amount of time that mothers spend with their children has been relatively stable, with mothers continuing to take the primary responsibility for children (Bianchi, 2000; Craig & Powell, 2012). For example, according to figures available from the U.S. Census Bureau (2012), the number of stay-at-home fathers in two-parent families has doubled over the last 10 years; however, even so they now constitute only 3% of stay-at-home parents. Ninety-seven percent of stay-at-home parents in two-parent families are women. Women also, of course, give birth to children and nurse them in a manner for which their physiology and nervous systems include multiple specializations (Carter, Grippo, Pournajafi-Nazarloo, Ruscio, & Porges, 2008). Given the concept of monotropy and the facts-on-the-ground of child care, it is not surprising that attachment theory and research, and most other developmental research as well, have focused on mothers.

But attachment theory has always contemplated a role for fathers and for others as attachment figures in the lives of children. A *father* paired with a *mother* who are together raising a *child* is a part of a romantic *pair-bond*, an embodiment of the moderate monogamy that is characteristic of humans. Paternal care and a degree of monogamy are found in only a small handful of other mammal or primate species, and in that sense our way of forming sexual relationships and raising our young is something of a rarity in nature. The long developmental period of a human childhood makes children an extraordinarily costly undertaking for a mother in biological terms and in terms of other resources. Romantic pair-bonds may be natural selection's way of connecting fathers to mothers and children for extended periods (Brumbaugh & Fraley, 2006; Fernandez-Duque, Valeggia, & Mendoza, 2009) and of thereby securing the benefits of paternal care for improving the well-being and survival of offspring (Jaffee, Moffitt, Caspi, & Taylor, 2003; Padilla & Reichman, 2001; Weitoft, Hjern, Haglund, & Rosén, 2003). The role of fathers in parental care appears, in the long view of natural selection, to have been powerful enough to be selected for and made part of the expectable environment for a developing child.

Bowlby did not have a great deal to say about fathers in his earliest works, though he did make clear that what mattered in terms of who the child preferred and made primary as an attachment figure depended not on the sex of the parent but on who was most present, available, and responsive to the child. Although this was most often the mother, it was, in his observations and those of others, sometimes someone else—a father, grandmother, older sibling, or other caregiver. But these were treated both by Bowlby (e.g., 1969/1982) and by Ainsworth (1964) as exceptions to the usual pattern. When such an exception did apply, the person who was actually the primary attachment figure for the child—father, grandmother, older sibling, or other caretaker—was considered to be *the* attachment figure for all theoretical and practical purposes. Thus, in family situations where a father functions as the primary attachment figure, attachment theory treats him as such. But in the pattern of caregiving that attachment theory (and most developmental research) takes as predominant, the father is usually considered a potentially important secondary attachment figure.

As secondary attachment figures, fathers have been the subject of some significant attachment research (for recent reviews, see Bretherton, 2010; Grossmann, Grossmann, Kindler, & Zimmermann, 2008). There is, first of all, considerable evidence that a child may have the same or a different degree of attachment security with each parent, thus emphasizing that attachment is a relationship with a particular other person and is also related to a set of characteristics of an individual (Lamb, 1976, 1977a, 1977b; Main & Weston, 1981; Tracy, Lamb, & Ainsworth, 1976; van IJzendoorn & De Wolff, 1997). The differences or similarities between a child's attachment to his mother or his father may be additive in advancing security (if attachments to both are secure), deepening insecurity (if attachments to both are insecure), or each moderating the influence of the other to some intermediate degree (when one is secure and the other insecure; Main & Weston, 1981).

There is also evidence that attachments to mothers and fathers may influence different emotional and behavioral domains of the child's life and functioning (e.g., comforting and closeness vs. play and exploration; Grossmann et al., 2002; National Institute of Child Health and Human Development in Early Child Care Research Network, 2004). Attachments to mothers and fathers may have consequences for different areas of functioning, depending in major part on the kinds of emotional states, activities, and experiences around which each parent engaged with the child most frequently and intensely (Bretherton, Lambert, & Golby, 2005; Grossmann et al., 2002, 2008; Lamb, 1977a).

The idea of secondary or multiple attachment figures who may influence the developing person with distinctive or overlapping effects in different domains of feeling and behavior is an extremely useful perspective for clinical work and for the perspective that I take in this book. It points toward a more nuanced and complex understanding of the attachment influences on an individual that goes well beyond simply assigning an individual to one of the broad attachment classifications of secure, avoidant, or anxious. This more subtle understanding must necessarily be grounded in an individualized appreciation of each person's personal history of attachment relationships and present functioning. It is linked to the idea, which has long been part of attachment theory, that multiple secondary attachment figures produce within an individual corresponding multiple internal models of attachment that govern expectations, behavior, feeling, and communication in relationships. It paints a picture of attachment experiences as not having a monotonic influence on development and personality but rather shaping an individual in complex ways. This is a subject to which I return several times.

3

THE NEURAL SCULPTING
OF THE SELF

The human brain and nervous system are extremely malleable. This chapter describes the neurophysiology and function of key parts of the brain and nervous system that are most affected and shaped by our early relationships, including important hormones such as cortisol and oxytocin. As a result of these early experiences, the body and nervous system learn to process and respond to relationships in specific ways. This chapter describes how this plasticity in response to relational experience underlies our attachment behaviors and characteristics and affects how we feel when we are with other people and when we are alone. Fortunately, the nervous system retains significant plasticity throughout life.

http://dx.doi.org/10.1037/14185-003
Attachment-Based Psychotherapy: Helping Patients Develop Adaptive Capacities, by Peter C. Costello

NEUROPLASTICITY

Neuroplasticity is the ability of the human brain to change its neural pathways and synapses in response to experience. It is the biological basis for the shaping of the self through attachment experiences.

We all are born relatively unformed, dependent and helpless, able to do almost nothing of what we need to do to survive. Our helplessness and our period of greatest dependency last, relative to those of other species, for a very long time. From birth, a human infant will remain almost totally reliant on the care of adults for at least a decade (and, as the socialization demands of industrial societies have increased, this period has in practice grown longer). This extended dependency of children is intricately woven into our evolved characteristics as a social animal. For example, the formation of *pair-bonds*—the romantic adult attachment relationships that figure so large in human lives and that often enough are the reasons that bring patients to therapy—appears to have evolved partly in response to the benefits to children of paternal care and the role that a pair-bond plays in creating and maintaining paternal engagement (Fraley, Brumbaugh, & Marks, 2005). In other words, the extended dependency of the child is implicated not only in the formation of an attachment relationship between the mother and the child but also in the formation of romantic attachments for the adult that the child will grow to be (Brumbaugh & Fraley, 2006). Humans are born into a dependency on others, and though we may acquire autonomy and great individual competence, our need for others will last throughout our lives. This is one of our special characteristics and strengths as a species.

This lifelong dependency holds two great advantages for us. First, that which makes human beings so successful as a species is precisely our capacity for social complexity and intensity—our mutual dependency—the degree to which we are able to coordinate our activities with each other through communication and through shared attention, shared purpose, and shared meaning (Tomasello, 1998; Tomasello, Kruger, & Ratner, 1993). It is the complexity of our social activities and interactions that accounts for the evolution of such a distinctively large brain in humans (Boyd, 2007; Dunbar, 2007; Flinn & Alexander, 2007; Miller, 2007; Stanford, 2007), just as in our primate relatives the size of their cortex corresponds to the size of their social group (Kappeler & Pereira, 2003). Our social dependencies are a central characteristic of human adaptations and a key strength.

A second critical advantage that follows from our extended helplessness at birth and our long period of dependency is that our relatively unformed brain and nervous system at birth make culture possible. It is culture that allows us to adapt rapidly to varied environmental demands through a process of learning and cultural variation rather than to be rigidly constrained by behaviors that are more fully developed at birth but also more narrowly fixed and invariant because of their biological form (Flinn, 2005). We assume our cultural form-in-the-world through our social dependencies, which shape our initially unformed nervous system.

Although this long period of learning, cultural acquisition, and slow physical development combined with dependency creates many difficulties and vulnerabilities for us, its advantages outweigh these difficulties. In a neurophysiological sense, the infant is helpless because his brain is still relatively amorphous and unformed. But it is exactly this initial lack of fixed form that makes it possible for us to take our final form in response to a particular social group and a particular environment. We do this through the processes of communication that we engage in with the members of our social group and that we each engage in most intensely with our mother. Our strongest social dependency is on our attachment figure, an influence that is at its peak during the early postnatal years when our nervous system is most plastic and is undergoing the most rapid development. This places our attachment relationships at the foundation of who we become socially and culturally in the world.

As the evolutionary developmental psychologist David Bjorklund (1997) pointed out, unlike that of other animals, including all of our primate relatives, the human brain continues to grow very rapidly after birth. Brain growth slows dramatically at birth for other primates, but the brain of the human infant continues to grow at the prenatal rate of development through the child's second year of life. This is a rather stunning fact about human development. It means that for us, the brain continues to develop at a pace of biological change as though we were fetuses even while we are experiencing not a fetal environment but rather a very active social life with our human family. In this sense, our initial social life is part of our fetal development.

It is in this way that these social and communicative experiences become coded into the biological fabric of the human nervous system. We each therefore can be made by these experiences into an individual with ways of thinking, feeling, and relating that are unique and special to those with whom we have had our first relationships. We can be especially well fitted to the specific individuals upon whom we are most dependent and to the challenges and opportunities of our immediate social and physical environment. We can wire ourselves neurophysiologically with the culture of our social group. This capacity for being specifically fitted to a particular social group and culture makes it possible for our species to live in so many different ways under so many different conditions. We and our nervous systems can be custom made, each one a kind of experiment in living.

Our mother is the leading edge of this process of custom-tailoring and of self-making. The primary attachment figure, in her role of shaping the developing person, is the agent of a specific culture, a specific family group, and specific individual variation in the development of the child. What she selects to attune to and respond to in her interaction with her child is selectively integrated and reinforced in her child's ways of relating to others (Kärtner, Keller, & Yovsi, 2010). Mothers are the rising voice of cultural adaptation and ways of thinking and feeling within our own minds and bodies. This is part of what makes them so important to the trajectories of our lives. It is the source of the influence of our early family relationships on whom we become as adults—the shaping of the self.

The relationship of our unformed neurophysiology and of culture works in both directions. The plasticity of the nervous system makes flexibility in culture and behavior possible for humans, but as part of actually growing up and living within a culture, culture and experience influence our neurophysiology and give it a more specified and, eventually, less plastic form (S.-C. Li, 2003). Thus, for example, the brain is most plastic with respect to language during the first years of life. Although we easily learn one or more languages during this sensitive, very plastic phase, we subsequently lose the ability to so effortlessly learn a new language as the brain becomes less plastic with respect to language acquisition. The same pattern—of an initial plasticity followed by learning through experience followed by reduced plasticity—obtains for other important aspects of the ways in which we communicate and form relationships. Early experiences scribe deep.

The degree to which the brain is malleable and the specific ways in which it is malleable vary at different points in our life. The periods of greatest malleability are critical periods in determining the kind of person we become. The brain undergoes the most rapid change and development during our first years, when we are forming our capacity for attachment to others. It is in these years that the greatest degree of neural shaping takes place. But the brain does remain changeable and at least somewhat plastic throughout our life. We continue to form new neurons and new synaptic connections and to alter old ones. There is strong evidence that the underlying mechanism of action by which the SSRI class of drugs (e.g., sertraline or fluoxetine) works is by increasing the plasticity of the brain with respect to emotional learning. SSRIs do this by increasing the formation of new neurons in a part of the hippocampus that is central to the formation of new emotional memories (Boldrini et al., 2009; Duman, Nakagawa, & Malberg, 2001; Krishnan & Nestler, 2008; Launay, Mouillet-Richard, Baudry, Pietri, & Kellermann, 2011; Mouillet-Richard, Baudry, Launay, & Kellermann, 2011; Nakagawa, 2010). SSRIs also shift neurons in the amygdala, the site of anxiety and fear conditioning, to a more immature state in which they become more plastic and better able to benefit from new experiences that reduce anxiety and fear, such as those that are provided in psychotherapy (Karpova et al., 2011). This increased neuronal plasticity is a key reason why these medications may work so well in concert with therapy (Welberg, 2012). But, whether drug assisted or not, change in adults is usually more gradual and less fundamental than what happens to the nervous system in childhood.

HOW THE BRAIN AND NERVOUS SYSTEM CHANGE

The complexity of the human brain defies its own capacity for appreciation or understanding. It is often described as the most complex entity in the universe. With 100 billion neurons, each forming between 10 and 100,000 synapses with other neurons, the brain contains approximately 1,000 trillion connections or switches (Steen, 2007). This number is essentially incomprehensible. The number of possible permutations of these connections, it is often said, exceeds the number of atoms in the universe (e.g., Ramachandran & Blakeslee, 1998). But perhaps even more stunning is the degree to which this enormous complexity continuously remodels and reshapes itself in an orderly and adaptive way, largely in precise response to its encounters with other people and its experiences in the world.

Three broad processes underlie the brain's ability to change and to adapt: the formation of new neurons (*neurogenesis*); the formation or changes in the strength of the synaptic connections that connect neurons into networks (*synaptogenesis*); and *neuronal pruning,* or the elimination of neurons or synapses through cell death (apoptosis) and through competition with other synaptic connections. Neurogenesis is most extensive during fetal development. At birth, an infant already has most of the neurons (about 100 billion) that he will need throughout his life. The course of neural shaping then shifts its emphasis to synaptogenesis, the creation and alteration of synaptic connections between neurons. Synaptogenesis occurs most extensively in the years before adulthood. This is why our childhood and adolescent experiences are fateful to whom we become and why change, like learning a foreign language, occurs more slowly for adults. Apoptosis takes place throughout life but occurs, somewhat counterintuitively, most extensively during the periods of rapid development in gestation and infancy. The competitive elimination of synaptic connections is most extensive during adolescence, when periods of extensive neuronal pruning take place, eliminating millions of connections between brain cells. The strengthening and weakening of synaptic connections take place throughout life. All of these processes of neuroplastic changes in the brain and nervous system are highly responsive to the effects of experience.

The shaping of the brain's connective networks involves both the creation of new synaptic connections and the elimination or pruning of others.

The role of cell death and synaptic pruning in development points to the way that development involves losing some potentials and specializing in others. There is an explosion of new connections from birth until about age 6; we have more synaptic connections at age 6 than we will at any other time in life. But then the process of pruning and elimination of less used synapses begins to accelerate. Millions and millions of the developing mind's synapses wither away. Through the period of latter childhood and adolescence this process takes a greater and greater toll, until at about age 16 we have only half the synaptic connections that we did at age 6. But don't fret; there are still about 100 trillion of them. And even when we are older adults our brain continues to create new neurons and to form new synaptic connections, especially in areas related to learning and memory, including the formation and processing of emotional memories (Kempermann, Wiskott, & Gage, 2004). This is the neurophysiological process that makes psychotherapy possible (Cozolino, 2002).

USE IT OR LOSE IT: THE PRINCIPLE OF THE USE-DEPENDENT DEVELOPMENT OF THE BRAIN

What determines which neurons and synapses survive and which are destroyed? This is decided primarily on the basis of the degree of activity and use. For example, before birth there are about one trillion neurons in the fetus's developing brain, but by birth 90% of these—900 billion neurons—will have died. What happens to them?

These lost neurons—actual particles of living tissue—are culled from the brain in a process that represents an extreme form of the neural shaping that will continue throughout our life. This sculpting takes place in a competitive process for survival—cell against cell, synaptic connection against synaptic connection—that Gerald Edelman (1987) described as "neural Darwinism." The essence of this competition is that neurons that become more used and active than their rivals (during fetal development, for example, by completing their migrations within the brain and becoming actively connected to other cells via axons and dendrites) will survive. The others will die.

The rule, a very important rule, is be active or be gone. The same rule—that structural changes in the brain reflect activity or nonactivity by neurons and synapses—applies generally to assemblies and networks of neurons in the brain; neurons that fire together wire together and survive (Foehring & Lorenzon, 1999; Hebb, 1961). These complex wired-and-fired-together networks of neurons and synapses are the neurophysiological basis of our perceptions, cognitions, feelings, and behaviors—the stuff out of which human lives are made.

The formation and elimination of synapses determines what we are able to do. Behaviors and experiences that are repeated become part of the brain's wiring. They are written in our neural anatomy. For human beings, the most important experiences are those that we have with other people. Social experiences and communications that take place during the periods when the brain is most plastic and is most actively pruning unused neurons and synapses are written most deeply. One can see these periods of rapid brain change mirrored in the quick developments of childhood and the transformations of adolescence, leading ultimately to the more stable and more slowly changing form of adults. Language is an excellent example—but only one example—of this. We need to learn our language during the sensitive period of our development when the language areas of the brain are most plastic and responsive to linguistic experience. We learn the very specific language that we use in our communications with the other members of our social group. Once learned during the appropriate plastic period, the language is deeply coded in our neurophysiology. Languages learned outside of this plastic period are learned with more difficulty. The way we use language to communicate will make us different from people in other language groups. This use-dependent formation of the brain's structure accounts for many of the differences between individuals. The use-dependent formation of our neural anatomy is how we become uniquely who we are.

What is actually happening during periods of synaptogenesis and synaptic pruning is that the brain is becoming more specialized in terms of what it is able to do, in part by losing the capacity to do things that is has not done often enough. As the brain loses the capacity to do some things, it becomes more efficient at doing others. For example, the developing infant or child learns and specializes in the specific sounds that are made in the language spoken by his caretakers. The neurons and synaptic connections in his brain that fire when these sounds are made become stronger and stronger. They are winning a competitive struggle for survival. But the learning and the increased specialization come at a cost. This cost is the pruning away of the capacity to hear sounds that will now be lost or never completely realized. This is why infants and young children are able to perceive and distinguish between spoken sounds that adults are literally unable to hear. The synapses that respond to sounds that are not used in the particular language heard by the developing child are culled, taking with them the capacity to hear the sounds to which they once responded. We lose some potential abilities (to hear and perceive all sounds) while developing and strengthening others (the ability to notice and focus on the sounds that are used in the language spoken around us). Like a sculptor's block of stone, the human brain achieves form and meaning in part through what is removed.

The sculpting and shaping of the physical structure of the brain occurs in us through our experiences with others. Every experience we have, every learning, is coded in the biology of our nervous system. The connections in the brain that are used are strengthened, and those that are not used are weakened (Jones, 2000; Maguire et al., 2003). "Use it or lose it" is one of the organizing principles on which the brain is built, and it is the biological basis for the influence of the past on the present (Abbott & Nelson, 2000). This record of all our experiences is rendered in a unique and personal form as one of the most intricate, complex, and dense entities on the planet, a three-dimensional sculpture of who we are and what has happened to us in life.

THE NEUROLOGICAL WIRING OF RELATIONAL, COMMUNICATIVE, AND EMOTIONAL CAPACITIES AND BEHAVIORS

The winnowing and the loss or diminution of some potentials and capacities and the strengthening of others, a topic to which I return in other chapters, is a key principle of development. What happens with language—the loss of the ability to perceive some sounds as we increase our ability to focus on others—is similar to what happens in other areas of our communicative, relational, and emotional behavior, for example, in our perception and responses to facial expressions and our expression or suppression of emotions. We are born with the potential to become many different kinds of person—to form relationships, to communicate with others, and to experience and use our own emotions in many different ways. But our early experience culls our capacities to those we need to form relationships with our principal social partners.

The neurons and synapses that get used the most and strengthened the most in the very malleable infant brain are those that are used in relationship to the mother and other early caregivers. Our mother is the one who surrounds us, who is the most important part of our environment during the first years of life. The first sculptors of our rapidly changing brain and nervous system are our early caretakers. Mothers are neural sculptors—as are fathers, and siblings, and friends and all the others we will interact with in our life.

This shaping of the brain and the winnowing of potentials occur at a neurophysiological level early in life, when human neural plasticity is greatest. This is why change in psychotherapy can be so difficult as an adult. The physical structure of the brain is conservative; in adults, it changes slowly and reluctantly. Some changes, like the acquisition of language or of basic attachment security, are easy to achieve during a particular period of brain formation but occur only with effort later in life. In order to change, one must produce an actual rewiring of already established parts of the brain (Brody et al., 2001; Schwartz, Stoessel, Baxter, Martin, & Phelps, 1996) during a period of life when the plasticity of the brain is reduced compared with its malleability at the time of childhood events. Whether the concern is with automatic thoughts, conditioned behaviors, or unconscious conflicts, a basic concern of all psychotherapists is how to produce conditions and experiences in therapy that enhance the malleability of the adult brain and how to target the changes that are most likely to produce meaningful differences in a patient's life.

Through our experiences with attachment figures early in life, some of our potentials are diminished and others are emphasized. Some of what we lose or fail to develop in these early relationships may be something that we need, and some of the learnings we have specialized in—for example, some of the ways in which we respond to our own emotions—may be learnings that we would now be better off without. Through psychotherapy and other experiences, some of our specializations can be modified and some of our lost but needed potentials can be restored in order to change the way we live with ourself and others.

We learn to be in the world and to have relationships in very specific ways, and the deep motivation to be attached to a particular other is a very potent teacher. Sometimes, what we have learned how to do in order to "fit" with our attachment figures does not serve us well in our intimate adult relationships and in the rest of our life.

PSYCHOLOGICAL AND EMOTIONAL DIFFICULTIES AS MALADAPTATION

Attachment theory has always been a theory of normal development through infancy and adulthood and also a theory of psychopathology (Sroufe, Carlson, Levy, & Egeland, 1999). The link between the two is the way in which development within a particular relational niche with one's primary attachment figures can lead to an adaptation to these attachment figures that is the best that can be obtained with them but that is suboptimal for the circumstances and relationships encountered elsewhere in one's life. Bowlby thought that "adaptation is always the joint product of developmental history and current circumstance (never either alone)" (Sroufe, Carlson, et al., 1999, p. 1). Thus, psychopathology should not be thought of primarily as a quality or trait of the individual but as a degree of maladaptation between the individual and his environment. Maladaptation in one circumstance might be ideal adaptation in another. Bowlby was concerned with how the developmental trajectory that was started in the childhood environment would play out for the functioning of the individual in the environments to come.

From the evolutionary perspective in which attachment theory is grounded—a perspective that emphasizes *reproductive fitness*, or the successful transmission of genes to the next generation—an insecure attachment style was not always a mistake. It depended on what the circumstances were in the developmental niche and which circumstances were to be later encountered in the wider world. In circumstances in which a mother is highly stressed, as has often been the case through human history, a child who was avoidant enough not to drive his mother away or who was anxious enough to successfully insist on attention might have a better chance of surviving and flourishing (K. E. Grossmann, 1995; Simpson & Belsky, 2008). Similarly, girls in homes that are significantly distressed, that are short on resources, and that engender insecure attachments appear to reach sexual maturity earlier in what may be an optimal reproductive strategy adapted to the circumstances at home (Belsky, 2010; Belsky, Steinberg, & Draper, 1991).

The implication of all this is that we have been designed by evolution to make an adaptation to our developmental niche—the circumstances in which we find ourselves during infancy and childhood—on the expectation that those circumstances are likely to reflect what we will encounter as adults. When circumstances in our childhood and in our adulthood are similar, we are well adapted. But if the childhood circumstances and opportunities are more constrained or more distorted from an optimal norm than those we encounter as adults, our own capacities also may be constrained and distorted in ways that do not serve our interests, that no longer fit the environment we are in, and that constitute maladaptation.

This view of psychopathology as a form of maladaptation created by childhood experience lies at the heart of Bowlby's clinical framework (Sroufe, Egeland, & Carlson, 1999). The child is powerfully motivated, in a process that begins prenatally, to establish an attachment to his mother. In doing this, he learns how to communicate with her, express emotions in a way to which she will respond, and form relationships in the way that she will form one. The patterns that the child acquires in regard to attachment, communication, and affect with his mother become his personal and idiosyncratic form of these powerful processes as he continues his life.

THREE NEUROPHYSIOLOGICAL SYSTEMS THAT ARE SHAPED BY EARLY ATTACHMENT EXPERIENCES

The developmental experiences that we have with our early attachment figures always have biological substrates. All of the emotional and psychological experiences that we have are based in the biological elements of our body. In this sense, it is always our own body that we directly feel when we are interacting with the external environment. When we experience others, we experience them through the effects that they have on us physically and biologically. The presence to us of others is always their presence or their impact within our own body. We can, if we direct our attention, feel these physical effects especially acutely when we come into the presence of a beloved or an enemy, or when we hold an infant or child.

Some of the impacts that others have on our body are transient or trivial, but others are profound and long-lasting. Some of the effects of others, especially those that occur early in life, while our brain and nervous system are developing, have such a powerful impact on the body's nervous system that they become a more or less permanent part of its structure.

The attachment behavioral system begins to operate in a preliminary way from a very early point in our development, even before we are born, as we begin to acquire an ability to identify and to prefer our mother (Winberg, 2005). This happens as specific physiological capabilities—such as the ability to hear and to process sound—begin to come online during fetal development and are turned toward the fundamental task of establishing a close relationship with the human beings who are the members of our immediate social group. From these early beginnings, the attachment system continues to develop as additional neurophysiological capabilities become available and begin to mature. The attachment system can be viewed as an assemblage and integration of the multiple subsystems that come online during development (Polan & Hofer, 2008) and that are related to social behavior and to the effect of social behavior on our physiology: our ability to identify our mother, our strong motivation to form a relationship with her through communication, to imitate her expressions, to make sounds in the way that she makes sounds, to engage her emotions with our emotions, to be soothed and comforted and regulated by her responsiveness. The development of social behavior in general is especially subject to influence by the experiences that we have while development is taking place—the neurophysiological systems that enable social behavior are dependent on social experience for their development—and so each of these subsystems is shaped and contoured by the very specific experiences that we have with others early in life. The specific types and characteristics of the attachments that we have to others as infants, children, and adults are constructed from the varying characteristics of these subsystems, and these varying characteristics are themselves caused by the effects of social experiences on these physiological subsystems as they develop (Hofer, 1987, 2004, 2006).

There are several very specific examples of this relationship-driven neurophysiological shaping that I would like to consider, clarifying the ways in which early attachment experiences shape our socially oriented nervous system.

The Amygdala

My emphasis here is on the emotions and the communications that occur in attachment and other close relationships and on how these experiences are neuroplastically sculpted into the brain and so become a part of the self and a part of future relationships with others. In these regards, the amygdala is a good place to begin a tour of the attachment-related brain because of the central role played by the amygdala in our social, emotional, and communicative behavior (Kukolja et al., 2008). The amygdala is in the limbic system, the part of the nervous system that is most involved in both emotional experience and emotional learning. It plays a central role in recognizing and interpreting emotional expressions in faces and relating these expressions to other stimuli in the situation in which they occur. It learns about emotional expressions and what they mean in the context in which they occur. In general, the amygdala assigns emotional significance and intensity to social and communicative stimuli, and it does this in a way that is heavily influenced by experience-dependent learning (Kandel, Schwartz, & Jessell, 2000). So, it is central to the way in which attachment experiences shape our capacities for interactions with others.

In fact, the amygdala and a closely interconnected brain center to which the amygdala delivers its neural output, the striatum, appear to support the two fundamental dimensions of attachment style (Vrticka, Andersson, Grandjean, Sander, & Vuilleumier, 2008). A too easily and too strongly activated amygdala appears to underpin the phenomenon of attachment anxiety; an underresponsive, difficult-to-activate striatum appears to underpin an avoidant attachment style. When the amygdala and the striatum are tuned just right, with the amygdala not anxiously overresponding and the striatum not avoidantly underresponding, a secure attachment style is present.

The amygdala is located deep and low within the temporal lobes of the brain (about level with the tops of our earlobes and halfway in toward the midline of the brain). The amygdala is phylogenetically the oldest of the basal ganglia, and its ancient status accords with its central location in our brain and with its very important role in our social behavior and emotional experience.

The amygdala receives input from the thalamus, which itself is a central processing and routing area for all types of incoming sensory data about the external world. It is also well connected to the sensory association areas in the temporal lobes that assemble coarse sensory data into complex and subtle perceptions (e.g., of faces). The amygdala is therefore well informed about events in the external world, and it is exquisitely responsive to these stimuli. The amygdala's connections to the sensory data about the external world and to motor nuclei in the brain stem are so direct and immediate that it can begin to respond to external events even before we consciously perceive them (LeDoux, 2009). It is a neuronal trip wire for things that make us react with fear before we consciously know that we are afraid. When we leap suddenly at a loud sound before we have had time to consciously think that we have heard a sound, or when we leap away from a furtive movement in our peripheral vision before we consciously register or think about that movement, it is the amygdala that has catapulted us into action.

The amygdala specializes in appraising whatever we encounter, including subtle expressions on the faces of others, and then creating learned emotional responses to these encounters. Its fundamental role is to connect a sensory stimulus, such as a facial expression, with an emotional response. Through its strong connections to the hypothalamus, it propagates an emotional response throughout the body, profoundly affecting our physiological state. It generates this emotional response to a stimulus and thereafter, because of its strong connections to the centers of learning and memory in the hippocampus and basal forebrain, it keeps that specific emotion assigned to that particular stimulus, so that we have the same emotional response when we encounter the stimulus again. It does this both with stimuli arising from the external world (other people, events, situations, places—external stimuli generally) and with those arising from the internal world (our thoughts, plans, intentions, body and visceral states, and emotional responses). It also specifies the *intensity* of the emotional response that we have to what we encounter, creating, for example, the difference between mild anxiety and mindless terror or between irritation and rage. Although it also plays a role in pleasant and positive emotions, it is especially important in generating the experience of anxiety and fear in relation to external or internal stimuli. It is the amygdala that does the work of making us feel afraid of particular things, based on the experiences we have had with particular people, situations, or stimuli, as well as on our innate fears, such as a fear of heights or of being alone in a strange place. It is the amygdala that calms our fears by becoming less active; as its activity decreases, our happiness increases, as though subtracting fear and anxiety produces contentment.

The amygdala is particularly sensitive and responsive to the social signals contained in the faces, voices, and body postures of other people, and it is also an important part of how we make our own facial and vocal expressions of emotions for communication with others. It reads faces and other social signals and simultaneously assesses their relevance for us personally. It also measures the intensity of the emotions being expressed by others. The amygdala pays a lot of attention to the areas around the eyes of our social companions. It is highly sensitive to where others are looking, whether they are looking at us and have intentions toward us and whether their pupils are dilated (a signal of emotional arousal). Without requiring our conscious effort, it registers the emotional valence of others' intentions and keeps us tuned for making a response to them. It is able to register facial expressions and their significance both consciously and unconsciously and to generate physiological, cognitive, and behavioral responses with or without awareness.

Its sensitivity to social signals like facial expressions, its function of appraising the personal relevance for us of these social signals, and its dual role in relationship to increases and decreases in anxiety and fear all make the amygdala an important component of the attachment system. The baby studying his mother's face for signs of feeling and social intent is training his amygdala.

The neural networks that process fear and the neural networks that process facial expressions overlap in the amygdala. This tells us something very important about the role of other people in our environment. One of the things that humans have most to fear is the loss of social alliances and group membership, and this is especially true with regard to our attachment figures. We become experts at reading the faces and minds of others in order to know what we should fear, both from our environment and from disapproval, rejection, or exclusion by others. The amygdala becomes most sensitive to and expert at decoding the facial expressions of those to whom we are closest (K.-U. Lee et al., 2008; Richeson, Todd, Trawalter, & Baird, 2008; Van Bavel, Packer, & Cunningham, 2008; Vuilleumier & Sander, 2008). It learns what to fear in ways that are influenced by the social practices and cultural beliefs of our group (Chiao et al., 2008), thus demonstrating the cultural tuning of an automatic and unthought neurophysiological response. This trains our mind to communicate and interact with others in specific patterns of interaction so as to maintain our relationships with them. This process of communicative and relational training and its connection to anxiety and fear of displeasing or distancing ourselves from others occurs most strongly with our attachment figures.

Emotionally geared learning about the people, situations, facial expressions, and other stimuli that are personally important to us for our survival and well-being is the amygdala's essential function (Kandel et al., 2000). The amygdala is a central component of an extended network of neural circuits connecting socially relevant information to key systems in the body that control our thinking and our physiological and behavioral responses. It participates in shaping these responses in a way that becomes automatic, so that the responses—thoughts, behaviors, and physiological body states—become more or less permanent parts of us (as, for example, in the acquisition of conditioned responses). In addition to having connections to the thalamus, which keep it informed about events in the external world, the amygdala has extensive connections to the areas of the cerebral cortex responsible for conscious thinking and planning and choosing among alternatives; thus, it is influenced by the content of our cognitions and plans. It has reciprocal connections to the orbital medial prefrontal cortex, which is strongly involved in social behavior, emotion regulation, and communication (Minagawa-Kawai et al., 2009). It is well connected to the hippocampus, which plays a key role in long-term emotional learning and memory (e.g., how we feel about a particular person, situation, or place or about something that happened to us) and to our conscious experience of emotion. The amygdala also has two-way connections with the hypothalamus and thereby with the pituitary and adrenal systems of the body. These systems control socially relevant endocrine secretions and the remarkable alterations in physical and psychological state that accompany variations in hormones, such as norepinephrine, cortisol, oxytocin, and vasopressin (about which I say more below), that are driven by our experiences in communicating with others.

As a baby interacts with his mother, he learns to read her face and her intentions and feelings toward him, and he learns from a very early moment both how to imitate her facial expressions and how to initiate facial expressions that are successful in influencing her. He learns to recognize anger, sadness, happiness, engagement and intimacy, disengagement and lack of interest. He learns what he does that produces these responses. He learns what to be afraid of in his mother's face because it leads to her anger, insensitivity, and withdrawal or because it signals that she is herself afraid. He learns what to welcome in her face because it leads to sensitive responsiveness, communication, and safety. The baby's amygdala learns how to recognize the mother's communications, gives them emotional impact and significance, and neuroplastically turns his recognition of them into biologically encoded, long-term communicative sensitivities and forms of interaction with others. His amygdala helps the infant to learn how to make the facial expressions that are acceptable, influential, and appropriate to his social partner, their social situation, and his own needs and emotional state. It triggers in him responses to his mother's communications that affect his entire body, his emotional experience, his cognitions, and his behavioral inclinations. His amygdala helps to turn these communications and physiological states into things he automatically does on a long-term basis.

The amygdala thus connects social signals we receive from others to recognition of relational consequences and to profound changes in our physiological functioning. It learns about these social signals, such as facial expressions, tone of voice, and body postures, and the situations in which they occur and then makes our responses to them a permanent part of who we are, how we understand others, and how we interact with them (Skuse, Morris, & Lawrence, 2003; Tottenham, 2006; Tottenham, Hare, & Casey, 2009). Children who have been with depressed mothers since birth, as well as children raised in substandard orphanages, have an enlarged amygdala, suggesting that they have struggled over these issues of communication and anxiety in relation to their caregivers (Lupien et al., 2011). The amygdala is one of the principal neural sculptors of the self in relationship to others, and it is itself highly plastic, not only throughout life but especially during the early developmental period with the attachment figure. The intricate neuronal shaping of the amygdala, created through interactions with the attachment figure and other social experiences, is how the self assumes an emotional and communicative form.

The amygdala's major role in assessing social communications directly mediates the operations of human attachment systems and behaviors. It has been directly linked to the way our body responds and the way that we feel during experiences of attachment insecurity (Lemche et al., 2006). The amygdala also feeds the results of its assessment of social information forward to other brain nuclei that are part of the brain's limbic system and thus makes a major contribution to how we feel about the social communications that we are encountering. It is a central part of the emotional brain systems that underlie the actual experience of attachment relationships (Vrticka et al., 2008). The amygdala becomes more strongly activated in anxiously attached individuals than it does in secure or avoidant individuals when they experience an expression of social disapproval from someone they think of as an ally. Its activation corresponds to a state of hypervigilance to interpersonal threats and to heightened relationship anxiety. Correspondingly, the striatum, a brain structure to which the amygdala feeds the results of its emotional assessments and which is associated with the experience of reward, is activated when we experience social approval from an ally. At least it does unless we are avoidantly attached, in which case the communication of social approval, which does not mean as much to avoidantly attached individuals as it might to others, also does not activate the striatum to a normal degree (the striatum underresponds to positive social stimuli in those who are avoidantly attached).

In other words, the dimensions of high attachment anxiety and high attachment avoidance both seem to be related to variations in how the amygdala and the associated striatum area are functioning. These are two of the major brain areas that neurophysiologically underpin the states of anxious and avoidant attachment. These areas also underlie the brain and experiential responses of securely attached individuals. Secure attachment has increasingly been understood as the relative absence of attachment anxiety and avoidance (Bartholomew & Horowitz, 1991; Fraley & Spieker, 2003); that is, as neither a heightened nor a suppressed response to social communications from others. And correspondingly, normal levels of activation of these brain areas in response to social approval and disapproval—neither the hyperactive amygdala response found in anxious attachment nor the hypoactive activation of the striatum found in avoidant attachment—are found in securely attached individuals (Vrtička et al., 2008).

Early experiences with our caretakers neutrally sculpt the functioning of the amygdala and associated areas. These areas then guide and support anxious, avoidant, and secure ways of forming attachments.

The Hypothalamic-Pituitary-Adrenal Axis and Cortisol

The amygdala links the sensory, cognitive, social, and emotional parts of the brain with the visceral, muscular, and hormonal parts of the body. Through these connections, our thoughts and perceptions become closely integrated with our body's physical state, and our learned emotional responses to people and situations become part of our body's physical reactions. The amygdala is thus central to the process that Stephen Porges (2011) called *neuroception*—the specialization of the nervous system to continually evaluate risk and safety, to monitor whether a person, place, behavior, emotion, facial expression, sound, or other communicative signal indicates safety or danger. The different surges of physical feeling that we get when we perceive a threat or are hugged by a friend are created through these interconnections of the amygdala with our hormones, visceral organs, cardiovascular system, and muscles. These connections run both ways—the way our viscera, cardiovascular system, and muscles feel is fed back through neural networks to influence how we think and what we notice or do not notice in our environment. This close integration of our thoughts, perceptions, social interactions, and emotions with the rapid changes in our physical body state that occur as we experience life is effected through the pathways connecting the amygdala with the hypothalamus and with the hypothalamic-pituitary-adrenal (HPA) axis of the body. Like those of the amygdala, the operations of the HPA axis are an important part of our nervous system and physiological responding that is shaped by our early attachment relationships.

The *HPA axis* refers to the network of interactions between the hypothalamus, a part of our subcortical brain that links our nervous system to the hormonal system; the pituitary gland, which is stimulated by the hypothalamus to secrete the master hormones that trigger other hormonal processes in the body; and the adrenal glands, which sit atop the kidneys and are directly influenced by the signals of the pituitary to secrete cortisol and norepinephrine. Cortisol and norepinephrine activate multiple physiological processes that are related to a response to stress or danger and to heightened levels of physical activity.

Thus, the HPA axis is central to many of the body's most useful reactions to the opportunities and demands that we face (Jänig & Häbler, 2000). It links the amygdala's evaluation of persons, facial expressions, emotional communications, and other aspects of social interaction to multiple physiological responses in the body. It is the master control for our responses to stress and threat of all kinds, from a saber-toothed tiger leaping toward us to the frown on the face of our beloved. The HPA axis prepares the body in multiple ways to deal with the threat—by fighting, fleeing, freezing, or communicating. It directly brings into existence the physiological states that are part of what we experience as our mood and emotions (Collet, Vernet-Maury, Delhomme, & Dittmar, 1997; Ekman, 1999; Rainville, Bechara, Naqvi, & Damasio, 2006). These emotions then feed back through the body to further influence our thinking and our perceptions—producing happy thoughts, anxious thoughts, depressed thoughts, angry thoughts. The HPA axis also regulates our immune system (helping to turn our hair gray and to age us in other ways), our digestive processes (giving us an upset stomach when we are under stress), our access to metabolic energy (making us feel quick or slow), and our sexuality, preparing and triggering the physical processes that accompany reproductive stimuli. For human beings, sources of stress usually have more to do with social interactions than they do with the physical environment, and the HPA axis strongly responds to our encounters with other people, thereby incorporating all of the above processes as responses to our social relationships.

Each individual's HPA axis is shaped in significant ways by his or her attachment experiences (Carpenter et al., 2007; Pierrehumbert et al., 2009; Quirin, Pruessner, & Kuhl, 2008). This is because of the role that our mother and other early attachment figures play when we are distressed by calming us and reassuring us or by failing to do so. When a child experiences stress—whether because he is frightened, hungry, or angry or for some other reason—his HPA axis activates his body; stimulates multiple visceral, hormonal, and muscular processes; and produces a specific physiological state that corresponds to a particular emotion. A sensitive, responsive attachment figure effectively calms a distressed child by how she communicates and responds to him and thus provides a relational scaffold whereby the child eventually learns how to calm himself by modulating his own inner responses. The responsive, security-engendering attachment figure buffers the child from stress.

When a child does not have the experience of this buffering and soothing by a responsive attachment figure, he experiences chronic stress that is thought to lead to underdevelopment of the neural structures, such as the hippocampus and the prefrontal cortex, that play a central role in modulating the operations of the HPA axis (Labonte et al., 2012; Quirin et al., 2008). The operations of the HPA axis become dysregulated, and the individual becomes impaired in his capacity to respond appropriately to stress. The dysregulation of the HPA axis in this way is a part of the picture in many forms of psychological suffering, including borderline personality disorder, depression, susceptibility to posttraumatic stress disorder, dissociative symptoms, and anxiety disorders (Blair, Granger, Willoughby, Kivlighan, & the Family Life Project Investigators, 2006; Blair et al., 2008; Claes, 2004; Neigh, Gillespie, & Nemeroff, 2009; Shea, Walsh, Macmillan, & Steiner, 2005; Ströhle & Holsboer, 2003; Wingenfeld, Spitzer, Rullkötter, & Löwe, 2010; Zimmerman & Choi-Kain, 2009). The effect of early attachment experiences on the poor regulation of the HPA axis may be lifelong (though psychotherapy can recover these effects to a meaningful degree; e.g., Hsiao et al., 2011; Olff, De Vries, Güzelcan, Assies, & Gersons, 2007).

Thus, significant failures in responsiveness by attachment figures affect the HPA axis in ways that foster later psychopathology—especially depression, anxiety disorders, and difficulties in interpersonal relationships. Children who have not had reliable and sensitively responsive attachment figures to help them through periods of stress have difficulty learning to control and modulate their own degree of arousal. Driven by a poorly modulated stress response, their bodies may effectively fly out of control and their thoughts, perceptions, and memories then follow their bodies' dysregulated and disordered state. Their impaired HPA axis leaves such children impaired in their capacity to respond adaptively and effectively to challenges from the environment.

Via the amygdala's transmission to the HPA axis of information about the emotions and facial expressions of others, our own physiological and emotional responses to social situations, relationships, and communications with others become encoded in the operations of the HPA axis. Thus, we come to have a particular physiological and body response to specific social situations and relationships with others. Our body and our emotions are shaped to socialize with others in particular ways.

For example, we may feel uncomfortable or even experience uncontrollable anxiety when separations occur or when certain emotions–anger, for instance–occur in us or the other person. Or, we may feel hopeless and depressed when people fail to respond to us as we would like or even when they simply fail to reassure us as much as we need them to; we may feel frightened in situations requiring self-assertion, or we may automatically dramatize and overemphasize our needs in order to draw a response from an expected-to-be-unresponsive other. The specifics of the ways in which the amygdala and HPA axis appraise and respond to relationships and social situations are highly individual and nuanced and are derived from the interactional history of each person. But our attachment figures play a leading role in the encoding process.

The Hormones of Stress and Attachment: Cortisol and Oxytocin

Some of these long-term effects of our early experiences on our responses to stress in our life and our capacity to form secure attachment relationships are moderated by the lasting effects of early attachment experiences on the operations of the hormones cortisol and oxytocin, which are key components of the HPA axis (Bao, Meynen, & Swaab, 2008).

Cortisol and Stress

Cortisol might be thought of as the main hormone of stress and anxiety, and oxytocin might be thought of as the key hormone of attachment (Carter, 2003). Early social experience influences the activity of these hormones through alterations in the expression of genes that regulate their development; through changes in the distribution and density of the neuronal receptors for these hormones that thereby alter how and to what extent they can influence our physiology and behavior; and through variations in the amount of the production of these hormones in response to the things that are happening around us and to us (Champagne & Curley, 2009; Cushing & Kramer, 2005; Wismer Fries, Shirtcliff, & Pollak, 2008). The effects that cortisol and oxytocin are able to produce on our body and in our mental state in response to cues from the environment are a major pathway through which early experience with attachment figures shapes our future relationships (Kaufman, Plotsky, Nemeroff, & Charney, 2000).

Cortisol is a steroid hormone that is secreted by the adrenal glands in response to signals sent to it by the amygdala and the hypothalamus. Its primary role is to ready the body to deal with experiences of stress and anxiety, and it does this by altering a wide range of internal processes to prepare us to respond to a challenge or threat. For example, it breaks down stored fats and proteins to make them available for immediate energy by increasing the amount of circulating glucose in the blood, it enhances our cardiovascular output to oxygenate our muscles and nervous system, it inhibits digestive and reproductive processes in order to divert their resources to threat responses, it slows the immune system in order to inhibit inflammation in response to an injury, and it shapes cognition and perception to focus our attention and learning on important elements of the present situation to which we need to make an immediate response (Haley, Weinberg, & Grunau, 2006; Munck, 2000; Smeets, Dziobek, & Wolf, 2009; Smeets, Otgaar, Candel, & Wolf, 2008; Taverniers, Smeets, Van Ruysseveldt, Syroit, & von Grumbkow, 2011; Vedhara, Hyde, Gilchrist, Tytherleigh, & Plummer, 2000).

Cortisol levels fluctuate in response to what is happening at that moment in our life. For example, on weekdays but not on weekends (Rystedt, Cropley, Devereux, & Michalianou, 2008), our cortisol rises in the few hours before we wake, to ready ourselves for the challenges of the day, and increases again at first light. The relatively lower level of cortisol on days we do not face the stress of getting up and going to work is one of the reasons that our body may feel more relaxed as we wake on weekend mornings. In a similar way, the stress of an unpredictable commute raises our cortisol levels (Evans & Wener,

2006; Evans, Wener, & Phillips, 2002). So does the relational stress of a temporary separation from our attachment figure, as, for example, when he or she is traveling away from us (Diamond, Hicks, & Otter-Henderson, 2008). In these circumstances, the person who is being left typically experiences more elevation of cortisol than the one who is leaving. Our body deploys cortisol in a variety of situations and for ordinary as well as unusual stresses.

Chronic stress and persistently elevated levels of cortisol cause problems. Under these conditions, cortisol can begin to damage sensitive portions of our body and our brain. Chronically high levels of cortisol appear to damage the hippocampus. The hippocampus is important in the regulation of the HPA axis and of cortisol itself, so chronic exposure to high levels of cortisol in infancy and childhood may lead to a permanent dysregulation of our ability to respond to stress, making us unable to soothe ourselves and less able to obtain the help we need from others. The hippocampus also is responsible for the formation of memories, and sustained levels of high cortisol may be responsible for the memory impairments that are sometimes found in depressed or chronically stressed individuals (Hinkelmann et al., 2009; Marin et al., 2011). These difficulties with memory formation also impair behavioral flexibility and the capacity to adapt to changing circumstances because they make it more difficult to incorporate new experiences into thinking, emotional responses, and behaviors. In fact, one of the reasons that antidepressant drugs such as Prozac and Zoloft may work is because they restore the capacity of the hippocampus to form new neurons and thereby to create the new emotional learnings. This restores the ability to adjust to new circumstances or to learn from experiences in psychotherapy.

Cortisol is an important and usually beneficial part of how the body deals with stress, but if our stress-response system is impaired or does not operate properly because of the effects of early experiences on its development, we become less able to deal with stressors of all kinds. As they develop, neglected or insecurely attached infants and children find themselves in a circumstance of chronic stress and chronic cortisol elevation. They are always in danger of losing their attachment figure or of the figure not responding to them. Their attachment longings remain present, in part fueled by the higher levels of cortisol itself. But they do not experience the support of a responsive attachment figure in dealing with the other stresses and difficulties that occur in their young lives. This chronic relational stress disrupts the normal development of their stress-response system—the HPA axis and its production of cortisol—in a way that affects their long-term relationships and the way they handle stressors and challenges in their lives. Insecurely attached individuals show specific patterns of unusual diurnal variations in cortisol production (Dozier, Peloso, Lewis, Levine, & Laurenceau, 2008; Kidd, Hamer, & Steptoe, 2011; Quirin et al., 2008). Their cortisol levels are unusually high in infancy, and this leads to a suppression of their HPA axis. This produces lower than normal levels of cortisol in these children. This suppression of the HPA axis of insecure children persists into adulthood, and fearful and insecure adults produce less cortisol in response to stress than do secure adults. The effects of early attachment insecurity on the stress-response system are one of the biological routes by which early insecure attachment experiences may lead—in adults—to depression, anxiety, relational difficulties, and the underutilization of opportunities in the environment.

The effects of early attachment experiences in disrupting the HPA axis and the secretion of cortisol may be transmitted from one generation to the next through the effect of an insecurely attached mother on her children (Ben-Dat Fisher et al., 2007; Yehuda & Bierer, 2008). Unable to regulate her own stress, a mother with an impaired HPA axis is also unable to help her children to regulate theirs. The result is that her children, because of the effects of chronic stress described above, develop impaired HPA systems of their own. These children, without intervention or psychotherapy or an alteration in relational circumstances, may then pass on an impaired stress response to their own children. Disruptions of the HPA axis and of cortisol production by early attachment experiences are one of the biological routes by which insecure patterns of attachment are transmitted from one generation to the next, creating an intergenerational chain of insecurity.

Cortisol helps us to cope with stress because it stimulates biological changes that underlie coping behaviors. One of the responses it stimulates is the activation of our attachment system. The physiological route through which cortisol helps to activate our attachment systems is by stimulating increases in oxytocin.

Oxytocin and Attachment

Oxytocin is another of the key pathways through which early experiences shape our neurophysiology and our future relationships. Oxytocin is a key hormone of attachment that has been described as "the great facilitator of life" (H. J. Lee, Macbeth, & Pagani, 2009), and its operation activates an array of physical and social processes that are exactly those that are of interest to attachment researchers and to psychotherapists (and to everyone else as well).

In general, the release and activity of oxytocin in the body are caused by events related to reproduction (including sexual intercourse and childbirth), maternal care, social relationships, and the formation of alliances. They are associated in both animal and human studies with sexual activity, giving birth, breast feeding, the development of social and maternal behaviors during a critical period around birth, bonding to offspring, the development of trust, recognition of trusted individuals and treating some individuals as special to us and distinguished from all others, mate selection and the formation of romantic relationships, sexual fidelity, the formation of alliances and social bonds with both romantic and nonromantic others, fear reduction, communication, and stress and affect regulation (Campbell, 2010; Carter, 2003; Ditzen, Bradley, & Heim, 2012; Galbally, Lewis, IJzendoorn, & Permezel, 2011; Gordon, Zagoory-Sharon, Leckman, & Feldman, 2010a, 2010b; Heinrichs, von Dawans, & Domes, 2009; Insel & Young, 2001; H. J. Lee et al., 2009; Rimmele, Hediger, Heinrichs, & Klaver, 2009; Wismer Fries, Ziegler, Kurian, Jacoris, & Pollak, 2005). That is quite a list. The activities of oxytocin in our body across these diverse realms and the effect that early experience with our caregiver has on how our own body produces and handles oxytocin constitute one of the key biological links between our early experiences with our mother and our later experiences with our sexual and romantic partners.

Oxytocin is released in men and women by sexual intercourse and orgasm. During sexual intercourse, it increases the sensitivity of the nipples and penis, causes uterine contractions, and facilitates the transport of sperm. The release of oxytocin during sexual intercourse is linked to the stress- and anxiety-reducing effects of intercourse (Hiller, 2004, 2005; Meston & Buss, 2007; Neumann, 2008). In childbirth, oxytocin is associated with cervical dilation and uterine contractions during labor and is released by the movement of the fetus through the birth canal. In maternal care, the release of oxytocin is produced by stimulation of the mother's nipples during nursing, both by the baby's sucking and through the baby's massaging of the mother's breast in the pauses between nursing, when mother and baby are most likely to make eye contact with each other (Matthiesen, Ransjö-Arvidson, Nissen, & Uvnäs-Moberg, 2001). Oxytocin produces the letdown response that makes the mother want to nurse the baby and that makes her milk readily available. The release of oxytocin during nursing increases the mother's production of breast milk and thus her desire to nurse. Soon after birth, through conditioning, the mere sight or sound of her infant wanting to nurse will produce oxytocin release and the letdown response in the mother.

In terms of social behavior, the release of oxytocin (and the related hormone vasopressin) during mating is associated in animal studies with the formation of partner preferences and long-term relationships. Some animals "imprint" on mates through the experience of intercourse in a manner similar to the way that newborns in some animal species imprint on the mother through early experiences with her (Curley, 2011; Donaldson & Young, 2008; Heinrichs et al., 2009).

In human studies, there are clear indications that a similar process occurs. For example, the administration of oxytocin through a nasal spray markedly increases both feelings of trust and the actual behaviors associated with trust toward other individuals (Kosfeld, Heinrichs, Zak, Fischbacher, & Fehr, 2005). The availability of oxytocin during conflict with an adult mate tends to reduce the hostility of the conflict and to maintain the partners' social bond (Ditzen et al., 2009). The fact that oxytocin is released in humans by sexual intercourse and that oxytocin increases trust and feelings of closeness leads to the advice of anthropologist and love researcher Helen Fisher: Don't copulate with someone you don't want to fall in love with (H. Fisher, 2004; Haselton & Buss, 2001).

In adult social relationships, oxytocin levels are closely associated with attachment-related interpersonal behaviors and with responses to positive and negative emotions (Tops, Van Peer, Korf, Wijers, & Tucker, 2007). Early attachment experiences change the way our oxytocin systems work by changing the distribution and density of receptors, the production of oxytocin, and the responsiveness of the systems to relational and environmental events. For example, the oxytocin levels of securely attached women respond actively and fluently to experiences that involve positive emotions and positive social interactions, but the oxytocin levels of insecurely attached women do not—they remain flat. Conversely, in response to the experience of sadness, the oxytocin levels of secure women remain stable, suggesting a capacity for resilience and the psychological availability of attachment-related positive psychological resources. But the oxytocin levels of insecure women fall in response to sadness, suggesting less internal availability of attachment-related resources, greater emotional lability, and more suffering. It is as though the oxytocin mechanisms of the insecure women have become impaired and do not operate properly in response to current experiences (Turner, Altemus, Enos, Cooper, & McGuinness, 1999).

All of this is directly relevant to the effect of attachment experiences because the way in which the brain and body produce and handle oxytocin and vasopressin during social interactions is directly linked to early experiences of child care and either nurturing or neglect. The oxytocin system is one of the biological systems that is strongly shaped by early experience (Bales, Boone, Epperson, Hoffman, & Carter, 2011; Bales & Perkeybile, 2012; Opacka-Juffry & Mohiyeddini, 2012; Rinaman, Banihashemi, & Koehnle, 2011; Veenema, 2011), and it thus translates early patterns with the mother into long-term patterns of feeling, loving, and relating (Ditzen et al., 2012).

For example, children who spent their early years in conditions of significant neglect in substandard orphanages show long-term differences from family-reared children in the functioning of their oxytocin and vasopressin systems (Fries, Ziegler, Kurian, Jacoris, & Pollak, 2005). The vasopressin and oxytocin levels of the orphanage-reared and family-reared children were examined both before and after they spent time with their mother and with an unfamiliar adult. The family-reared children showed an increase in the elevation of their oxytocin levels after spending time with their mother, but their oxytocin remained flat in the presence of the unfamiliar adult. The neglected children, who were examined 3 years after they had been removed from the orphanage and placed in an adoptive family, showed no increase in oxytocin after 20 minutes with their adoptive mother; their oxytocin levels responded to the familiar and nurturing adult in the same way they responded to an unfamiliar adult. Also, the orphanage-reared children showed lower vasopressin levels overall; vasopressin appears to be critical for recognizing and acting distinctively toward familiar individuals. Because oxytocin and vasopressin connect social experiences to the nucleus accumbens, the "reward center" of the brain, these results suggest that neglected children develop a nervous system that finds social contact less rewarding and familiar and unfamiliar individuals less distinguishable from each other.

The failure to receive adequate nurturing during the first years of life appears to have long-term effects on the ability of these children to take comfort from positive social interactions with caretaking adults. This pattern is notably similar to that found in the oxytocin patterns of secure and insecure adult women that was noted earlier: The oxytocin levels of the secure women increased during positive social interactions (as for the family-reared children) and remained stable during sadness; the oxytocin levels of the insecure and interpersonally troubled women showed no response to positive social contact (as for the orphanage-reared children) and fell during sadness.

The effects of early experiences on the way in which the body manages oxytocin are related to the effects (discussed above) of early attachment experiences on the HPA axis and cortisol system. Cortisol is a hormone of stress and fear. Oxytocin is a hormone of attachment and alliance. Stress and fear activate attachment systems. One of the ways in which cortisol helps us to cope with stress is by increasing our production of oxytocin, thereby helping to activate our attachment system and prompting us to look for help from an attachment figure. When we are under stress or afraid, we seek allies and attachment figures (think of the frightened toddler running for his mother's arms). The activation of the attachment system, if it leads to a sensitive and helpful response from our attachment figure or ally, leads to a reduction in stress and fear and so to a reduction in cortisol. Thus, oxytocin in the context of a secure attachment reduces stress and cortisol and assists soothing and affect regulation (Onaka, Takayanagi, & Yoshida, 2012). However, children with early experiences of insecure attachment are likely to have a compromised HPA axis and cortisol system. Because the regulation of cortisol is linked to the regulation of oxytocin, the role of oxytocin in activating attachment behaviors and thereby reciprocally regulating cortisol is also disrupted (Dabrowska et al., 2011). Furthermore, as is the case with the intergenerational transmission of an impaired HPA axis, the dysregulation of oxytocin is transmitted through insensitive maternal caregiving from one generation of insecurely attached children to the next (Champagne, 2008; Champagne & Curley, 2009; Pedersen & Boccia, 2002; Rilling, 2009; Strathearn, Fonagy, Amico, & Montague, 2009; Weaver et al., 2004). Essential attachment behaviors involving sex, reproduction, maternal care, trust, affect regulation, and the formation of romantic attachments and alliances with others are compromised and impaired over succeeding generations.

Among our most profound experiences are those involving sex, love, nurturance, the birth of our children, physical contact and comfort, trust and a durable personal commitment to specific people. Oxytocin is a key hormone in the mediation of these experiences. It is central to the biochemistry of attachment, and its influence extends beyond reproductive relationships to include all social alliances and close relationships. Oxytocin's operations and characteristic patterns in the body and brain are shaped by our earliest attachment experiences and are transmitted via the characteristics of maternal care from one generation of children to the next.

4

ATTACHMENT

This chapter describes attachment theory and attachment behavior in detail, including the attachment, caregiving, and exploratory behavioral systems; the basic components of an attachment relationship—proximity, safe haven, secure base, and separation distress; and the fundamental attachment styles—secure, avoidant, anxious, and disorganized. The chapter clarifies the important idea of proximity in attachment theory and describes the key concepts of the trusted companion and internal working models of self and other. The existence and influence of multiple attachment relationships are described. An extended clinical case is included.

http://dx.doi.org/10.1037/14185-004
Attachment-Based Psychotherapy: Helping Patients Develop Adaptive Capacities, by Peter C. Costello
Copyright © 2013 by the American Psychological Association. All rights reserved.

THE ATTACHMENT, CAREGIVING, AND EXPLORATORY BEHAVIORAL SYSTEMS

A *behavioral system* is a neurophysiologically based set of physical and psychological states and behaviors that is automatically activated and that "runs" when the right stimuli are present in the environment. It is an evolved biological system whose operation increases the organism's likelihood of transmitting its genes to the next generation. Usually, it is important in helping the organism to survive, to compete for resources, or to reproduce. The attachment, caregiving, and exploratory behavior systems are interrelated and develop early in life. The experiences we each have with our early attachments will shape the ways in which we communicate with others and how we manage our emotional life. They will also determine the fundamental level of security and safety we feel in the world, and this will influence how confidently we approach the challenges of learning and work.

The Attachment Behavioral System

Bowlby described attachment behavior as resulting from an evolved and deeply embedded behavioral system with powerful motivational characteristics for human beings. Bowlby (1969/1982) proposed that in the "environment of evolutionary adaptedness" (Chapter 4, p. 50 ff.) in which humans evolved—during which our genetic ancestors lived in small, cooperative groups of migratory hunter–gatherers—natural selection favored the development of behaviors that maintained proximity and communication between children and their caregivers as a form of protection from predation and coordination against other dangers. At moments of danger and at times of migratory movement, infants and children who sought or were already in close communication or contact with a "stronger and wiser" caregiver would be more likely to survive. The attachment behavioral system modulates and controls proximity-related behaviors and communication between the child and the caregiver, and it relies on the emotional availability and responsiveness of the caregiver to the child's signals, especially signals of fear or distress.

In humans, the activation of the attachment behavioral system initiates changes in emotions, hormones, brain activity, the cardiovascular system, metabolism, cognition, perception, and memory, as well as changes in behavior and communication. It gives rise to a strong feeling of being motivated and of wanting to do something: to establish contact and communicate with someone to whom we have bonded and who is stronger and wiser—at least for the moment—than we are.

Bowlby (1969/1982) thought that the role of attachment as a motivational force was the main difference between his work and traditional psychoanalytic theorizing. For human beings, the impelling motivation to create and maintain an attachment overrides almost all of our other concerns and motivations. The fear of death is soothed by the presence of attachment figures, and one of the most reliable comforts we find in our last hours is the presence of those who love us. The primacy of attachment motivations means that we will give up almost anything else—especially when we are children—in order to maintain a primary attachment relationship. We are willing to bend and shape ourself to fit the requirements of the person to whom we are becoming attached. Children will endure abuse in order to stay as close as possible to their attachment figure, however imperfect this closeness may be. Attachment relationships constitute the powerful, intimate core of the sociality that is a defining characteristic of human nature. They form the foundation for all of our other efforts at relatedness and communication. Attachment begins to operate in rudimentary form even before we are born, and it continues to operate robustly and with powerful effect throughout our life until the day we die.

Attachment motivations are innate and biologically based. They are encoded in us through the operations of natural selection in the course of the evolution of our species. In its narrowest meaning, *attachment theory* says that natural selection has favored the development of behaviors that would maintain proximity between children and their special caregivers at moments of danger, and this seeking of a particular other in moments of distress and fear is the basis for our bonds of affection and loyalty to those who are most important in our life. In the so-called environment of evolutionary adaptedness in which we evolved—during which our genetic ancestors are thought to have lived in small, cooperative migratory groups of hunter–gatherers—infants and children who sought proximity to their "stronger and wiser" caregiver were more likely to survive the dangers of predation, the disruptions of migratory movement, and the assaults from others. Children who ran to their mothers when danger threatened carried genetic predispositions that inclined them to do so. These predispositions were differentially preserved via natural selection (because these young ones were more likely to live) and thus became more and more characteristic of our evolving human ancestors. This, in its most basic form, is our *attachment behavioral system*.

There is also a broader meaning of attachment behavior, which is certainly the conception that Bowlby intended, and it is the sense adopted here. In this broader meaning (Bartholomew & Shaver, 1998; Pederson & Moran, 1999), attachment theory suggests that mothers and infants are strongly motivated to form an intense and stable relationship with each other, that more than mere physical proximity they seek to maintain emotional availability, and that they do this in moments of distress but also whenever they need the help of a "trusted companion." Ethologists, who study the behavior of different species of animals, make a sharp distinction between the use of proximity simply for protection from predators, as occurs in the schooling of fish or the herd formations of animals, and the use of proximity as a means of making possible communication, parental caregiving, and social cooperation, as is the case for species in which parental care and social cooperation are prominent. Humans are preeminent in this regard, and it is this broader function of proximity and attachment that is intended by Bowlby's theory.

In part, the attachment relationship exists for the protective reasons just noted, and attachment motivations will always be very active when the child is scared or in distress. But the attachment relationship is also there because the biologically underdeveloped child needs an intense relationship with his mother to foster his development and to neurologically complete him. This is an even more important outcome of a close relationship with a specific individual than is protection from predators. The attachment relationship of the child with his mother develops the child's innate capacity for social relationships in a way that fits him within the social group into which he was born (e.g., in terms of language and social mores). This joins the child to his culture, which is itself a critical adaptation for human beings, and makes his social group a part of him.

In general, the close relationship with the mother nurtures, protects, and fosters the child in a wide variety of ways, as all mothers know. All of these ways require the mother's interest in and responsiveness to her child and the child's close attachment to his mother. The stability and responsiveness of this relationship are the basis for its protective function. They are the reasons the child expects protection from the particular other who is his attachment figure.

This broader conception of attachment, with its emphasis on general responsiveness as well as protection and its implications for learning and exploration, points directly to the two other behavioral systems that are closely interwoven with attachment: the *caregiving behavioral system* and the *exploratory behavioral system*.

The Caregiving Behavioral System

The caregiving behavioral system is the part of the caregiver or attachment figure that understands and responds to the goals and needs of the person who is attached. Bowlby thought that the process of caregiving should be conceptualized as separate from attachment itself, though the two are closely interlinked and complementary. The caregiving behavioral system includes the ability of a caretaker to understand what the other person is feeling and to intercede in a way by which the other person feels helped. Thus, it includes our abilities for emotional and communicational competence, our capacity for empathy, and our abilities to be effective in dealing with real problems in the world.

Our caregiving behavioral system is shaped by the attachment experiences that we have had when others were taking care of us. In a direct way, our caregiving responses to others are the reciprocal of the attachment experiences we had with our own caregivers. We respond to the attachment behaviors of others as our own were responded to, and, unfortunately, we do this even if we know that our own early attachment relationships were flawed in significant ways. Without intervention or events that produce a process of personal change, we care for others as we were cared for. In this way, by a chain of repeated reciprocals of attachment and caregiving, attachment styles are transmitted from one generation to the next.

The Exploratory Behavioral System

Ainsworth (1964, 1979) recognized the close relationship between attachment and learning and emphasized the exploratory behavioral system. The exploratory behavioral system is the part of the child that wants to explore his environment and to learn how to be an effective agent acting on the world around him. Exploration can really take place only when the child is not afraid. The exploratory behavioral system is intertwined with attachment because exploration and learning take place most exuberantly and competently when the child knows that his attachment figure will be there if he needs her and when the attachment figure actively supports the exploration. There is a sense in which a securely attached child has his most powerful allies with him—or within him—at all times. The knowledge that his attachment figure is a secure base to which he can reliably retreat makes it possible for the child to feel free to explore and to engage and face down some of the inevitable anxieties of exploration, learning, and taking action with respect to the world. In a child, the exploratory system is active when the child is curious, engaged, and actively seeking mastery; in an adult, the exploratory system is active in confident approaches to work and achievement and the opening of new opportunities. For those who are securely attached, these explorations and engagements can be made confidently and with unfettered interest.

Thus, our experiences of love, need, and fear and our ability to act effectively in the world are closely interrelated. Where we experience love, our fears are reduced and made more manageable and our natural competencies are able to express themselves in action.

THE MOTIVATIONAL PRIMACY OF ATTACHMENT

As a biologically embedded, naturally selected behavioral system, attachment behavior is primary in terms of motivation: It derives from nothing deeper, requiring no other motivation than itself, and the motives that are attached to it arise out of the very biological stuff of which we are made. It was designed into us by natural selection, and it is characteristic of our species in the same way and for the same Darwinian reasons as the adaptations of other animals. Bowlby (1969/1982) considered the motivational primacy of attachment behavior to be a crucial aspect of his theoretical position. In considering the many differences between his own approach and that of Freud, Bowlby thought that the critical difference concerned the role of attachment motivation in human psychology. The impelling, motivational primacy of the need and desire for attachment to a particular individual—with all of the specific patterns of affective communication and relating that characterize the particular other—is a foundational principle of attachment theory.

The motivational force of the attachment behavioral system, especially during the first years of development, is such that it has the capacity to shape other behaviors and systems that develop in the infant and child and that remain active and influential throughout adult life. Attachment experiences shape the way we form relationships, how we regulate and express emotions, how we communicate and interact with others, and how we explore and learn about the world. It is not enough to understand the effects of early attachment experiences only in terms of attachment style itself—for example, whether we are primarily secure, anxious, avoidant, or disorganized in our attachments. It is also necessary to understand how our attachment experiences and attachment styles influence the ways in which we regulate affect, communicate or don't communicate with others, think and feel about ourself and others, and explore and learn in the world. The effects of early attachment experiences are broad, and these effects last throughout our life.

Although Bowlby originally described the role of physical proximity for attachment motivations, he came to underscore that the process of communication was itself a key form of proximity (thus we talk about "getting in touch" or "making contact" or "feeling a connection" with others). He also came to focus on a particular kind of communication as the main process by which a secure attachment is established—communication that is characterized by openness, sensitivity, and responsiveness. To be communicatively coordinated with someone who was capable of taking care of us and of helping us in the way that we needed to be taken care of and helped was for Bowlby the essence of the experience that formed a secure attachment. Emotional availability was the key. Mere physical proximity was not enough: It is possible for a child or an adult to be standing right next to an attachment figure who engenders only insecurity and fear. And it is possible for us to be with others, even very familiar others, and to feel only loneliness.

The attachment behavioral system is the basis for the formation of all important affectional relationships in our life. It remains active, as Bowlby put it, "from the cradle to the grave." Attachment motivations are so important because of the central role that close relationships and alliances in general play in human life. Our alliances and our communication are central to what we are as a species. It is what we are designed to do better than any other species. Attachment theory speaks to the essence of what is most evolved and most human about us—the importance of relationships and communication in our lives.

THE CENTRALITY OF FEAR AND ANXIETY

The attachment figure is a source of security. Attachment motivations are especially powerful when they operate at the intersection of our feelings of fear and anxiety and our ability to feel connected to someone. This has important implications for our ability to act competently in the world, because attachment security also confers courage in the face of challenge. The nexus of love, competence, and fear is central to attachment theory.

Fear and anxiety are imperial, peremptory emotions. They are the psychological equivalent of a burn, signaling us that something is intensely dangerous. As the emotional equivalent of physical pain, they interrupt and displace all other feelings and activities; they drive all other thoughts and concerns out of our mind.

There is good reason for this. In the hardheaded calculations of natural selection, there is always more survival advantage in responding immediately to a danger than there is in doing anything else; the predator about to strike or the fall we are about to take must be attended to before anything else can be done. We can no more ignore our fear and anxiety than we can make ourself keep our hand on a hot stove.

So, fear and anxiety displace all other concerns, except one. When we are afraid, nothing else matters—except whom we are close to. This is true in even the most frightening and disorienting of circumstances, even at the ultimate moments of life. On the morning of September 11, 2001, people who had gone to work in the World Trade Center suddenly and without warning found their world turned to heat and flames as the once-solid building shook to pieces around them. We know they were terrified, and we know that many of them knew they were going to die. Time and again, their last act was to reach out to their closest life companion, by phone, by voicemail, by e-mail, by taking a picture from their wallet or desk. This is the operation of the attachment behavioral system. (The operations of the caregiving and exploratory behavioral systems can also be seen on that day: Hundreds of rescue workers ran toward those who were endangered, many of them climbing 50 stories of stairs before the building collapsed; families, intimate partners, and friends tried frantically to get in contact with those in the buildings, and they looked desperately in the days that followed for those who had not returned; this is the operation of the caregiving and attachment behavioral systems. No one continued with the ordinary work of the day or could think about anything else, and schools and businesses suspended activity; this is the suspension of the exploratory behavioral system.)

The same interaction of fear in relation to the closeness of a beloved other operates in less drastic circumstances; for example, with a baby in arms or a child with his mother in a shopping mall. The fundamental motivating properties of the attachment behavioral system are the same both in infants and in adults. When we are afraid, we feel an intense and compelling motivation to seek out the person with whom we have the strongest bonds of intimacy and whom we believe would want and would act to protect us. When our fear is great, we seek out and cling to that person, just as a frightened child does to his mother. We simply want that person.

The centrality of fear and anxiety and the motivational importance of maintaining the availability of the attachment figure are two of the most important ideas in attachment theory. The impelling, motivational primacy of the need and desire for attachment to a particular individual—with all of the specific developmental and lifelong effects that flow from learning how to communicate with and relate to that particular individual—is a fundamental principle in the construction of an attachment-based psychotherapy. These efforts to maintain availability are powerful enough to shape our nervous system, our emotional life, and the ways in which we each communicate with others. Together, these create our future relationships and the ways in which we work in the world.

THE COMPONENTS OF ATTACHMENT

It was noted above that one of Bowlby's most evocative terms for a secure attachment was to describe it as the experience of having a *trusted companion* (Bowlby, 1973). He described this experience in terms of the presence of four components of an attachment relationship: *proximity maintenance*, *separation distress*, a *secure base*, and a *safe haven* (Bowlby, 1969/1982). Although these are described below as they occur between a mother and her child, they are also present and essential whether one is describing the formation of the first attachment relationship with the mother or thinking about an attachment within an adult romantic relationship.

The character and quality of a particular attachment relationship depend on the way in which each of these components exists and operates within that relationship. When these processes are operating in a strongly positive way, they create the experience of felt security that is a hallmark of secure attachment (Sroufe & Waters, 1977). When they are operating suboptimally, they define the experiences of insecure (anxious, avoidant, or disorganized) attachment. These components are key interpersonal and intrapersonal processes that are activated and addressed in an effective attachment-based psychotherapy.

Separation distress is a central concept in attachment theory. It was the observation by Bowlby (1940, 1944a, 1944b) and others of the distress and difficulties of children who were separated from their caregivers—for example, in the wartime evacuations of children from London (A. Freud & Burlingham, 1942) or by the hospitalization of children in an era that sharply limited the access of parents to the sick child (Bowlby & Robertson, 1956; Bowlby, Robertson, & Rosenbluth, 1952; Robertson, 1953)—that led to the development of attachment theory itself.

Separation from our attachment figure when we do not wish to be separated, especially when we are frightened or anxious, is an intrinsically aversive physiological and psychological event (Hofer, 2008; Hofer & Sullivan, 2008; Winberg, 2005). It results in a form of anxiety that seeks to avoid the loss of the other and that therefore impels activity that might prevent her loss, including the activity of suppressing our own feelings, thoughts, and communications if these are what we feel threaten to take away our attachment figure. Bowlby observed that separation distress, if extended in time, led to a regular sequence of reactions to the threatened and continuing loss (Bowlby, 1960a, 1960b, 1960c; Bowlby et al., 1952). Our initial response to an unwanted separation is to *protest*—a communication to the attachment figure, like a baby crying, that she is wanted urgently. If our protest is unsuccessful in bringing the return of the attachment figure, protest is followed by what Bowlby called the stage of *despair*, which looks like depression and is an intensely felt state of feeling that we are not going to get what we deeply need, no matter what we do. If the absence of the attachment figure is prolonged still further, we enter the stage of *detachment*, in which we appear to have returned to normal and not to be troubled or to care about the absence of our attachment figure; we may even appear uninterested if she does return. But this is only because we have suppressed and deactivated our attachment longings in a way that separates us from our most important other. This is not a return to normal but rather a profound form of disengagement.

Separation distress does not only occur in children. It is what an adult feels at a separation from or the loss of a romantic partner (e.g., Fraley & Shaver, 1998). Separation distress is also the sharp pang of anxiety that we may feel when we think we have done or said or felt something that is causing our attachment figure to withdraw. The potential for the experience of separation distress is a defining characteristic of an attachment relationship.

Proximity maintenance means that the child seeks to maintain emotional access to and coordination with the attachment figure, so that the attachment figure will be helpfully responsive to the child. It is what the child does to avoid separation distress. Although the word *proximity* suggests physical nearness, Bowlby (1973) made clear that what he meant was emotional availability and responsiveness. Proximity in Bowlby's meaning includes the availability of truthful, accurate communication with the attachment figure and the assurance that the attachment figure will understand and will respond in a sensitive way. A good way to think of proximity in Bowlby's sense is to think of it in terms of feeling in contact with someone about what is most important to you. The contact may include physical nearness, like a toddler running to his mother and clutching her leg, but it also includes the experience of talking to someone if we feel that we can talk openly and accurately about what is most on our mind and that the other person will understand and be responsive. What the contact must include is emotional communication about important experiences that are understood and responded to by the attachment figure. Proximity maintenance, understood in this sense, is the key characteristic of a secure attachment relationship (Ainsworth Blehar, Waters, & Wall, 1978; Behrens, Parker, & Haltigan, 2011; Dykas & Cassidy, 2011).

Open emotional communication is not always easy or accepted within a relationship, and most relationships include at least some communications that are suppressed or excluded. Bowlby emphasized that children learn what will keep their attachment figures emotionally available and responsive and what will drive them away. In other words, children learn what they can communicate and what they must avoid communicating. Depending on the psychology of the attachment figure, a child may be more or less constrained in terms of what he can bring into the relationship without driving the mother away or making her less understanding and less communicatively responsive. His communication may be more or less candid, extensive, and accurate. The more open the relationship with the attachment figure is to the child's real emotional experience, the more secure the child will feel within the relationship (Dykas & Cassidy, 2011). The degree to which the emotional communication between the child and the mother is open and truthful—the extent to which the relationship allows communicative, emotional, and physical proximity—determines how well the other components of attachment will operate.

The attachment function of *safe haven* means that when the child is distressed or frightened he can retreat to the caregiver as a haven of safety and that he experiences a sense of protection and security when he does so. Whether a child (or an adult) experiences his attachment figure as a secure safe haven depends on how the attachment figure responds to the request for haven. If the mother, for example, is annoyed or dismissive of the child's distress or fear, as avoidance-engendering mothers often are, the child is likely to learn to suppress his need for protection and his feelings of distress and not seek the active protection of the attachment figure, because seeking that protection makes him feel worse. If the mother is distracted or is inaccurate in perceiving or understanding the child's distress, perhaps because she is preoccupied with her own pressing needs and emotions, as anxious mothers often are, the child may amplify his distress and need for a response to try to overcome his caregiver's inattention. His emotional reactivity increases, and his focus may shift from his own concerns to the problem of getting his attachment figure's attention. If the mother is frightened by the child's distress or seems too helpless or fragile to protect the child, as mothers who engender disorganized attachment often are, the child may become more frightened by the very contact that he is seeking. He may become unsure about whether to move toward or away from her. He may seek to take care of his mother, to reassure her, and to control her emotional responses as a way of making her more able to take care of him. The emotional and cognitive load of these tasks and the unalleviated fear and uncertainty that he feels may overwhelm him and make it difficult for him to function at all.

But if the mother sees and understands what the child is communicating to her about his distress, if she conveys her understanding in such a way that the child feels understood and feels that his distress is seen and is important, and if she acts emphatically to address and to relieve the distress, the child feels comforted and reassured and secure. His emotional distress and reactivity diminish. He has reached a safe haven.

The *secure-base* component of attachment is reciprocal to the safe haven component, and each depends on the other: A caretaker can be a secure base because the child has experienced that she will be a safe haven, and it is the presence of the secure base that allows the autonomy and exploration that may make a safe haven necessary. A secure base means that the child has a sense of the attachment figure as reliably available, responsive, and capable, so that the child feels free and safe in exploring and learning about the world. He can depart from her a bit and move out into the world. He can leave anxiety behind in the pursuit of his own interests and experience, because he knows his attachment figure is there if he needs her and that he needn't worry about her own internal state or readiness to help. She's got him covered. He feels safe even while he is taking some chances and being guided by his curiosity and other self-actualizing motivations. In the relational context of the security-engendering attachment figure, he can turn his mind to the activities at hand. It is not that fear and distress become impossibilities or are artificially, defensively denied. But the child does not need to be constrained by hypervigilance, to worry about where his attachment figure is, or to be ready to handle his fears on his own. In an optimal relationship, he feels and knows without thinking about it that if he becomes distressed or afraid, his attachment figure will be there to help him. This unconscious sense of safety—forgetting to be afraid—is an enormously valuable internal state.

THE BASIC ATTACHMENT STATES OF SECURITY, AVOIDANCE, ANXIETY, AND DISORGANIZATION

When we are young, our need for nurturance is so great and our mind is so malleable that our experiences with our attachment figures set in us a basic level of anxiety or security about whether caretaking and protection will be available to us when needed. One of the ways in which our attachment experiences become a permanent part of who we are is through the cultivation in each of us of individual variations of the basic attachment states of security, avoidance, anxiety, and disorganization. Although researchers often categorize individuals as falling predominantly into one of these states, for clinical purposes it is more useful to think of these as tendencies that are primed and evoked by different circumstances, by different emotions, and within different relationships. It is probably useful to think of them as potential vulnerabilities or strengths that we all have in varying degree. So, one can be more secure in one relationship and more avoidant or anxious or even disorganized in another—one way with mother and another with father, and even a third with grandmother. Similarly, different types of situations may evoke or induce different basic states. For example, situations requiring autonomy, separation, or anger may evoke states of disorganization, but situations involving cooperation and following may not.

These basic attachment states are considered in detail later, but for now I will say the following:

- *Secure attachment.* To the extent that we are secure, we trust that others will be available to us and will respond when we need them; we trust that we can communicate openly to these others and that they will remain connected to us while we do so. Although we know our own mind, we also enjoy closeness with others; we do not fear their abandoning us, either because we are different or because they are neglectful. We expect that relatedness and open communication will generally lead to a good result. We feel and think that we are good and that others are generally trustworthy and valuable as relational partners. We can be a good relational partner—attentive, able to really listen to the other person, and reliably helpful. Relationships are important to us, and we invest in them. We can also exercise our own autonomy and concentrate on our own goals and purposes. We are capable of anger and jealousy but also of gratitude, love, and forgiveness.

- *Anxious attachment.* To the extent that we are anxious about attachment, we are uncertain that others will be available when we need them. Our experience is of inconsistency of attunement and often of intrusiveness: The others might respond or might not. When they do respond, it may be difficult to hold their attention, or their response may have much more to do with their own needs than with our own. We fear their absence or their misattunement when they are wanted, and we also fear that when we get a response from them that it will not match what we need and will therefore not be helpful. We are always worried about whether the others will be there in the way we need them or whether they will abandon or reject us just when we need them most. We may often be angry at our attachment figures, but we also may seem to be excessively clingy and constantly pursuing or chasing them. We may struggle with unreasonable jealousies and fear that our partners will be drawn to others because we are not good enough for them. We may offer forgiveness because we fear losing the other if we do not, and being offended against will make us feel badly about ourself; we may offer gratitude but in part to seek reassurance from the other. We tend to see ourself as deficient and to see others as better and more valuable, possessing qualities and resources that we do not have. Relationships are very important to us, but we spend much time within them struggling to get our own needs met. We are often disappointed in our relationships and feel that they have not met our needs.

- *Avoidant attachment.* To the extent that we are avoidant, our early experience led us to expect the other not to respond to us or perhaps to respond to us with annoyance and anger, dismissiveness, or increased distance. So, we seek not to need others by suppressing and managing our feelings on our own and by dismissing the significance or helpfulness of relationships in general. In our experience, expressing a need to others drives them away. So, we tend to avoid closeness with others. Closeness does not seem particularly important to us; it makes us uncomfortable, and we may carve out a life where we can be on our own a lot of the time. If the anxious state brings with it a fear of the other's absence, the avoidant state brings with it a fear of our own feelings. We don't think there is much of significance in feelings. We don't have much expectation of others helping us when we are upset, and therefore we try to avoid focusing on feelings as a means of calming ourself. We often don't think highly of others—we see them as needy or defective, selfish or incompetent. We think we are better off on our own, and we often think we have the qualities that make us strong enough to be on our own. We don't feel especially grateful to others, nor are we especially inclined to forgive them. We don't invest much in our relationships, and we are only weakly committed to them.

- *Disorganized attachment.* To the extent that we suffer with disorganized attachment, we anticipate that the other to whom we would like to turn may create in us feelings of fear and of confusion. Our attachment figure may actually threaten us, or she (or he) may be herself so fearful and fragile that she can provide us with no sense of safety. We may feel that our demands or approach to her will frighten or damage her further. Instead of feeling helped, we find this other to be a source of increased fear within ourself. The longed-for other is there, but she increases our anxiety and distress, and we do not know whether to turn toward the other or to turn away. So we may fluctuate between urgently pursuing our attachment figure (in a way that looks like anxious attachment) and avoiding and distancing ourself from the attachment figure (in a way that looks like avoidant attachment). We may even reverse roles and try to take care of her. We experience both anxiety about the absence of our partners and discomfort in their presence. We feel confused and very uncertain about how to proceed with others, unable to communicate clearly or to establish a calm relationship with them. We sometimes feel confused and anxious, experiencing a kind of psychic vertigo that makes us simply want to retreat.

These basic attachment states are the sense of the world, ourself, and other people that hums in the background of our mind. Even while we sleep, these attachment states are influencing our sleep and dreams and the state of our body, through their effects on the levels of stress and affiliation hormones and through the distribution in our body of receptors for these hormones. Because these basic states reflect our general degree of trust or anxiety about the availability and helpful responsiveness of others, our individual tendencies toward one or another of these states—and especially the circumstances and relationships that tend to evoke them in us—directly and strongly influence our most important relationships. These basic states also influence the way in which we approach and explore the world, for example through our freedom or inhibition with regard to work and productive activity.

One useful way to think about how these basic attachment states are constituted is to think of them as based on different levels or intensities of two dimensions: *avoidance*, or the tendency to avoid closeness, to suppress feelings, and to minimize our own needs and the needs of others; and *anxiety*, or the tendency to be anxious about whether our needs and feelings will be recognized and responded to and about whether others want to be with us as much as we want to be with them (Griffin & Bartholomew, 1994; Ravitz, Maunder, Hunter, Sthankiya, & Lancee, 2010). Some people are high in avoidance and relatively low in anxiety: They are avoidantly attached. Some are high in anxiety and low in avoidance: They are anxiously attached. To the extent that people are high in both avoidance and anxiety, their attachment is *disorganized*: Such individuals want both to avoid and to seek after others, to suppress and to accentuate their feelings and needs. These impulses are contradictory, and thus such individuals have not been able to work out a coherent way of handling their feelings or of relating to others. To the extent that individuals are low both in avoidance and in anxiety, they are securely attached.

MULTIPLE ATTACHMENT FIGURES AND MULTIPLE DOMAINS OF INFLUENCE

Attachment theory generally takes one individual to be our primary attachment figure within any developmental stage or life situation, a quality that Bowlby referred to as *monotropy* (Bowlby, 1958) and a position that he and Ainsworth both maintained (Ainsworth, 1979; Bowlby, 1969/1982). For example, Bowlby pointed out that even in a situation like primary school or during a hospitalization, a child who needs reassurance will seek out one particular teacher or nurse for a special relationship, thus showing the tendency of the attachment behavioral system to look for a specific individual with whom to form a primary attachment. One way to experience this quality of monotropy in your own life is to ask yourself whom you would call first if you were in a serious traffic accident or suddenly became ill: That person is likely to be your primary attachment figure. However, there has also always been recognition that there are secondary or subsidiary attachment figures in each person's life—for example, fathers, grandparents, siblings, nannies, friends—and that these secondary figures may be extremely important developmentally or in present life circumstances. Indeed, one of the major developmental processes that generally occurs in adolescence and young adulthood is the shift of the primary attachment relationship from a parent to a romantic partner; individuals who cannot do this are constrained in their adult relationships. Most people will have multiple attachment figures in their lives. We might therefore think of all attachment relationships as having a level of importance, either developmentally, during the periods of transition and growth that have formed us, or presently, in the current life circumstances that continue to affect and shape us. One relationship is likely to be primary, but the others are influential and significant (Bretherton, 1985, 2010; Fraley, Heffernan, Vicary, & Brumbaugh, 2011; K. Grossmann, Grossmann, Kindler, & Zimmermann, 2008; Howes & Spieker, 2008).

These different attachment relationships may specialize in different emotions, domains of activity, or aspects of the self. It is possible for aspects of the self to be sectioned off among different attachment figures or, alternatively, for there to be a great deal of consistency and integration among multiple figures (Fraley et al., 2011). Therefore, in understanding any one individual's attachment characteristics and history, it is important to recognize the role of specific secondary attachment figures and the domains in which they may be important. For example, there is some evidence that although mothers are usually primary and especially important for feelings of closeness and comfort when frightened, fathers may be especially significant as attachment figures for exploration, play, and friendly affiliation. The same may be true for adults, who may be able to fully express and comfortably experience specific aspects of themselves—closeness or sexuality or exploration in the world—in some attachment relationships rather than in others. In both individual and couples therapy, addressing such restrictions in communication and mutual experience may be an important part of clinical change.

It is also possible that patterns of multiple attachments from early in life—including a pattern of having or emphasizing multiple attachments—may repeat themselves in the present. For a good and bravely told personal example by a leading attachment researcher of a pattern repeated from early childhood of "a lingering tendency to get involved with one woman while keeping another in the wings," see Goodman (2006, p. 7). One of the qualities of resilience that may make interpersonally skilled children better able to survive a less-than-optimal primary caregiver is the ability of these children to find and make good use of secondary attachment figures. Many children discover that they can have some types of important emotional experiences with one parent rather than with the other. Other children may find people outside of the immediate family setting—a grandparent, a regular babysitter, or the mother of a childhood friend—with whom to develop a secondary attachment that may be extremely important in preserving aspects of the self and of security, albeit in a somewhat split-off form, from constrictions in the primary relationships. Patterns of having such "second mothers," as one patient described them to me, may persist in adulthood and may be an important focus for clinical attention.

INTERNAL WORKING MODELS OF SELF
AND OTHER IN RELATIONSHIP

In addition to cultivating a sense of basic security, avoidance, or anxiety with regard to relationships, our attachment experiences create within each of us a set of basic templates of how relationships work—an internal working model of self and other in relationship. How many of these exist in an important way for each of us depends on the variability, consistency, and integration of our attachment history and our current relationships. Internal working models include aspects of the basic attachment states outlined above, but they also include more detailed expectations about what happens in relationships. These expectations are based on our past experiences with our attachment figures, and they are written in the neurophysiology of our body. Internal working models are a kind of guidance system that tells us what to do and what to expect when we are with another person. They are scripts for social interaction. They include a sense of what we are like, what other people are like, and what is most likely to happen in the interaction between us and the other person. They include the "lines" or the communications that each of us is likely to speak in the course of the interaction. They have a specificity that exceeds the basic attachment states, because internal working models include lots of details, such as what attributes we believe ourself to possess, what attributes we believe are present in others, and what is likely to happen in the relationship between ourself and others. For example, am I a valuable person? What do others value in me? What do they not value or even actively dislike? What about me puts others off? What attracts them? What do I do that leads others to come closer to me or to move farther away? Are others resilient and flexible? Or are they fragile and prone to sadness or anger? Are they safe and helpful or uncaring and unreliable?

Internal working models also include the recognition of different types of relationships or categories of interactive situations. There are, for example, situations in which we seek the help of others, situations in which we are competing with others, and situations in which we give help to others. There are relationships characterized by enmity, friendship, or indifference. These categories of relationships or settings in which we interact with others in a particular way are also part of what has been internalized through our attachment experiences. When we encounter these settings and relationships as adults, our expectations and relational behaviors are shaped by our internal models.

Moreover, internal working models also incorporate the codes, signals, and rules that we use for communicating with and interpreting others. On the basis of our formative experiences with our attachment figures, we become adept at reading certain states in the other and in communicating certain aspects of ourself. Thus, our internal working models include the signals we are skilled in sending to others and the messages we are skilled at receiving from them. For example, we may become particularly good at noticing signs of anger, fear, or sadness. We also become skilled in performing behaviors that have been useful or necessary parts of our attachment relationships and of the interactive situations that we have come to recognize and understand in a specific way. These behaviors become automatic, unthinking responses to particular types of situations. Thus, in addition to including specific cognitions, attitudes, and beliefs about self and other, internal working models shape our ability to perceive, communicate, and behave. Someone with an often-angry father may become adept at noticing the smallest signs of anger in another; someone with a depressed mother may be highly attuned to sadness but miss seeing expressions of happiness or warmth.

Thus, through our attachment experiences, via our internal working models, we each acquire a social or relational self that is skilled and specialized in particular and well-practiced ways and that has specific kinds of interpersonal expectations and expertise. This self includes our basic levels of attachment security, and it becomes who we are with other people, and our internal working models guide us in our interactions with them.

And, like any actor with a script, we look for others who also know how to play their parts, who fit their role in the script and who know what lines to play back to us. We look for and find others who fit our own internal working models. To the extent that the attachment figures who were engaged with us during the formation of our internal working models were problematic (e.g., were unresponsive or frequently distracted), the people whom we find to play the role of others in our adult relationships, including our most important adult relationships, are likely to be problematic in the same way.

5

COMMUNICATION

This chapter describes the key role of communication in attachment relationships and in the creation of psychopathology. Communication is how we each experience the presence of the other. In attachment relationships, the goal of the child is to achieve a particular kind of communication—a *coordinated state*—that enables the child to feel securely connected to the mother. The way in which a mother responds to her child's signals determines the attachment style that the child will learn to have.

FROM PROXIMITY TO COMMUNICATION

Bowlby originally described proximity (meaning physical proximity) to the attachment figure as the primary, biologically driven motivation (i.e., set-goal) of the human attachment behavioral system. Like the baby

http://dx.doi.org/10.1037/14185-005
Attachment-Based Psychotherapy: Helping Patients Develop Adaptive Capacities, by Peter C. Costello
Copyright © 2013 by the American Psychological Association. All rights reserved.

geese in Lorenz's experiment (see Chapter 2, this volume), human infants and children sought to be close to their mother, especially at moments of alarm, in order to protect themselves from malign forces in their environment. But it quickly became clear that proximity seeking was too limited a concept to explain what the human infant sought from his or her attachment figure, and the conception of the set-goal of human attachment began to shift. The limitations of proximity as the set-goal of attachment were addressed by shifting from a concept of physical proximity (Bowlby, 1969/1982) to one of communicational proximity (Bowlby, 1973). Physical nearness was seen to give way to communicational access, physical contact to the exchange of signals. In other words, proximity was progressively replaced by communication in understandings of how the attachment system operated. This changed in an important way the conception of the underlying purpose of the attachment behavioral system and in fact enlarged its purpose considerably.

The quality and characteristics of the communication between mother and infant now became crucial, and in the second volume of his attachment trilogy, Bowlby (1973) augmented his understanding of attachment processes in two critical ways. First, he shifted from the description of proximity as the set-goal of attachment behavior to an emphasis on the experience of emotional availability and responsiveness from attachment figures. Second, he emphasized the role of the internalization and psychic structuralization of actual attachment experiences via the internal working models that played a critical role in making appraisals of self and other and that became a permanent part of the self.

Emotional availability and responsiveness is a very different set-goal than mere proximity, and a very different set of behaviors and processes is required in order to accomplish it. The change is less in emphasis than it is in meaning. The significance of this change marks a critical transition in attachment theory (Bretherton, 1992; Kobak, 1999; Kobak & Madsen, 2008).

Proximity requires motor behaviors, either for following or for clinging, and perceptual modalities, primarily for locating and tracking the attachment figure to whom proximity is sought. It does not involve communication except for the purpose of tracking and maintaining proximity. Availability and responsiveness in the extended sense defined by Bowlby (1973) calls for a set of processes that are about communication that is responsive to the motivations, goals, and emotional state of the individual who is seeking attachment. It requires of the caregiver an understanding of the interiority of the attachment-seeking child, primarily in terms of the child's affective communication about his goals in their interpersonal interaction and in the environment within which the child is operating.

AINSWORTH AND THE CENTRAL IMPORTANCE
OF COMMUNICATION

This conception of specific qualities of communication as the fundamental process that creates a secure or insecure attachment was a key finding of the foundational research by Ainsworth, Blehar, Waters, and Wall (1978) that created the attachment categories of secure, avoidant, and resistant, as we use them today, and founded the profound and vigorous tradition of developmental research within the attachment theory perspective. Ainsworth had started her research working within Bowlby's original (1969) model of proximity as the set-goal of the attachment behavioral system, as a study of the effect of actual physical separation of the child from the mother. But she concluded by placing the development of secure and insecure patterns of attachment firmly in the context of the quality and characteristics of mother–infant communication.

Ainsworth began by studying the reaction of children to an unexpected separation and reunion with their mothers in an unfamiliar setting, the strange situation. The patterns in the children's reactions became the categories of secure, avoidant, and resistant attachment. The interesting question was then how these patterns of attachment in the Strange Situation were related to the interactions of mothers and infants in everyday life.

Ainsworth's research team spent thousands of hours creating detailed observations of interactions between a mother and her infant in ordinary situations at home. In doing this, Ainsworth shifted from an emphasis on proximity and physical separation to an emphasis on the qualities of maternal behavior and communications when mother and child were actually present to each other and interacting. Ainsworth and colleagues studied variables such as the mother's availability to the baby, the promptness and effectiveness of her response to the baby's distress, and the amount of interaction offered to the baby. Their observations emphasized moment-to-moment interactions involving a wide variety of affective communications between mother and infant across a broad range of situations. Ainsworth et al. (1978) summarized their findings as follows:

> The most important aspect of maternal behavior commonly associated with the security-anxiety dimension of infant attachment is manifested in different specific ways in different situations, but in each it emerges as sensitive responsiveness to infant signals and communications. The highly significant differentiation between B [secure] and non-B [anxious] mothers . . . that is provided by a global measure of this variable occurs, we believe, because of the pervasive effect of this quality of maternal behavior throughout many specific kinds of interaction. This and correlated measures of maternal behavior thus do not reflect maternal behavior in

absolute terms, but they do tap the extent to which a particular mother is able to gear her interaction with a particular baby in accordance with the behavioral signals he gives of his states, needs, and, eventually, of his wishes and plans. . . . *The sensitive responsiveness of mothers to infant signals and communications seems to be the key variable in accounting for environmental influences on the development of a secure versus an anxious attachment relationship* [emphasis added]. (p. 152)

In other words, it is the mother's capacity to enter into a coordinated and responsive communication with her child in terms of his needs, intentions, and emotional state that more than any other factor determines the security or insecurity of the child's attachment.

THE MOTHER'S SENSITIVITY TO THE CHILD'S SIGNALS AND COMMUNICATIONS

A mother's sensitivity and appropriate responsiveness to her child's signals and communications is the most important factor in determining the qualities of her child's attachment. Although there are many other factors that shape attachment relationships, nothing matters more than this single element of the child's contact with his mother (Ainsworth et al., 1978; Bakermans-Kranenburg, van IJzendoorn, & Juffer, 2003; De Wolff & van IJzendoorn, 1997; van IJzendoorn & Bakermans-Kranenburg, 2004). The attachment-enhancing mother is able to read her child accurately, and she is also able to read him relatively completely. She is *open to* and *accepting of* (though not necessarily assenting to) whatever her child is communicating to her. She notices and she responds, treating the child's communications as important, valid, and worthy of a response. This does not mean that she gives her infant the scissors he wants to play with or that she lets her child stay home on his first day of school; it does mean that she substitutes for the scissors something else that the infant is likely to be enticed by and that she perceives accurately her older child's anxiety and finds a way to soothe it and to facilitate the task that he must undertake. She notices and responds. She is able to *see* her child and to act in a way that specifically addresses what the child is feeling and communicating. Her ability to perceive her child is unimpaired by her own anxieties and needs. The most common source of the ability to do this is that she herself has been well mothered.

The mother's appropriate response makes manifest and makes felt both her understanding of what the child is communicating and the importance that she attributes to what he wants and to his internal state in general. The fact that she understands and responds appropriately has enormous consequences inside the child. He experiences that his own goals, feelings, and thoughts matter; they matter in the sense that the world has been changed by his communications in a way that entails at least the partial (toy instead of scissors) realization of what he has been striving for. He gets a version of what Winnicott (1971) called a "moment of omnipotence" (p. 38) or what Bandura (1997) might call an experience of self-efficacy and agency—an experience of his inner state influencing or even creating an external reality. Winnicott thought this was the origin of a strengthened spontaneous impulse that made creativity and vitality in living possible: the sense that one can make or change a world.

The child also learns that his inner experience affects a very important other in his interpersonal world; his attachment figure is changed by and responds to what he is experiencing. His interpersonal world is responsive to him. The child discovers that he himself and what he himself wants exist in and influence the mind of his mother, the most important other person in his world. He matters and can affect and influence other people, especially the one who matters most to him. When he feels and expresses something, she reacts. She will respond to him benevolently and helpfully, especially when he is in distress. This is the essential basis of a secure attachment.

No mother (nor anyone else in the child's life) can do this perfectly. Everyone's understanding and responses are imperfect. But some are better than others, and it is this variation in attuned responsiveness, more than any other factor, that produces a variation in the quality of the attachment relationship and the communicational and affective processes that occur within it. Some mothers are relatively calm and centered; they are not preoccupied or distracted or hardened by their own lives. They are emotionally unburdened (at least relatively speaking), and their cognitive and emotional resources are freer to flow naturally into attentive responses to their child or partner. Their own concerns and methods of soothing themselves do not interfere with their ability to see their child and to respond to him.

Ainsworth's research and her conclusion created an emphasis in several decades of attachment research on the role of maternal sensitivity to infant communications (Behrens, Parker, & Haltigan, 2011). The significance of communication between mother and infant in the functioning of the attachment behavioral system has steadily emerged as central in evolving conceptions of the set-goal of attachment behavior and in the understanding of how patterns of communication create patterns of attachment (e.g., Beebe et al., 2010; Beebe & McCrorie, 2010; Bowlby, 1991; Bretherton, 1990a, 1990b; Fonagy, Steele, Steele, Moran, & Higgitt, 1991; Kelly, Slade, & Grienenberger, 2005; Kobak, 1999; Kobak & Madsen, 2008; Lyons-Ruth, 2006; Tronick & Beeghly, 2011).

In the research literature, maternal sensitivity is most predictive of attachment security when it is defined in a way that emphasizes the quality and responsiveness of interactional communications between mother and child (Nievar & Becker, 2008). Communication has also been a focus of intervention programs and protocols aimed at improving the attachment security of children in distressed mother–infant couples. The most effective of these programs target improving the abilities of the mother to read her infant's signals and communications and then to respond in a sensitive way, often using videotape of the mother and child to teach the mother how to interpret and respond to her baby's signals (Bakermans-Kranenburg et al., 2003; Moss et al., 2011).

Even so, some attachment theorists and researchers (Kobak, 1999; Kobak & Madsen, 2008) have suggested that the significance of this conceptual shift from proximity to communication has never been fully incorporated into attachment theory or into attachment-based clinical work with adults and older children:

> Although attachment researchers have made exciting advances in understanding the cognitive and personality processes involved in child and adult attachment, less attention has been given to the formation, maintenance, and repair of attachment bonds across the lifespan. Much of Bowlby's (1973) Separation volume directs attention to the continuing importance of open communication in maintaining a secure attachment bond. Similarly, Mary Ainsworth's seminal study of infant attachment highlights the ongoing quality of mother–infant communication as the context within which working models and attachment strategies initially develop. . . . This focus on communication holds considerable promise for extending attachment research to older children and adults. (Kobak & Madsen, 2008, p. 24)

ATTACHMENT AND DYADIC REGULATION

Sensitive responsiveness has two components. Sensitivity involves the ability to quickly and accurately read what the child is communicating. Responsiveness requires both communication and competent action; it calls for the ability to communicate back to the child in a way that is closely coordinated with what he has expressed and the ability to act competently to address and further the child's goals.

The goals and emotions to which the attachment figure is sensitively responding have a physiological form. They give rise to body states that carry physiological force, and the child feels his goals and emotions as pressures in his body, as pressing and immediate physical imperatives. In fact, this is true whether we are looking at a hungry and uncomfortable infant, a frustrated toddler, an ambitious 10-year-old, an anxious adolescent, or a sad and lonely adult. Their goals and emotions always have a physiological component, and this physiological component is part of what makes the goals and emotions so impelling. They are felt.

In all cases, the state within the individual that requires a response from the attachment figure has a physiological form. The individual's body is doing something that he wants help with. In this sense, what the child (or any of us at any other age) is asking for from the attachment figure is help with a physiological state of arousal. It is these physiological pressures to which the attachment figure responds.

The term for the help that the mother provides in relation to the child's physiological and emotional state is *dyadic regulation*; she communicates and otherwise responds to her child in a way that enables him to manage his physiological arousal (Sroufe, 1997). A mother may do this by facilitating the action that the child wants to take; for example, by helping him to reach something that he wants. If the child is distressed, the dyadic regulation may involve soothing; in more positive states, it may involve the maintenance or even an amplification of the state. Think of a mother playing peekaboo with her baby and of the ramping up of excitement and interest that occurs in him as his mother plays the game; then, if the baby finally feels too excited and becomes uncomfortable, think of the attuned mother's ramping down of the excitement of the game until the baby is once again relaxed.

The child needs the attachment figure to respond and communicate with him in a way that modulates his physiological state in relationship to his goals and emotions. In all cases, this necessarily involves the mother's understanding of the child from within his own experience, seeing and feeling through his eyes but with the resources and judgment of someone who is older and wiser and stronger (Fosha, 2001; Tronick, 2005). She brings these resources to bear on behalf of the experiences that the child is having.

Something goes wrong in the child's body and with his pursuit of his own goals if his attachment figure is not there to help him. This is true whether he is injured, frightened, sick, or in distress or if he is interested, excited, and joyous.

The absence of dyadic regulation is part of what makes the infant miss the mother and become anxious at the prospect of separation from her. This is especially true when the child is afraid, but it is also true in the case of other emotional states. This need for help with physiological regulation from an attachment figure begins very early and at a very basic level. To develop physically and neurologically, the infant needs physical warmth and feeding; tactile, auditory, and visual contact; holding and carrying; soothing and excitement. These early regulatory processes have a direct effect on development. In animal studies, researchers have discovered that there are specific interactions between a mother and her infant that regulate the infant's physiological states (Hofer, 1994). Each of these regulatory interactions with the mother is linked to a specific set of developmental outcomes in the infant.

For example, if the mother's physical warmth is not provided, the infant undergoes a gradual decline in his general activity level, and this falling off of activity looks a lot like depression. If milk sufficient to sustain growth is not provided, the infant's cardiac rate declines by half. The regularity and periodicity of the mother's milk supply and of the associated feeding interactions between her and the infant are directly related to the duration of sleep and waking and the smoothness of the transitions between these states. If the tactile stimulation that is normally provided by the mother is absent, this leads to states of hyperarousal (which looks a lot like anxiety) in the infant when he encounters novel circumstances. If all of these regulatory interactions are withdrawn because the mother is unavailable, the infant protests, cries out, and experiences distress. The distress that we feel at separation or nonresponse from our attachment figure is intrinsically related to the disruption and dysregulation of a physical process. This physiological dysregulation is the anatomy and inner working that underlies separation anxiety (Hofer, 1995, 2006; Polan & Hofer, 1999).

The process of dyadic regulation lives within and instantiates the process of attachment. In this sense, what we call *attachment* might be accurately thought of as an umbrella term that collects a number of separate processes, all of which require sensitive responsiveness and dyadic regulation by the attachment figure. Hofer (2006) called these processes *hidden regulators* that collectively create the need for the attachment figure and give rise to the experience of attachment as well as the experience of separation anxiety. The loss of the attachment figure is the loss of something biologically actual that is desperately needed. The absence of the attachment figure truncates normal development and causes intense distress.

The process of dyadic regulation is how we feel the other person's presence and involvement with us. The attachment figure becomes connected to our physiology, and our own physiology becomes connected to that of the attachment figure. That person becomes relevant to and facilitating of our goals. When our attachment figure acts in a way that alters our physiological state in the way we want it to change, we feel in a deep and noncognitive way that we have been understood and responded to; we feel helped with something that we needed help with. This is not something we think or know; it is rather a physical and emotional experience, and so it is available both to immature infants and to fully developed adults. We feel understood and responded to by another person because our physiological state changes in the right way. This is how we *feel felt* by another person (Siegel, 2007).

This experience of feeling felt and understood by the other person can be accomplished through direct physical means, and it often is. But it also can be accomplished by the kind of communicational exchange that we have with another person. When we consistently experience open communication and direct contact with another person, and it leads to a state that feels physiologically good, we then have one of the fundamental components of secure attachment.

A COORDINATED STATE AS THE SET-GOAL OF THE ATTACHMENT BEHAVIORAL SYSTEM

In regard to human attachment, this analysis suggests that the goal of attachment behavior is the attainment of individualized maternal caregiving through the achievement of a coordinated interactive state via sensitivity of mother and infant to each other's signals. This is the interactive state that Bowlby described as "availability" or "presence"; its variations have been described by Ainsworth and her colleagues and have been at the center of research on security-engendering mothers for 30 years (Bakermans-Kranenburg et al., 2003; Behrens et al., 2011). The achievement of a coordinated interactive state through communication, rather than proximity, might then be taken as the immediate objective, the set-goal, of the attachment behavioral system. The concept of a coordinated state, when joined to the extensive literature on mother–infant communication, gives specificity and operational clarity to Bowlby's and Ainsworth's extension of the meaning of proximity to denote "ready accessibility," being "willing to respond in an appropriate way" (Bowlby, 1973, p. 201), and "sensitive responsiveness of mothers to infant signals and communications" (Ainsworth et al., 1978, p. 152). The availability and sensitive, helpful responsiveness described by Bowlby and Ainsworth can only be based on a highly developed and textured coordinated state. This state must precede the responsiveness because it makes the responsiveness possible; it is how whatever degree of responsiveness that exists is created. The creation of a coordinated state is a child's primary and preemptive goal with his mother. It precedes and is more fundamental than any other task because all other tasks depend on it, as Eibl-Eibesfeldt's (1989) account of the evolution of maternal care emphasizes. Nor is it separable from attachment motivations, because it is how the child knows that the mother is accessible and available to be responsive. It is what Bowlby originally defined as proximity.

The ways in which coordinated states may be achieved by a human mother–infant pair are extremely variable, and this variability is accommodated to by the child in learning how to be with his mother and how to obtain her relatedness. The child adapts to the conditions the mother imposes for the creation of communicative understanding and responsiveness. And the child also learns the mother's way of constructing and conducting interpersonal and emotional transactions. The attachment-motivated need for the coordinated state is in this view the underlying goal that motivates the child to make the necessary adaptations to the characteristics of the caregiver. It drives the process of adaptation to the mother and in so doing shapes the child.

The child does not only enter coordinated states with his attachment figure, and he is actively communicating with his mother only some of the time, perhaps as little as 30% of the time they are in each other's presence. But the coordination with the mother has a primacy and shaping power over the child's developing mind because it is driven by attachment motivations. It is this coordination that will take on the qualities of an imprinting and that will remain with the child as he grows.

The vicissitudes of the attachment process are the vicissitudes of mother–infant communication. The child experiences disruptions and constraints in communication as a separation from the attachment figure. Disruptions or constraints on communication with the mother that are created by insensitivity, an inability to understand the child's signals, or emotional disengagement all create disruptions and constraints in the child's sense of the mother's availability and thereby compromise security of attachment (Kobak & Madsen, 2008). The child very quickly comes to appreciate when—under what conditions, within what kinds of situations, with what contingencies to his own communications and emotional state—these disruptions occur. Because the disruptions are directly painful to him (MacDonald & Leary, 2005), the child then seeks to avoid those disruption-triggering conditions by constraining his own communication and its associated emotional state.

If coordinated communication is seen as the set-goal of attachment behavior, individual variations in coordinated communicative states become the object of attention and the basis of an understanding of attachment pathology. The detailed processes of affective communication and their very extensive role in adult relationships are placed at the center of infant and adult attachment processes. The attachment classifications imply types of coordinated states, with different qualities and degrees of coordination defining each classification. The problems of attachment anxiety and of attachment avoidance are seen as the result of trying to manage communications and emotional states that have been made problematic—provoking either anxiety or avoidance—by the ways in which coordinated communication has been disrupted in the attachment relationship with the mother.

In this way, conceptualizing coordinated states as the set-goal of attachment helps attachment theory to retain much more individual variation and texture that is of great clinical significance and utility in working with individual patients. Ainsworth originally identified nine attachment classifications. Others have since been added, but most have fallen prey to the practical constraints of empirical research, to the detriment of attachment theory's clinical utility. Focusing on coordinated states as the goal of attachment restores clinically vital individual variation to attachment theory, because it focuses attention on exactly how disruptions of coordination occur.

In thinking about a particular mother and child, questions arise: Under what circumstances and to which communications and emotional states is the mother sensitively responsive, and to which does she respond with insensitivity or disengagement? And how does the child change himself in coordinating with these variations of sensitive responsiveness? The child learns the answers to these questions in a deep and automatic way—physiologically, cognitively, and behaviorally—that becomes the form of his future relationships and way of being in the world. The clinical question while working with a patient becomes how did this individual enter into a coordinated state with his or her attachment figures, and how has this influenced the individual's emotional life and relationships with others?

THE IMPORTANCE OF COORDINATED COMMUNICATION

A coordinated communicative state gives a child what he needs most: an ally in his social environment who is ready and willing to help him with whatever needs arise. In attachment theory, the dangers from which a child needs protection are often described as predators or accidental injury or getting lost and left behind. But for human beings, the most important part of our environment is the social environment; our most powerful adaptation in the face of an impersonal and dangerous world is our set of social relationships and our continuing acceptance in our social group itself. And the greatest threat to our survival comes either from a loss of our social group or from direct aggression and competition from other human beings.

It is not a biological accident that the human amygdala, which processes fear-related information within the nervous system, reacts to angry or fearful facial expressions as actively as it reacts to direct physical threats; it treats social dangers in much the same way that it treats physical dangers (Heywood & Kentridge, 2000). Similarly, the human nervous system processes social exclusion in the same way that it processes physical pain; social exclusion is a form of physical pain (MacDonald & Leary, 2005).

For the somewhat xenophobic species of humans, nothing is as safe as being with others who consider us to be a member of their group, which is defined in distinction to others. Nothing is more dangerous to us or makes us more subject to mistreatment or indifference than to be defined as a member of an outgroup. The long and brutal history of ethnic warfare and violence is one instance of this. But in all circumstances, exclusion from the group is practiced as a form of punishment: for example, the religious practices of excommunication and shunning; the secular practices of exile or imprisonment; and, for those already imprisoned, the further punishing exclusion of solitary confinement. To not have somebody with whom we can enter into a coordinated state is a terrible thing for us.

An attachment relationship with an older and wiser adult gives a child exactly what he needs in such circumstances: a way of learning how to be a member of the social group and an alliance in the intense and often competitive politics that are part of all human societies. Allies are always critical in social terms. A mother provides her child with essential resources for a successful social life. She socializes him transformatively (i.e., she makes him into someone who speaks the language, experiences the emotions, perceives the world, and enacts relationships in the way that is mandatory in his social group). She also provides the relational resources that give him status and power within his social world through her own alliances with other women and men—her pair-bonded mate and relatives and friends (Hrdy, 2005a).

In his studies of chimpanzee politics, Franz de Waal (1982/2007) has described the difference a powerful and active mother can make in the survival and social fortunes of her child. The same is no less true of a human parent in her arrangement for her child of social contacts, her invocation of her own alliances for his support, her advocacy for his entry into privileged contexts, and her tutelage in social behaviors necessary for his success. Indeed, the maternal alliance may be more important for humans than for any other primate or animal (Hrdy, 2005b). But in the subtle and rapid give-and-take of social relationships, the effectiveness of the attached mother's social alliance with her child depends directly on her close coordination with him—both in terms of her early fostering of his social nature in a way that is specific to his group and of playing an active and allied role in his unfolding life within the social group. It is precisely these elements that make her attached coordination with him crucial. An alliance with a highly motivated adult provides protection from what we have most to fear—either rejection by the social group or the attacks and competition of other people.

A good attachment relationship, with its qualities of coordination, offers a primary social alliance—an unearned commitment that is usually forged before the child is born, that is extensively one-sided in terms of the provision of support and resources, and that is abrogated only rarely and in the most exigent circumstances. Within the social group, the primary attachment relationship offers a haven and network of alliances in what is otherwise an often indifferent world (Ford, Goodman, & Meltzer, 2004; Lasch, 1976).

It is the ultimate refuge and is taken as the location of ultimate safety and comfort, the place we flee to from the fear of the dark, the schoolyard bully, and even the specter of death (Florian & Mikulincer, 1998). In the natural world's calculus of survival, the economics of natural selection apparently dictate that it is better for a child to remain attached to a highly imperfect caregiver than to risk life without the support of this primary alliance. But all of this works only within the context of an ongoing coordination, to whatever degree this may be present.

MOTHER–INFANT COMMUNICATION AND ONTOGENETIC TUNING: THE WINNOWING AND SHAPING OF COMMUNICATIVE POTENTIALS

In humans, the process of achieving individualized maternal bonding and caregiving through coordinated communication is more complex than in other species because the processes of human communication are themselves so much more complex and variable—dependent on experience for their form and development—than is the case for other species. The human communication process is less innately fixed biologically and is much more extensively shaped by individual and cultural variations. It therefore requires a much more extensive process of learning and of adaptation. It calls for a process of adaptation both to a particular and idiosyncratically variable individual (the mother or attachment figure) and to a particular sociocultural group (the family, the extended family with its social network, and the community).

In describing the operations of the attachment behavioral system, Bowlby (1969/1982) emphasized this tuning and winnowing of the signals to which the behavioral system responds. As it develops during early attachment experiences, the attachment behavioral system gradually begins to focus on some signals and to ignore others. This tuning and winnowing occurs partly as a result of physical developments that make it possible to perceptually discriminate more precise information (e.g., a baby becoming able to see faces more clearly and therefore to make finer discriminations of facial expressions). But major aspects of this winnowing and tuning of signals result from experience and learning that take place in interaction with other people. We are genetically coded to be shaped by experiences with our attachment figures. These experiences teach the developing child's attachment system that some communications and interpersonal approaches are more likely than others to elicit a desirable response from the caretaker. These then become the ways of communicating and handling relationships in which the child learns to specialize for constructing his own relationships.

He learns to "speak" a certain kind of relationship in the same way that he learns his mother tongue as his native spoken language.

The principal communications channels by which we construct and conduct relationships with others are through vocalizations and facial expressions, both of which carry an enormously influential and powerful set of signals that connects us to others. In interpersonal communication, nothing is more important than the face and the voice. And in both the voice and the face we see the direct shaping and narrowing of communicational capacities and sensitivities through interactions with the attachment figure. We see it, for example, in the acquisition of language sounds and in learning to read facial expressions and emotions.

Voices and Vocalizations

Learning how to speak a language requires that a child learn how to produce and recognize the particular sounds that are made in the language he or she is acquiring. The child must also understand the context of meaning in which the sounds are used. Languages use different subsets of the sounds that the human vocal apparatus is capable of making; no language uses all of these sounds. It is the specific subset of sounds used that gives a language its particular tonal properties. So as babies and children learn their first language, they must also learn to produce and recognize the particular sounds that are made in their language.

This process begins early. By their fourth day of life, babies are able to distinguish between adult utterances in their maternal language and those in another language (Mehler et al., 1988). By about 6 months, the infant will engage in conversations with his mother made up of babbling sounds—phonemes and intonations but without words. The strings of sounds and tones and changes in pitch are strung together so that they sound very much like sentences (e.g., rising in pitch at the end of the string so that the utterance sounds like a question). Without the content of words, the conversations are essentially about relatedness, emotion, engagement, and responsiveness between the child and the other person. But the child is also learning which sounds are meaningful in the language spoken by his attachment figure. Even before they begin to form words, babies learn to babble in a way that is recognizably characteristic of the sounds and intonations made in the language they are acquiring (de Boysson-Bardies, Halle, Sagart, & Durand, 1989; de Boysson-Bardies, Sagart, & Durand, 1984). In other words, the baby learns the particular phonemes and intonational contours that are used in the language that he is acquiring as these are distinguished from all the speech sounds he can initially make and hear. The mother and others who speak to the baby make some sounds and not others; they respond meaningfully to some of the baby's sounds more than others. From this winnowing process, the infant is left with the sounds that are used in his language. What is interesting about this process for our present purposes is that as a baby becomes better at making and responding to the sounds used in his language, he simultaneously loses the ability to produce or even to perceive sound differences that are not used in his language.

Faces and Expressions

A similar process of winnowing and specialization occurs in regard to face processing—the recognition and interpretation of individual faces and of facial expressions—during the development of the first attachment relationship. Faces play a very special role in human interaction. They are the basis of both the instant identification of specific individuals and the primary nonverbal communicator of emotion, relationship, and intention, all of which are crucial for human social life. The brain is specialized to identify and interpret faces—this is why faces are so easy for us to remember, much more easily remembered than numbers, for example, or even names—but the process is not entirely innate. There appears to be a sensitive period for the learning of faces—whose they are and what their expressions mean.

The infant shows recognition and preference for his mother's face by 4 days after birth, even before he can see faces clearly, by focusing on the outline of the head (Bartrip, Morton, & de Shonen, 2001; Pascalis, de Schonen, Morton, Deruelle, & Fabre-Grenet, 1995). This ability is supported by specific regions in the brain that are specialized for interpreting faces (the amygdala is especially important for interpreting facial expressions), and these regions develop in the infant in response to social experiences during the period when the child's first attachment relationship is developing (Quinn, Yahr, Kuhn, Slater, & Pascalis, 2002). We have to learn about the faces and facial expressions of those who surround us, and we are then specialized to perceive and understand these faces and facial expressions better than others. (This is the origin of the *other-race effect*, in which adults and children find it easier to recognize and interpret faces from within their own ethnic group, as long as these are the faces among which they have been raised. The effect is entirely dependent on experience during development: Children adopted cross-ethnically are better at the faces of the ethnic group in which they were raised.) Infants get better at recognizing some faces than others, and they also get better at reading and interpreting some facial expressions rather than others. The sensitive period for this training of face processing seems to occur from about 3 months to about 3 years (see Pascalis et al., 2005, and references therein).

Which faces and which expressions they learn best depends on their social environment and especially their experience with the face and the facial expressions of their attachment figure. As is the case with language learning, when this sensitive period for learning faces and expressions closes, the child is left with a lifelong specialization in face interpretation that is based on his experiences with his attachment figure.

Facial expressions are extremely rich in social and emotional information, and the face to which the infant or child is most attuned is that of his attachment figure. It is important to note that as part of the process of face learning, the nervous system of the developing infant becomes tuned to recognize and discriminate the specific emotion signals that are expressed by his attachment figure. Some basic emotional signals seem to be innate and universally recognized across cultures and situations. But others are specific to the culture and the particular social group in which the infant is developing. As part of his attention to the faces of others and especially to the face of the attachment figure, the infant is learning how to interpret the emotional state of the other, the attitude of the other person toward the infant's self, the relationship between the infant and the other person, the intentions of the other, and the emotional and intentional meaning of the situation in which the interaction is occurring. Infants are specialized for this type of social cognition. They learn it quickly and naturally, and their nervous system is altered by this learning as it occurs and so becomes specialized for it. The result is a child who is a part of a specific social context and set of relationships, who knows how to automatically "do" that social context and those relationships, and who will carry that automatic "knowledge" forward into the rest of his life.

FITTING THE SELF TO THE SOCIAL ENVIRONMENT

The winnowing of signals and stimuli is a part of the process of ontogenetic tuning within a specific environmental niche that converts a set of genetic potentials in the individual (the genotype) into a more specific version that has been adapted to a very particular environmental niche through the effects of experience (the phenotype). For humans, the most important part of the environment to which we adapt during development is always the social environment. So, this fitting to a specific niche means learning to fit and to communicate with a specific social group and to acquire this group's culture—the group's way of thinking, feeling, expressing, relating, and doing. This process of shaping the infant's way of communicating and relating is led by the infant's mother or primary attachment figure. "By the time the first birthday is reached, each mother–

child couple has already developed a highly characteristic pattern of inter-acting. The magnitude of the differences between one couple and another can, moreover, hardly be exaggerated" (Bowlby, 1969/1982, pp. 344–345). The development of this pattern of interaction continues until it reaches a major developmental transition in early adolescence—the point at which Bowlby thought the predominant attachment patterns in an individual became well established and less susceptible to change. The tuning of the attachment behavioral system is based on which signals are most effec-tive in producing the behavioral system's desired result. The desired result from the baby's point of view is the availability and responsiveness of the mother. The signals that influence this responsiveness are the baby's com-munications. The baby therefore learns to send and to respond to those signals that keep his mother most available and responsive. As emotion-sensitive brain circuits in the orbitofrontal cortex and the amygdala are developing, they become sensitized to some facial expressions and other signals of emotion more than to others (Leppanen & Nelson, 2009). This means that a mother and a baby will gradually narrow in on the signals that they use to communicate with each other—that they will create their own interactional world and their own form of coordinated communication. They will become specialized in terms of facial expressions, vocal sounds, and other means of communicating emotional and relational informa-tion. This restricted set of signals and stimuli comes to be their familiar and preferred way of relating to each other, and it comes to be the baby's way of communicating and relating within close relationships. The baby becomes communicatively coded with the types of interactions he has with his mother.

Each of these means of communicating with another person is inextri-cably tied to emotional expression and regulation, and as these forms of com-munication are shaped, so is the child's way of having emotional experience also formed. Attachment, communication, and affect develop together, with attachment motivations shaping nuanced developments in the other two. The attachment relationship forges the child's way of communicating and having emotional experience.

OPENNESS VERSUS CONSTRAINTS AND DISRUPTIONS IN COORDINATED STATES

This gradual winnowing of signals to which a response will occur gives a particular character to each individual attachment relationship. The qualities of an attachment relationship might be thought of in terms of the types of signals to which the attachment figure will respond and the circumstances under which she will respond to these signals. The concept of a coordinated communicative state is clarifying in this regard because it directly points to what communications are coordinated with (resulting in an experience of availability and responsiveness) and what communications are rejected or ignored or punished (resulting in an experience of loss of attachment). A child becomes a specialist in sending signals to which his attachment figure will give the most optimal response. He learns to "speak" the relational language of his attachment figures. The way in which a child communicates within his most important intimate relationship becomes the pattern by which he effects coordination and intimacy—or the lack thereof—in future relationships. This is the essence of attachment psychopathology and of the intergenerational transmission of patterns of attachment.

What disrupts or constrains communicative coordination in the first attachment relationship? Why would coordination ever be suboptimal or incomplete? Usually, this occurs either because the mother is unable to pay attention to her child's signals, as her attention is elsewhere, or because something in what the child needs and is signaling sets off disruptions within the mother's own emotional state, so that she needs to suppress the child's signals and her own responses to them. In the first case, the mother may be distracted, self-preoccupied, or overburdened. She may be overwhelmed by circumstances that make it difficult for her to pay attention to her child. Or she may be so distracted by her own thoughts and feelings and need to spend so much of her psychological time and energy attending to her own needs for emotional regulation and soothing that she does not see or register what her child is expressing. She then either ignores him or superimposes her own needs and emotional communications over his own. She takes care of herself rather than her child, because she must. When this happens, the mother's response to the child's communications is likely to be inconsistent and sometimes intrusive: She may sometimes be available enough to respond and sometimes not. Or she may force a particular kind of coordination and communication on the child that suits her own emotional needs rather than respond to those of the child.

From the child's perspective, coordination with this mother requires a particular kind of effort. The child may find that he has to amplify and exaggerate his emotional communications in order to get his distracted or preoccupied mother's attention. He may discover that some types of emotional communications drive her away and so seek to suppress his expression of those feelings or needs. He may try to evoke a response from a troubled mother by trying to take care of her so that she can take care of him.

A critical component of this process of adapting to the mother's way of communicating and coordinating is the child's experience of the conditions under which his attachment figure will be available and responsive to him. The child experiences disruptions and constraints in communication as a separation from the attachment figure (Kobak, 1999; Kobak & Madsen, 2008), and so he seeks to avoid the conditions that disrupt their communication. These conditions include the child's implicit understanding of what aspects of himself are acceptable or unacceptable to the caregiver (Bowlby, 1973). This understanding is used as the basis for predicting and interpreting the signals and behavior of the attachment figure and for constructing the child's own communications and behavior. They become a part of the child's attitude toward himself, his goals, emotions, and behaviors. Bowlby proposed that those aspects of the child that lead to the nonresponsiveness or nonavailability of the attachment figure are "defensively excluded" from the child's awareness and behavior. (Defensive exclusion is discussed in detail in Chapter 7, this volume.) Bowlby emphasized that the child's understanding of how to communicate with and relate to his mother is constructed on the basis of actual experience with the caregiver and in that sense constitutes a record of the actual transactions between the two. These patterns become the template for his future transactions with others.

Sensitively responsive mothering leads to an open style of communicative coordination that permits a child to have access to a wider range of emotional and motivational information about both himself and others. This occurs because more sensitive responsiveness means that there is less defensive interference with the child's experience of his own emotions and emotional communication (Bretherton, 1990a, 1990b; Haft, 1990; Haft & Slade, 1989). This greater access to emotional self-experience enhances the coherence and competence of the individual's behavior by making it more accurate and reflective of what is actually happening. Securely attached children (and adults) communicate openly and comfortably across a wide range of emotions.

Secure attachment can be understood as a communicative relationship that is open to a wide range of affective communications without major distortions, rendering the attachment figure accessible and sensitively responsive to the person attached. Information flows freely between the two, and the attached person has relatively unimpeded access to his or her own feelings, thoughts, intentions, and needs because there is no anxiety about how the attachment figure will respond to their expression. Insecure attachments can be understood as communicative relationships that operate under constraints and distortions that leave the attached person in limited contact with his attachment figure and also with his own mental and emotional state. These constraints and distortions constitute necessary strategies for getting as much coordination and contact with the attachment figure as possible, given the attachment figure's pattern of responses to communications in the past.

As a child develops an internal template for interactions and for understanding himself and others, his access to affective experience is also shaped and delimited. This delimitation on affective experience plays a crucial role in shaping and controlling interactions, cognitions, and behaviors. Understanding the consequences of this shaping for psychopathology and psychotherapy requires a consideration of the role of affect in human behavior and experience.

6

AFFECT

Our emotions—how we experience them, how we control them, and how we let them affect our behavior—are, along with communication, one of the main aspects of the self that are affected by attachment experiences. This chapter describes what emotions are, both physically and psychologically; why they are so much a part of what we are able to do in the world; and how they are shaped by our attachment relationships. Specific emotions and their functions in our lives are described in detail. Each attachment style is described in terms of its characteristic way of regulating our emotional state and communicating it to others.

WHAT IS AN EMOTION?

There is a sense in which emotions are the felt meaning of life in a form that is both physical and psychological. Our emotional states can make us soar with joy, freeze us with fear, inflame us to the point of wanting to harm

http://dx.doi.org/10.1037/14185-006
Attachment-Based Psychotherapy: Helping Patients Develop Adaptive Capacities, by Peter C. Costello
Copyright © 2013 by the American Psychological Association. All rights reserved.

another, lift us with spiritual awe and a sense of transcendence, warm us with love for our children and partners so that we melt in their presence, weight us with sadness so that our hearts are heavy in our chests, or drown us in a despair so deadening that we withdraw from living a life we once found full and meaningful. The emotions that we have in response to different stimuli determine, in a moment-to-moment way, the meaning and the experience of our life.

The reason emotions are so powerful is that they are a synchronized response of virtually everything we are—in mind and in body—to what is stimulating us and presenting itself to our attention at the moment (Scherer, 1993). When we have an emotion, all the components of our physical and psychological being—central nervous system; autonomic nervous system; hormonal, cardiovascular, sensory, muscle, skeletal, and digestive systems; brain; cognitions, perceptions, and memories—participate in creating the experience. These systems all change in a coordinated way. They try to do the same thing, in the sense of producing a particular result, at the same time. Our emotions are the fine-grained texture of our experience in living, because they are themselves the fine-grained variations in the state of our physical being through which we experience all of life.

The effects that these variations and synchronizations produce in our state of being are profound. Emotions can transform us from one way of being in the world to another. They almost make us into a different person. They do this primarily by altering, by degrees either subtle or profound, the state of our nervous system, which then alters the rest of our body. This changes our responses to the situations in which we find ourself, and these changes in our responses are the evolutionary purpose of emotions: They are adaptive physical and mental schemas for responding quickly and efficiently to circumstance that have been important in human survival and flourishing. The changes that emotions create in the mind and body are all coordinated around the function of our having an adaptive response to something that is happening that has significance for us.

THE PROCESS OF HAVING AN EMOTION

Emotions begin as our nervous system senses or perceives a stimulus—something that is happening around us or in us. This something might be as definite and external as the appearance of a familiar or unfamiliar face, or it might be as internal and vague as a thought or memory that flits through our mind, a slight physical sensation, or, indeed, even the feeling of another emotion. This initial sensing is usually preconscious because our physiological reactions to a stimulus often begin before we are consciously aware of it

(Bechara, 2004). We do not always become conscious of what our nervous system is processing, because our consciousness is only a small part of what is happening in our nervous system, and our nervous system constantly registers but filters our awareness of our environment so that we are not overwhelmed with information. Usually, our nervous system has begun to perceive something before we become consciously aware of the perception.

This initial preconscious perception of an event immediately ignites a low-level physiological reaction. If the low-level sound is the faint tinkling of keys as our partner approaches the door, our body might, for example, begin to respond with an initial level of pleasurable interest even before we are aware of hearing the sound. If, while we are driving, the movement of cars in a traffic pattern suggests that sudden dangerous changes are about to take place, our body begins to respond with increased tension even before our mind fully focuses on the cars around us. As our preconscious perception of an event gets stronger, so does the low-level physiological reaction that is brewing in our body, and both move closer to conscious awareness.

This happens because the initial and just barely begun physiological state feeds forward through our central nervous system to the association centers in our cortex. This stimulates more and stronger cognitions and perceptual expectancies, such as similar traffic patterns from the past and heightened awareness of the location of other vehicles, which fit with our initial physiological reaction. The cognitions cued by our incipient physiological responses also include our memories of the consequences of feeling a particular emotion in our past—what has happened when we felt angry or frightened or sad. In this way, our emotions and physiological responses actively shape our knowledge of our environment and of our options because they cause us to look for some kinds of things and not for others. They cause us to look for the things in the environment that are relevant to the emotion we are beginning to have.

At the point where the preconscious perception and low-level physiological reaction become strong enough to enter our consciousness, a full-scale emotional reaction is ignited. Our body moves toward actually taking the actions that our body has been preparing us for, and our conscious cognition actively focuses on interpreting the stimulus and making choices related to it. Is that shape a cat or a raccoon, a stick or a snake; is that sudden sound in the night an intruder or our own dog; did that person intend to bump into us, or was he distracted and looking in the wrong direction; did we really lose our keys, or are they in our other pocket? These processes of perception and physiological response closely intertwine and influence each other. Our initial preconscious perception of the stimulus event (e.g., the traffic pattern) helps to cue our physiological response. The physiological response then further shapes our perception and cognition (Blanchette & Richards, 2010).

The two-horned neural anatomy of the amygdala, the almond-shaped structure in our brain that is central to emotional experience, reflects this interaction between our body state and our cognitive processes. The amygdala receives perceptual input from the thalamus; this is how it "knows" what is happening around us. One branch of its neuronal connections then goes toward our body and our autonomic nervous system, generating physiological responses, and another branch of its connections goes to our prefrontal cortex, where complex perceptions and conscious thought are generated. Neural information resulting from our cognitions enters the amygdala and influences its output to our body, thus changing our physiological state; neural information resulting from our physiological states enters the amygdala and influences its output to our cortex, thereby changing our cognitions. Through this two-horned switching and integrating station, impulses from both our physiological state and our complex cognitions loop back and influence each other in a reciprocal and ongoing process (LeDoux, 2009).

This reciprocal intertwining of cognitive reactions with physiological reactions means that emotions are forms of both knowledge and action. They give us something to think about and something to do. Because our thoughts, perceptions, and physiological reactions influence each other reciprocally and repeatedly, our reactions and emotions in response to a stimulus unfold over time. They continue to change as we think about what is happening and as we take action in response to it. If we think a stick is a snake and then realize it is only a stick, our emotional state changes rapidly in response to this cognition; if we think a stick is a snake and we successfully leap away from it, our emotional state changes rapidly in response to our body's own actions. Our emotions change in response to what we think and what we do. This means that the behaviors we take on the basis of our emotional states are also one of the ways in which we can regulate and modify our emotional states. We take actions because of our emotional states, and we also take actions in order to change our emotional states.

It is possible for the links between the physiological changes that are part of an emotion and our conscious cognitions about the emotion and its sources to be distorted or suppressed. This may happen simply because we are distracted and our attention is focused elsewhere, but it may also happen because will distract ourself or suppress and redirect our attention if there is a reason for us not to become aware of or to act toward certain types of stimuli (Atkinson et al., 2009; Warren et al., 2010). This is a key aspect of the defensive processes that Bowlby indicated could arise from attachment experiences and impair our ability to function effectively in relationships and work, about which I say more below. If for some reason we suppress awareness of the stimuli that are causing our feelings, or if our attention is focused elsewhere, we may experience an emotion in terms of its physiological changes and its promptings to action without becoming fully conscious of its source. We may direct our conscious attention away from the stimulus and so suppress our awareness of it. We may even have the emotion for a while before we become aware of what we are feeling, let alone why we are feeling it. We have all had the experience of becoming aware that we are feeling a certain way and have been feeling that way for a little while but not knowing what is stimulating that feeling in us. In such circumstances, we may misattribute our feelings to a stimulus other than the one that is actually moving us and so direct our emotionally prompted responses in the wrong direction. We may, for example, be rude to the taxi driver instead of recognizing and directing our anger at someone else who has actually caused our anger. Similarly, we may take action to regulate or modify an emotional state without fully recognizing the relationship between the action we are taking and the emotional state we are acting on or attempting to modify. So, we may decide to move from one job to another or one city to another rather than to address the life situations about which we are feeling uncomfortable but about which we also, for one reason or another, are unable to act.

THE EMOTION OF ANGER

Each emotion has a unique profile in terms of the ways in which it alters and adjusts our physical and psychological state (Ekman, Levenson, & Friesen, 1983; Friedman, 2010; Kreibig, 2010; Lench, Flores, & Bench, 2011). The different pattern of each emotion defines our experience of the emotion. For example, when we say that we are feeling the emotion of "anger," we feel it because our body is changing in a specific way. The specific body responses that may occur during anger include the following:

- Our respiration increases, filling our blood with oxygen.
- Our heart beats faster and pumps more blood with each stroke, raising our blood pressure and making energizing and strengthening hormones and oxygen-enriched blood more available to our muscles, brain, and other parts of our body.
- Blood flows to our hands, making them feel warm and giving them an energetic readiness to move and to act, perhaps to strike.
- Blood flows to our face, reddening it, giving it a feeling of heat that is characteristic of the experience of anger.
- As our facial muscles become more suffused with blood, our facial expressions become more vivid, active, and intense.
- Our adrenal glands secrete more of the energizing hormones adrenaline and noradrenaline, increasing their levels in our blood and tissues and making us more active, more ready to act.

- The rising levels of these energizing hormones and the increased oxidation produced by the oxygenation of our tissues cause our metabolism to rise, making more energy available to our muscles.
- Our increased metabolism raises our body temperature, adding to the feeling of the heat of anger.
- The proportion of the androgens that are available to our tissues as free testosterone increases, boosting our tendency toward dominance and aggressiveness in our motivations and behavior and decreasing our ability to trust; simultaneously, the increased levels of available testosterone reduce our capacity to empathize with others, coaxing us to see our own point of view more than the other person's.
- Our perspiration increases, more efficiently cooling our over-heating body, increasing the conductivity of our skin and making it more sensitive to touch, and releasing scents that affect both us and the others who are with us.
- In our brain, blood flow increases in the anterior paralimbic regions, activating specific neuronal tracks in the orbital frontal cortex, the right anterior cingulate cortex, and the bilateral anterior temporal poles.
- With this increased blood flow, the neurohormones adrenaline, noradrenaline, and testosterone flow to the brain regions that have become most metabolically active. Our mind begins to work differently as a result of these changes within our brain.

THE EFFECTS OF HAVING AN EMOTION

Emotions create motivations, action tendencies, and communication.

Motivations

The physiological and neurological changes taking place in our body and our nervous system under the influence of an emotion predispose us to think about things in a particular way, and they prepare us psychologically and physically to take specific types of actions. They make us *want* to take particular kinds of actions. Our cognitions, perceptions, and memories are altered. In the case of anger, our psychological state changes to become more aggressive and dominant. Other neurological and hormonal changes make us less empathic and sympathetic to others. The speed of our thinking increases, and the thoughts that we have, the memories that come to us, and the perceptions of our environment all focus on issues relevant to anger. When we become angry, other thoughts are suddenly driven from our mind; our mental decks are cleared and made ready for action. We think of why we should be angry, and we remember other things that have made us angry in the past and that justify our present anger. We also remember other occasions when aggression has been enacted by us or by others in our presence. These images and memories become available to us as models for our own behavior.

Action Tendencies

Changes in motivation create tendencies to take particular kinds of actions. There is a different type of action tendency for each emotion. Emotions make the body want to do particular things. In close concert with the changes arising in our nervous system and the psychological state that is emerging in our mind, the other changes in our body are making us physically ready to take the actions that we suddenly want to take. In the emotion of anger, the blood flowing to our hands makes the muscles there want to move, to form themselves into fists, or to grab something—a lapel, an arm, or even a weapon. Our increased respiration, pulse rate, and blood pressure all boost the energy that is available to our large muscles, tensing them and making them spring-loaded for movement. The dilation of the capillaries in our skin brings blood closer to the surface, warming our skin, fueling nerve endings, making our skin more sensitive to input from the environment and thus making us more alert to that environment.

Communication

Our facial expressions, vocal qualities, and body postures change under the influence of an emotion, either signaling our state to others or causing us to try to conceal our state from others. In anger, our eyebrows are lowered and pulled sharply together; our forehead creases vertically, radiating lines upward from the area close to where our eyebrows meet; and our lower eyelids are tensed and straightened. Our lips are tensed and turned inward so that they appear thinned. The corners of our mouth turn down, and the muscles at the tip of our chin are pushed forward and up. Our mouth may be open in a snarl or closed with the lips pressed tightly together. Making an emotional expression, as Darwin first suggested, appears to increase the extent to which we experience the emotion that corresponds to the expression. Others see our emotions, unless we successfully suppress their expression, and this affects their own feelings, thoughts, and behavior in the situation. For each of our emotions, there is a very specific pattern of physiological and neurological changes. In each, the body responds in different ways; in each, different regions of the brain become more active. In each major emotion, different facial, vocal, and postural expressions appear; these communications of our emotional state are sensed and responded to by others. These changes are extremely fine-grained and fluid in a way that research is only beginning to uncover (see Kreibig, 2010, for a review). For example, there are many forms of anger and many ways in which we may experience it—outward directed, turned inward, suppressed, focused on someone who is not present, and so on—and each of these seems to have varying physiological processes and changes associated with it (Lerner & Tiedens, 2006). But each emotion has underlying physical and psychological patterns, and each has a general function that natural selection has distilled as effective in dealing with commonly encountered circumstances in our life.

SADNESS CONTRASTED WITH ANGER

Compare, for example, the changes wrought by anger with those that take place in us when we experience the sadness of irretrievable loss (Freed & Mann, 2007). Anger insists on creating a change in our situation. It has a future orientation that is its leading edge. Sadness, rather than a demand for change, is about withdrawing our involvement and resources from something that has been lost when it is not possible to reverse the loss. The physiology and neurology of sadness slow us down and make us less active, less alert, and less able to engage our environment. Somatic and metabolic processes in our body decelerate and become sluggish, making us feel tired and heavy, without energy. We may wish merely to sit alone, or we may seek to be held by others. The muscles throughout our body lose their strength and tone. Our arms and legs become leaden. Our head feels too heavy for our neck muscles to support; it falls forward, casting our eyes down toward the ground rather than out toward the world. Even the muscles in our back lose their strength, and we slump or slouch, our shoulders curving forward, bringing our head further forward and down. Our face changes: Our eyelids droop and the inner corners of our eyebrows move together and rise, altering the pressure on our tear ducts; the corners of our mouth turn down and the lower lip pushes up and forward, forming a pout. In our brain, opioids and oxytocin—both associated with attachments and pleasurable interactions with others—decline. We talk less, and we look other people in the face less often. If we cry, the lachrymal glands behind our upper eyelids secrete tears into the space between the lid and the eyeball. There is pressure behind our eyes. Our throat feels full. It becomes more difficult to talk. We blink repeatedly, squint, or close our eyes to clear the tears away. Our tears may run down our face, becoming another signal to others of our distress. These tears have a different chemical composition than those produced for lubrication or by an irritant, reflecting the different biochemical environment of our body when we are in a state of sadness. The effect of many of these changes is to make it more difficult for us to see. A diffuse physical pain, akin to what we feel when we are socially excluded, throbs in our viscera and face; we may clutch our abdomen with our arms and hold and hide our face in our hands. We feel more subject to harm and more risk averse. We feel hopeless and ineffective. Nothing we do can retrieve our loss. Our thoughts and attention turn inward. As we become more introspective, we may ruminate about what we have lost and how the loss will affect us.

What is all this for? There are two effects of these changes: We are much less able to take actions—to do anything—and we no longer face toward the world. Instead, we are drawn in on ourself, and we see our own body rather than the events around us. Other changes that occur in sadness have similar effects.

EMOTIONS ARE DESIGNED BY OUR EVOLUTIONARY PAST BUT ARE SHAPED BY OUR PERSONAL HISTORY

Our emotional reactions have two sources: natural selection and personal experience.

The Natural Selection of Emotions

The biological origin of basic emotional patterns and the types of stimuli that elicit them lie in our evolutionary past. The emotional reactions of anger, fear and anxiety, sadness, depression, guilt, surprise, disgust, joy, interest, excitement, shame, embarrassment, and shyness are templates of reactions that have served to promote our survival and the survival of others allied with us in our ancestral past. Each of these emotions has an adaptive function to serve in helping us to deal with the events that are taking place in our life (Plutchik, 2003). Each reconfigures our body for a particular adaptive challenge or opportunity that throughout the evolution of our species has been recurrent and also critical to our competent functioning in our environment (Nesse & Ellsworth, 2009). Our responses to these situations have become biologically encoded, and this encoding of adaptive responses is much of what we mean when we refer to "human nature." A tour of the functions of emotions is a tour of the essential situations and circumstances that are important in any human life.

For example, anger demands change in what is happening; it helps us to confront obstacles to our goals and to prevent the aggression of others from interfering with our goals. Happiness inclines us to approach and to continue our involvement with what is causing us pleasure, making us want to do more of it. Typically, what makes us happy is what natural selection has calculated is good for us, and so natural selection has woven garlands of happiness around what it is good for us to do. Shame makes us want to stop doing something that is causing us pleasure, because someone else sees us and strongly disapproves of what we are doing. It is an essential component of our sensitivity to social approval and disapproval, which Darwin (1871/2004) believed was one of our strongest instincts. Fear and anxiety, like the physical pain to which they are neurologically related, make us avoid or flee something that can harm us. Embarrassment alerts us to the danger that our social group may perceive us as incompetent or dishonest and therefore less valuable as a group member. Lust and erotic love set off our reproductive and partnering behaviors. Sadness prompts us to withdraw from an activity or an involvement that was important and beneficial to us in the past but that will no longer repay continued investment of resources. It represents a disengagement from a valuable but no longer possible activity, a process that may be seen at its most intense in our mourning of the loss of a beloved person. Guilt prompts us to make reparations to others for a harm we have done to them and to thereby restore or preserve our relationship with those who may have become hostile to us because of what we have done. Feelings of interest lead us to explore and to seek to know more about someone or something that may be related to our goals in an important way. Surprise clears our mind of other thoughts and rivets all of our attention on an unexpected and possibly important event. Disgust leads us to convert an appetitive response, like the desire for food or for touch, into the rejection and expulsion of something noxious and potentially harmful that has gotten too close to us and that may damage us. Shyness prompts us to avoid the evaluative scrutiny of other people, especially the situation of many people evaluating us simultaneously—a situation that in our evolutionary past may have signaled a potentially dangerous degree of critical or envious scrutiny.

The Personal Experience of Emotions

Natural selection sets our genotypic emotional potential and prescribes the basic pattern of each emotion, but this genotypic potential is turned into a phenotypic and individual actuality by the experiences of emotion. These experiences lead individuals to vary in their *emotional profiles*—the degree to which they experience different emotions, the ways in which they control these emotions, the specific situations that occasion these emotions, and how open, accurate, and comfortable they are in communicating their emotional states to others. These patterns of emotional experience vary by culture, by family, and by individual, and these patterns are nested within each other like

Russian dolls. Families live within but also instantiate cultures, and individuals develop within and also instantiate families. Although we all participate in broad communities with which we share important emotional patterns, we all possess individual and idiosyncratic emotion profiles. Each of us is emotionally triggered by different particular circumstances and situations, each of us struggles more with some emotions than with others, and each of us seeks to manage and resolve our emotional states in a different way.

Individual emotional profiles have consequences for how people form relationships and live their lives in the world. People need their emotional endowment to live their lives as fully and completely as possible, but their early emotional experiences can constrain those capacities if their emotional processes become distorted or deformed in the course of their developmental experiences. No experiences are likely to be more important to the shaping of our emotional potentials and experiences than those we have with our attachment figures.

AFFECT SUPPRESSION AND AFFECT HEIGHTENING IN INSECURE ATTACHMENT

Children who are securely attached have a different pattern of emotional communication with the mother than do children who are insecurely attached (Bretherton, 1990b; Cassidy, 1994; Isabella, Belsky, & von Eye, 1989; Pauli-Pott & Mertesacker, 2009; Sroufe, 1997). Mother and child talk and respond to each other in a different way, especially in regard to the emotional content of their interactions. It is through these differences in the communication of emotion that attachment relationships exercise a profound influence on the processes of emotion socialization, and these differences shape the way the infants and the adults they will become use and experience emotion in life (Kochanska, 2001; Sroufe, 2005; S. F. Waters et al., 2010). As a consequence of these differences, securely attached children and adults have fuller access to the powerful and enlivening biological functions of emotion. They are better informed about their own emotional state, they know more about what actions they can take in response to stimuli in the environment, and they view other people as more likely to be helpful to their purposes and needs. They are more fluently and expansively alive and alert to the events and possibilities in their environment.

Mothers and children in secure dyads communicate with each other in ways that are characterized by the qualities of *openness, accuracy, balanced expressiveness, responsiveness, sensitivity,* and *mutuality.* These qualities are absent or are not found in the same degree in the communication between the insecure child and his mother.

The communication between the securely attached child and his mother is more emotionally open and diverse in the sense that it encompasses more complete and balanced information about the actual experience and emotional state of both individuals in regard to what is going on between them and around them at the moment. They are honest and nondistorting with each other. As a result, the child has the opportunity to think and feel more clearly about his own emotions, his relationships with others, and the experiences that he is having in the world.

This greater openness in secure dyads includes the ability to engage fluently and comfortably with both positive and negative emotion. Although mothers of avoidant children actually seem to spend more time in a state of apparent positive emotion with their children, they do this by suppressing and ignoring negative affective communications, both their own and the child's. This has been described by some authors as *defensive idealization*. Such a mother avoids engaging with negative feelings, and she becomes unavailable in a way that threatens attachment security when negative feelings are present, thus discouraging the child from communicating negative feelings to her. Although the interaction may have a positive facade, the absence of negative emotion is artificial and distorting of the child's and the mother's actual experience. The psychoevolutionary functions and the usefulness of the emotions that are suppressed become unavailable to the child and the mother. Their interactions lack depth and emotional truth. This impedes their functioning in regard to what is actually happening at the moment and makes their interactions more shallow and less responsive to the child's needs. It also leaves the child in the situation of not only *not* being helped with regard to what he is distressed about but also being burdened with the task of suppressing, controlling, and regulating the negative feelings that are disturbing him without the help of his attachment figure. It is the equivalent for an adult of not being able to tell your most intimate other that you are upset about something. The child becomes insecure about the experience of his own emotional state: His emotions, when they are negative, lead his mother to withdraw and become unavailable, and they thereby heighten his own attachment anxiety and insecurity. His own feelings become something to avoid, and he seeks to suppress them. The mother who avoids negative emotions therefore triply burdens her child: with the need to deal with what is upsetting him without help, with the need to suppress and regulate his emotions on his own, and with the need to control his anxiety about the withdrawal and unavailability of his mother.

The pattern of emotional communication in avoidant dyads leads the child to acquire a general pattern of emotional self-regulation and communication that involves the *suppression* of his own emotional experiences and of the signaling of his emotions to others. In the Strange Situation studies (see

Chapter 2), the avoidant child does not object when his mother leaves and may seem not to notice her departure; he continues to be involved with his toys in her absence and continues to play even when she returns. In general, the avoidant emotional pattern leads to a fear of feeling and to a shift away from relationships and toward play and work activities that distance oneself from others (think of workaholics, of chronic video game players, or of someone sitting remote from his or her partner while surfing the Internet).

Mothers of anxiously attached children also constrain and distort the emotional communication with their children, but they do so in a way that leads to an overemphasis on negative emotions. These mothers tend to be inconsistent in their availability and responsiveness to their children because they are often preoccupied with their own needs and concerns. They thus have difficulty decentering from themselves and focusing on their children. They are not consistently suppressive of negative affect, as are the avoidant mothers, but rather are frequently unresponsive and difficult to attract into sensitive interaction.

Because the child has to work harder to attract such a mother into interaction, he winds up relying on and amplifying his communication of negative affect to draw his mother's attention. The child's situation is like that of Natalie, described in Chapter 1, who had to cry for a long time and increase her emotional state to a level of intense distress before her mother would come to her crib. Such a mother is less likely to create experiences of closeness with her child when he is happy, and she is likely to become more available during those moments when he is distressed. So the child specializes in feelings of distress and unhappiness because these are what reliably bring his attachment figure into closer contact with him.

The problem is that this pattern also involves a distortion of the child's emotional experience that places him out of fluent and precise emotional contact with other elements and stimuli that are present within himself and in his environment. He tends to become preoccupied with the availability of his attachment figure, to track her whereabouts and to monitor her emotional state with a constant level of background anxiety about her availability and his possible abandonment. He becomes overattuned to what she is feeling. He also becomes overattuned to any of his own feelings of distress, anxiety, or unhappiness and readily communicates these as a way of engaging her. In his overattunement to her and to his own anxieties, he becomes underattuned to his other thoughts, feelings, goals, and explorations. His world narrows to his mother's emotional state and availability, which is fraught with uncertainty and anxiety. In his overattunement to his own feelings of distress, he experiences his environment as more threatening than it needs to be and becomes underattuned to his other emotional responses to interesting or meaningful stimuli that are present around him.

The pattern of emotional communication in anxious dyads leads the child to acquire a general pattern of emotional communication and self-regulation that involves the *heightening and overemphasis* of his own negative emotional experiences and of the signaling of these emotions to others. In the Strange Situation, the anxious child is so distressed when his mother leaves that he is very difficult to soothe and to reengage in play; in her absence, he plays only halfheartedly with his toys, unable to return to other interests, and continues to show signs of distress at her absence. In general, the anxious emotional pattern leads to a preoccupation with relationships, a fear of absence, and a failure to fully engage in work and exploration (think of people who often can't focus on work or their own goals because they are preoccupied thinking about their relationships).

INSECURITY AND THE NARROWING
OF EMOTIONAL COMMUNICATIONS

In addition to evoking patterns of emotional suppression and emotional heightening, the mothers of insecure children generally communicate to their children within a narrower range of emotional signals than do the mothers of children who will become secure adults (Bretherton, 1990a, 1990b; Cassidy, 1994). They attune to some emotional communications but not to others (Haft, 1990; Haft & Slade, 1989; Isabella et al., 1989; Malatesta, Culver, Tesman, & Shepard, 1989; Stern, Hofer, Haft, & Dore, 1985) in a systematic way that teaches children what can be safely expressed and what cannot.

Daniel Stern (1985) called this process *selective attunement*. He described this joining of the child in some emotional communications more than in others as one of the most powerful ways in which a mother shapes her child's internal and interpersonal life and one of the key ways in which the emotional and communicational ways of the mother become characteristic of the child—a process that is central to the intergenerational transmission of attachment.

Stern (1985) offered two examples of a mother selectively attuning to a child. In the first, the mother would join the child in the child's enthusiastic, expansive, excited states but was less attuned when the child was less emotionally excited. In the second, quite the opposite, the mother would attune to the child not when she was excited but only when her excitement had ended and she became depleted—a state that Stern called *exthusiasm*. For the first child, the enthusiastic state becomes overvalued as a means of connecting to the mother and becomes preferentially forced and overplayed. (This overvaluing of a positive state and underresponding to more negative states is characteristic of avoidant mothers.) For the second child, the state of enthusiasm and excitement is lost because it leads to the loss of connection with the mother.

(This underresponding to a positive state and overvaluing of more negative states is characteristic of anxious mothers.) Through selective attunement, Stern wrote, the parent shapes both the internal emotional experience of the child and his or her interpersonal communication with others.

The parent is providing a template for what is allowed and shareable, and the child adjusts his inner state and external communication to fit within this template. The child loses access to the emotional states and interpersonal communications to which the mother will not join and comes to depend on those emotions and signals to which the mother will respond. This shaping of internal emotional experience and of external emotional communications is motivated and enforced by attachment processes. To express something to which the mother does not attune is to lose communicative coordination with the mother and thus her emotional availability at the very moment that the child is trying to obtain such coordination and responsiveness. This creates attachment anxiety in the moment and leads the child to avoid the signals that his mother does not respond to, that she responds to by withdrawing, or that she responds to by herself becoming anxious and insecure.

Another way of saying this is that the parent offers forms of engagement along specific emotional channels. The child learns what these channels are and how to find these preferred emotional states within himself. He uses them in preference to other emotions that he might also feel as ways to connect with and attach to the mother. The child learns to exclude, conceal, displace, or distort emotional states to which the mother does not respond. Thus, the avoidant child in the Strange Situation suppresses his distress at his mother's departure and his need for comforting on her return because such expressions of distress tend to drive his mother out of engagement with him. So he keeps his attention on his toys and hides the distress even though physiological measures show that his suffering is quite real. The anxious child in the Strange Situation amplifies his anguish at his mother's sudden absence, because that is the emotional channel that is most likely to lead to her reconnecting with him. The repeated experience of her unavailability unless he is very upset drives his anguish into its higher registers, and he becomes dysregulated and very difficult to soothe.

The mother of an insecure child communicates with him (or her) along a much narrower bandwidth than does the mother of a secure child. She selectively attunes to less of what the child is expressing, and the child has to fit himself to a more rigidly constrained template of what experiences and emotions and relationships are allowed. As with the process of the winnowing of infant babbling sounds that become limited to the specific subset of sounds that are used by the infant's mother, so also allowable and shareable emotional states and communications become limited to those with which the mother attunes. The other emotional states, as with the other babbling sounds, are lost to the child. He routinely suppresses them inside himself and excludes them from communication to others, in a kind of forced self-regulation that consumes psychological and cognitive resources and that distracts him from other tasks (Mikulincer, 1997; Mikulincer, Shaver, Cassidy, & Berant, 2009; Mikulincer, Shaver, & Pereg, 2003). The ways in which he can connect to others and the emotional states he can draw on to respond to the environment are narrowed.

A security-engendering mother is more open and accurate with her child across a much broader range of emotional signals, and the result is that the child has a wider range of emotional experiences and communications to others that are allowable and within his interpersonal orbit. There are many more emotional channels open for communication with the parent, and thus many more forms of engagement are possible. The child has less need to suppress, conceal, displace, or distort his own emotional responses to what is happening to him and around him. His cognitive resources are not diverted to the onerous tasks of suppressing and hiding emotions and managing them without the help of others. Nor is he distracted from the emotions he actually has to the task of amplifying the emotional communications preferred and forced by his attachment figures. There is less distortion of his spontaneous emotional responses in order to fit what he takes to be the needs of others.

This role of the emotions in creating an effective and high-functioning self who is in a fruitful and coherent relationship to others is a crucial issue from the point of view of an attachment-informed view of development and adult functioning. Emotions that are distorted or excluded from the child's emotional capacities by early attachment experiences are lost to his adaptive functioning, and this loss diminishes the self that he becomes and the ways in which he can communicate and relate to others.

Bowlby (1980) referred to the process of excluding emotional states and communications from awareness and acknowledgment as *defensive exclusion*, a process that he placed at the heart of attachment-based psychopathology (p. 45) and to which I return in Chapter 7. It is also the process whose undoing lies at the heart of attachment-based psychotherapy.

II

ATTACHMENT-BASED PSYCHOTHERAPY

7

DEFENSIVE EXCLUSION AND THE FOCUS OF ATTACHMENT-BASED THERAPY

This chapter integrates the chapters in Part I by providing an account of psychopathology in terms of attachment, communication, and affect. Psychopathology is seen as patterns of relating, communicating, and feeling that were acquired during development, when they were useful in maintaining connections to caregivers, but that now constrain and distort the individual's ability to be with others and to explore the world—a misshaping of the self. A psychodynamics of attachment is described, and the effects of formative relational experiences on internal working models and on procedural knowledge—what we know how to do in relationships, automatically and without thinking about it—are considered. Several case examples are provided.

http://dx.doi.org/10.1037/14185-007
Attachment-Based Psychotherapy: Helping Patients Develop Adaptive Capacities, by Peter C. Costello

MOLLY VERSUS ALLEN

Recently, I was sitting and chatting with a colleague who had brought her 3-month-old daughter to the office with her. The mother and I were at first both focused on her daughter, Molly, who was happily engaged with her mother from a semireclined position in a baby seat. Molly was smiling and wriggling and making bubbles with her mouth. When Molly's mom and I became more engaged in a point of conversation with each other and her mother turned away from her, Molly began to kick more emphatically and wave her arms more jerkily, her smile faded, she pushed out her lower lip, her eyes squinted and began to tear up, and then her face simply crumpled and she began to cry. Molly was having the very aversive experience of losing attunement and coordinated communication with her attachment figure at a time when she wanted it. (Perhaps she especially wanted it then because I, a stranger to her, had come into the room and was staying.) The involuntary discontinuation of their communicative coordination had given Molly the experience of separation and loss of attachment—even though she and her mother were still in close physical proximity to each other. Molly's mother quickly reengaged communication with her daughter: She made eye contact, smiled, and touched Molly's belly while cooing in motherese. Molly took a moment to reregulate and right herself. One could almost see the distress flow out of her body as she once again began to smile and wriggle and bubble. Her relatedness with her mother was reestablished.

Molly's self and the course of her future relationships—her capacity to explore the environment and her emotional characteristics as a human being—are being shaped by interactions, like this one, that involve the ebb and flow of a coordinated state. Molly is discovering the "rules" for establishing a coordinated state with her mother. The discovery of the interactional rules and idiosyncratic contours by which a coordinated state with a particular individual is achieved constitutes an infant's developing attachment relationship and the first building blocks of an internal working model of herself in relationship with an other. Simultaneously, Molly is discovering how she has to control and shape her own internal affective state in order to be with her mother.

For example, she is discovering what states in her mother signal imminent separation and consequently the onset of an experience of loneliness. She is also discovering what she has to do in order to end the loneliness, to bring her trusted companion back to her side. She is learning how her mother likes to coordinate—what kinds of affective communications she is likely to send and which affective states she likes to share. For instance, Molly's mother engages her with a very gradual and smoothly rising intensity of affective signaling; there is a calmness and softness that characterizes her interactions with her daughter (and also her interactions with others). Molly is learning these affective contours, the shape and form of her mother's emotional transactions, as a style of affective communicating. She can decode the kinds of messages her mother sends—she is getting very skilled at reading them—and she is learning how to match the characteristics of these messages in her own signaling. She is learning how to recognize and how to handle her mother's communicational preferences, so that she knows how to keep her mother close when she wants her. Finally, she is also learning how much of what they will coordinate about will come from Molly and how much from her mother: Who will adapt to whom and when and how; whose experiences, communications, and desires will be most pressing—Molly's or her mother's?

Out of these experiences, repeated many thousands of times over the course of Molly's first few years, will come a pattern in the way in which Molly handles affective communication in relationships and affect regulation in herself. She is becoming skilled—by which I mean that she is acquiring specific procedural knowledge—in how to recognize, respond to, and communicate certain specific affects with her mother. This is her relational language; it is how others will come to know her. And she is learning how to handle affect states within herself and in interaction with others—and whether they can be shared with the all-important other or whether she needs to manage these states on her own, perhaps through the emergence of newly formed defensive processes. This is the process of affect regulation in the making, and it will determine what emotions Molly can draw on from within herself to evoke and entrain her own behaviors, memories, cognitions, and perceptions. The self that Molly will become is taking shape in these communicative and affective interactions.

For Molly with her mother, this shaping of the self is essentially an affirming and a graceful process because her mother is sensitively responsive to the signals that Molly is communicating. Molly's mother goes to some trouble to shape herself to Molly's most pressing needs. Although Molly does have to learn how to be with her mother, this mother is attentive and supple enough so that Molly's goals and affective states are regularly honored in their interaction in a way that is directly experienced by Molly. It is not that Molly always gets what she wants but rather that what she wants and needs is responded to in a way that takes account of her state of mind and her internal affective state. Although Molly can't think of this in self-aware and self-conscious terms, she nonetheless has the experience of feeling recognized and known and helped by her mother. For Molly, this means that when she communicates with her mother, she has the experience of finding that her own internal states directly influence the environment—through the process of communication, her own forceful and innate human charm, and the agency of her mother—so that her own internal state affects what actually happens in a way that is helpful to Molly. This is a paradigm of healthy development and the foundational instance of what is so important in human life—our alliances with others.

But not all children are as fortunate in their communication with their mother as is Molly. Consider another baby, now a 34-year-old adult in treatment, named Allen.

His mother was a tense and anxious woman who often felt overwhelmed and angry. These disruptive internal states regularly entered into her communicative coordination with Allen. In one of his paradigmatic memories—a model scene of his childhood that condenses and stands for thousands of similarly structured (if less drastic) interactions—Allen was in distress and crying for his mother. He was signaling not only unhappiness but also vulnerability and the need for help. As Allen remembers it, he was sitting in a chair, probably a high chair or a booster seat. Allen remembers that as he cried, his mother walked over to him and poured a glass of water over his head. He remembers that she laughed at his reaction after she did this. When he remembers this story, he feels humiliated, and it is a difficult story for him to tell, one he has never told other people, his wife for example.

What, then, in the original situation as it occurred, was Allen's experience of the consequences of communicating his internal state to another? What was his experience of the impact of his internal state on his environment? Allen's self—his capacity for adaptive, unhampered, fluid self-experience and the communication of that self-experience to another—was distorted and misshaped by interactions like this one. His expectations regarding what internal states can be fully experienced and fully communicated to another are very different from Molly's. For Allen, as an adult today, the internal states of vulnerability and dependence on others elicit feelings of shame and suspicion of the other; they are an occasion for defensive evasions and distractions, like maintaining a pretense of not needing the other or of spotting something that the other is doing wrong. In fact, Allen often communicates anger when he feels most vulnerable and dependent, and he easily becomes angry over slights or threats that others do not perceive. The direct communication of his internal state is a perilous undertaking, and so he rarely does it and in fact has difficulty knowing what his own internal emotional state really is beyond the defensive emotions that he uses to protect himself. And so his communication becomes much less direct and open, more distorted, much more hampered by feelings of anxiety and distress when he most needs to communicate to another.

USE THEM OR LOSE THEM: WINNOWING AFFECTIVE AND COMMUNICATIVE PATTERNS

As discussed in Chapter 5, the goal of attachment behavior is the achievement of a coordinated communicative state with the mother. A coordinated state is when, within a dyad, each partner's communication signals an awareness of and receptivity to the other's state of mind. The signals of one partner are directly reflected in the signals of the other. Each partner has the sense of having an immediate impact on the other. What is optimally coordinated with by the mother in fortunate development is the social and affective state of the child. This is the lesson of several decades of research on the characteristics of security-engendering mothers (and, as will be discussed, it is one of the touchstones of Bowlby's approach to psychotherapy). For Molly's mother, being able to establish and maintain affective coordination with her baby is what sensitive responsiveness and emotional availability mean. Coordination by the mother is constitutive of sensitive responsiveness and availability; miscoordination constitutes insensitivity (i.e., nonresponsiveness to the signals of the other and thus unavailability). The optimal mother fits herself to the shape of the child while flexibly and responsively shaping that self through her own affective messages.

The experience of coordination is directly tied to the infant's affective state and internal affective regulation and consequently to his ability to maintain a state of self-organization (Tronick, 1978; Tronick, 1989; Tronick et al., 1998; Weinberg & Tronick, 1998). Communicating with an appropriate other about what we are experiencing is a fundamental way in which we become able to fully and deeply experience life while also managing those aspects of our experience that are difficult or disruptive. Because coordination is so richly rewarding and miscoordination is innately aversive and anxiety provoking, the baby, and thereafter the child and the adult, is impelled to achieve a coordinated state. This is the internal (affective) and the interactional (communicational) process at the core of the attachment of a particular child to a particular mother. A coordinated state is how a baby or any other individual "knows" or experiences that attachment has occurred. The coordinated state is the experience that is sought by the attachment-seeking individual.

How we coordinate with others—through what particular behaviors, affects, and communications—has everything to do with how each of us experiences ourself in the moment-by-moment course of our life. In a coordinated state, the mother helps the infant to regulate his internal experience through coordinating with his affective communication. Their communicative interaction occurs cooperatively at the interface of *intraindividual* and *interindividual* affect regulation (i.e., the mother and the baby are jointly affecting the baby's emotional state and ways of regulating his emotions; what happens in affective communication influences subsequent affect regulation, and what happens in affect regulation influences subsequent affective communication). In failures of coordination, the infant is left to manage his experience on his own. This is disruptive and inherently aversive. It feels bad. The infant's efforts both to manage his internal state and to maintain relatedness to his noncoordinating mother are the origin of the defensive processes that lead to the distortion of the self and to psychopathology. That is, the baby (and the child and the adult) learns to defensively process and to exclude those internal states that cause the loss of coordination with the attachment figure, either because these internal states excessively disrupt the other or because they are not joined with and responded to by the other. In this way, the self-experience of the infant, child, and adult is impoverished and rendered less clearly related to the individual's environment.

So, for Molly (as for Allen and for all infants and children) there is a lot to learn: What affect states in Molly and signals from Molly bring her mother into synchrony with her? What affect states and signals seem to drive the mother away? And, if her mother has moved away, what affect states and signals will bring her back? By this process, Molly's self is shaped. She learns to be a self in relation to another, and she learns to regulate and control herself internally in order to be the right kind of self to successfully be with the only other she has ever known. She is learning her relational and affective mother tongue. In so doing, she is also shaping her own affective and interactional capacities and disabilities in a way that is profoundly consequential for her life. She is becoming fluent in some forms of affective experience and interactional behaviors and incapable of others. There is a process of the winnowing of affective and communicational potentials: This winnowing is very much like the ways in which the extensive range of sounds that babies begin to babble at about 6 months is gradually reduced to the specific set of sounds that are actually used in the language they are learning to speak (i.e., those sounds that are mirrored are kept while others are lost). What is not coordinated with is lost or disowned, remaining at best a potential.

AUTONOMY AND COMMUNICATIVE COORDINATION

It is important to note that coordination can include nonengagement with the infant. There are two reasons for this. First, the infant or child may seek to disengage from emotional involvement with the mother in the interest of affective self-regulation (as when a game of peekaboo has become too exciting, and the child needs to withdraw in order to calm herself; e.g., Tronick, 1989). The second form of coordinated nonengagement between mother and infant or child involves the child's exploration of the environment. This is an instance of what Bowlby termed the *exploratory behavioral system*, which will later express itself in more autonomous behavior and which occurs most fluently in the context of secure attachment. Appropriate autonomy and exploration are regularly facilitated by security-engendering mothers (Ainsworth, Blehar, Waters, & Wall, 1978; De Wolff & van IJzendoom,

1997). Interpersonal relatedness and self-definition are sometimes thought of as two distinct, although dialectically related, developmental lines (e.g., Guisinger & Blatt, 1994). But from the perspective of coordinated states (which include coordination with autonomy) and attachment theory (which includes a relationship between security and exploration), the relationship between relatedness and self-definition is more intrinsic: Self-definition best occurs and perhaps can only occur in the context of a relatedness that embraces it.

Autonomy occurs most fluently where relatedness permits it, and the securely attached child exercises autonomy as a natural extension of the safety he feels in coordination with his mother. The responsive relatedness of the coordinated mother is then for the child a given, and autonomy is exercised by the child easily and naturally. Søren Kierkegaard wrote a beautiful description of a mother helping her child to take his first steps alone that is immediately recognizable as coordination with a newfound and just developing autonomy and as the support of a trusted companion for emergent capacities in the self:

> The loving mother teaches her child to walk alone. She is far enough from him so that she cannot actually support him, but she holds out her arms to him. She imitates his movements, and if he totters she swiftly bends as if to seize him, so that the child might believe that he is not walking alone. . . . And yet, she does more.
>
> Her face beckons like a reward, an encouragement. Thus, the child walks alone with his eyes fixed on his mother's face, not on the difficulties in his way. He supports himself by the arms that do not hold him and constantly strives toward the refuge in his mother's embrace, little suspecting that in the very same moment that he is emphasizing his need of her, he is proving that he can do without her, because he is walking alone. (quoted in Sroufe, 1997, p. 205)

THE CONSEQUENCES OF ATTACHMENT PSYCHOPATHOLOGY FOR ADAPTIVE FUNCTIONING

Emotions, as I described in Chapter 6, are organizing experiences that are needed by the organism in order to respond adaptively, coherently, and quickly to events in the real world. They are highly efficient means of organizing processes of appraisal, physiological response, cognition, perception, behavior, and communication toward adaptive goals.

When an individual's affective communication and experience become distorted and inaccessible to him—are not fully processed—the individual loses the capacity for coherent and adaptive behavior in the situation in which he finds himself. Because appraisal rests on affective self-experience and these processes are disrupted, there is an important sense in which the individual does not know what is happening to him. Because affective communication is disrupted, the individual communicates with others inappropriately, miscuing both himself and them about what is happening and leading the interaction in a distorted and maladaptive direction. Unconscious physiological processes that may begin but not be fully processed or accurately appraised are not usable for the implementation of suitable action tendencies and behaviors; they may themselves become disorienting and confusing to the individual. Because of the strong human propensity to find a cognitive interpretation, the individual creates an understanding that incorrectly interprets what is happening both in the self and in others and then communicates and acts on the basis of the inaccurate interpretation. These interpretations are cognitive and representational but are built, as described earlier, on a foundation of procedural knowledge; they may be extremely robust and resistant to contrary information, unable either to assimilate or accommodate to it. A new iterative cycle of interaction with the environment begins (LeDoux, 1994) and incorporates and compounds this miscommunication and misinterpretation.

PRIMARY AND PREEMPTIVE EXCLUDED STATES

In the view elaborated here, nondefended affect is inherently adaptive because it gives the individual access to the information and internal resources that he or she needs to understand and to respond to the environment in a way that is accurate and congruent with his or her own goals. Nondefended affect is accurate and purposive; it reveals and informs us about our relationship to the environment in a direct and useful way. But when some affective experiences and communications have been placed off limits to an individual—through developmental experiences of systematic miscoordination in an attachment relationship—these adaptive affects and their associated processes, self-states, and responses are defensively distorted. When an individual begins to experience a defended-against affect in an incipient way, in response to a situation to which it could constitute part of an adaptive response, this leads directly to an experience of anxiety—what we should call attachment anxiety or coordination anxiety. It therefore immediately becomes subject to defensive processes and becomes defensively distorted.

The defended-against affect remains inchoate, not fully processed or accessible, not usable by the individual for adaptive purposes. The processes that are constituent of or recruited by the affect—appraisal, physiological responses, motivations, communication, perceptions, cognitions, memories, innate action tendencies—are also excluded and defensively distorted. Taken together, they constitute a defensively excluded affective state, what is called a *primary* excluded state.

A direct consequence of the primary excluded state is a maladaptiveness and a certain incoherence in the individual's behavior. The inability to fully process the affective response to the situation means that what one is experiencing remains to a significant degree out of awareness and unconscious. In this sense, as Izard (1993) suggested, "unconscious motivation may be an emotion experience (motivational/feeling state, action tendency) that is not cognitively tagged or articulated" (pp. 633–634). Because the individual is responding to unconscious motivations and defensively distorted appraisals and cognitions, his behavior and communication acquire an incoherence with respect to the adaptive task. He is not responding to what he thinks he is responding to. In the iterative cycle of emotional processing, the situation gets worse instead of better.

In such a situation, the individual's management of the defensively distorted affect becomes maladaptive with respect to his or her own goals. For example, if people defensively distort anger, they may indeed express anger but in a misdirected, situationally incoherent, maladaptive way. They may throw tantrums, find an array of faults with the other that are not related to the central issue, or withdraw from engagement with the situation, making excuses to leave. Or they may direct their anger at themself, becoming guilty, depressed, and convinced of their own inadequacy.

Individuals in a primary excluded state cannot feel without distortion what they need to feel in order to act effectively. Their functioning and the way in which they interact with others become overly patterned, rigid, and constrained. A stiff, false, or overly conventional quality may enter into those interactions that evoke the excluded emotion—a kind of confabulation to replace affective and interactional qualities that are not available. Similarly, individuals may seek to control their environment and interactions in order to avoid the possibility of events or stimuli that would threaten to evoke the excluded state. Situations and people that are likely to require the excluded affect are sources of anxiety and must be avoided or dreaded.

More generally, the individual may adopt an interactional style and a style of living that is shaped in order to prevent the need for the excluded, anxiety-eliciting affect. One instance of this phenomenon is the artificial suppression of some aspects of affective communications and experience and the artificial heightening of others (Cassidy, 1994; Dozier & Tyrell, 1997, 1998; Fraley, Davis, & Shaver, 1998). This defensively driven suppression and heightening of affect and affective communication is taken here as a basic process that occurs in many ways along many dimensions of self-experience. For example, an individual who experiences anxiety, exclusions, and defensive distortions in relation to the experience of anger may adopt an interactional style that stresses friendliness, that is hypervigilant to interpersonal cues that avoid conflict, and that is overly pleasing and accommodating to the desires of others in order to preserve their goodwill. But there is more than one way to avoid or at least reduce the likelihood of experiencing an anxiety-eliciting, defensively excluded affect. The same difficulty with defensively excluded anger might be managed with an interactional style that emphasizes not wanting things from others, by not imposing adequate boundaries, or by staying out of close interactions with others.

In each of these cases, the individual is pursuing what might be described as a strategy of *preemptive* exclusion, and this may be described as a preemptive excluded state (i.e., a state that excludes not the presently evoked experience of an affect but rather the relationships, situations, and events that may be anticipated as occasions for the evocation of the excluded emotion). Such preemptive states depend on the existence of a primary excluded state, which is what the individual seeks to avoid. They operate in a manner similar to a phobia (McCullough et al., 2003), and they may exercise a similarly powerful and constraining influence on an individual's life, foreclosing possibilities for adaptive, fluent action and full experience both in the moment and in the life choices that operate across the many years of the individual's life.

As with a phobia, a preemptive excluded state leads the individual to map his or her relational and situational world in terms of what must be avoided. Part of this is a search for ways to reach goals that do not take the individual into affectively excluded territory. The individual's pursuit of goals becomes both complexified and compromised because the direct route may not be taken. Similarly, the individual's conduct of relationships becomes "neurotically" intricate and shaped by the avoidance of some interactional experiences, the false heightening of others, and indirection and disavowal with regard to purposes.

THE MISSHAPING OF THE SELF

Taken together, primary and preemptive excluded states lead to a misshaping of the self. This position assumes, of course, that each individual has, at least inchoately, a true shape. The argument here is that the true shape of the self is that which is not defensively distorted. It is an individual who has relatively full access to his or her own internal resources and affective experience; who is able to understand the real constraints, difficulties, and opportunities that are present in the environment and can bring his or her understanding and resources to bear; and who is able to affectively communicate with others in a sufficiently open and accurate way to permit the evolution of close alliances and of intimacy. This is not an ideal type: Securely attached children, for example, in Crittenden's (1994) descriptive system, are characterized by their relaxed, intimate, and direct expressions of feelings and desires and by their ability to negotiate conflict and disagreement in relationships (Crittenden, 1992, 1997).

But for others, there is a distortion of affective communication and affective self-experience that impedes fluent, intimate, effective functioning. They are contorted by their defenses. In terms of primary and preemptive excluded states, this deformation is experienced as something that the individual is doing, but it actually occurs because of something the individual cannot do. In each moment of misshaping there is, in addition to what the individual does do, something that the individual cannot do and that if done would prevent the misshaping from taking place. Just as with a phobia, the thing that cannot be done is what produces the actual circumstantial distortion, incoherence, and sometimes chaos. The thing the individual cannot do is the affective communication and its associated self-experience that are defensively excluded. For example, Allen cannot communicate or let himself fully experience a sense of vulnerability and dependence on others. In this sense, when a patient brings a therapist an account of a difficulty, the clinical problem is not in the difficulty itself but in what did not happen just before the difficulty unfolded; the focus in terms of psychopathology is one moment before what the patient wants to talk about; it is what the patient leaves out without knowing that he or she is leaving it out; it is what the patient doesn't know that he or she is unable to do. It is the source of the misshaping. This is the region of the excluded state.

ATTACHMENT PSYCHODYNAMICS

Psychodynamic understandings of behavior and psychotherapy emphasize the interaction of conscious and unconscious processes. Attachment experiences shape the way in which these interactions occur.

Internal Working Models

In a relationship with an insufficiently responsive attachment figure, pathology arises through the construction of internal working models of the self and other that incorporate the beliefs, explanations, and expectations that are necessary to navigate the other's excessive unavailability and nonresponsiveness (see Chapter 4). These internal working models include the attributes of the self that occasion nonresponsiveness in the other and the possible conditions or relational strategies under which such responsiveness as is available might be obtained. For example, if the attachment figure is impatient with expressions of distress (as the mothers of avoidantly attached children often are), the child may learn to not communicate and to actively suppress his own internal affective experience of distress.

In this sense, internal working models are strategies and rules for achieving a coordinated state with a particular caregiver that evolve from interactions with the attachment figure as the child's developmental level advances. They both leave out and leave in particular affective communications, relational configurations, and self-states. They do so on the basis of what in the self has been successfully coordinated with by the principal caregiver in the past. Patterns of affective communication in the coordinated states that have been successfully achieved in the past are available for coordination in the future. Patterns of affective communication that have not been coordinated with in the past are subject to defensive exclusion and are left out of interactions in the future, with delimiting and distorting consequences for the individual. This is what produces problematic consequences for the individual's adaptive functioning. For example, a child whose distress is not coordinated with loses the capacity to rely on others as sources of support.

Patterns of communicative inclusions and exclusions are not only woven into the fabric of our relational configurations, they are its constitutive foundations. Once we are "trained" in a particular internal working model, we meet it everywhere—through what we are sensitive and insensitive to in others and through the ways in which we are most practiced in communicating and in regulating the self. Fatefully, for children and adults, self-experience that was communicatively excluded remains excluded; therefore, communication about interactions and relationships becomes delimited and constrained. It becomes difficult to know and to talk about one's relationships; it becomes especially difficult to talk about precisely those aspects of one's relationships that are problematic because they incorporate exclusions. As these communicative exclusions are incorporated into internal working models, they delimit the possible relational configurations that the once-infant, now-adult can have with others.

Consider the ways in which the internal working model of close relationships that Allen developed in interaction with his mother has influenced his close relationships as an adult. Allen experienced coordinating around closeness, dependence, need, or vulnerability as dangerous and shameful, as reflected in his memory of his mother's responding to his distress by pouring a glass of water over his head. The internal experiences of need and distress and of desire for care were virtually impossible for him to communicate. These internal experiences were shaped through an internal working model that led him to expect that his own experiences of need or distress would be ignored by the other or would be used to humiliate him. So, when Allen became anxious and insecure about his fiancée's departure on a business trip, he was unable to communicate his vulnerability to her in a way that might elicit responsive care. He was very angry at her for needing to go and also worried, even suspicious, about whether she might become involved with another man while on the trip, something his fiancée had given him no reason for concern about. But he could not tell her how scared and vulnerable he felt about her going away. He could not even fully and openly experience those feelings within himself. He could only indirectly feel and express an inarticulate anger, claiming that she didn't really need to go—a position that made no sense to the fiancée and that felt like an unreasonable and controlling demand.

When Allen, in the course of a psychotherapy session, did become aware of his own fear and vulnerability about her leaving him, his immediate reaction was that the last thing he would ever do would be to tell his fiancée that he was scared of her leaving him or her coming to prefer another man. He was shocked at the thought that the therapist seemed to think that might be a useful communication to her. For Allen, awareness and communication of dependence and vulnerability were very dangerous. Consequently, he could not bring his own affective experience to bear on his situation in a clear and effective way. As a result, his communications with his fiancée about this issue were indirect, unclear, vexed, and filled with frustrated struggle. He was not able to talk about, or even within himself to know, what was at issue. As a result, he doesn't get comforted, and his fiancée remains confused by his reactions within their relationship.

Internal working models incorporate pathology because they guide the behavior and expectations of the individual in regard to how the other will respond to his (or her) desire for attachment. They therefore guide the individual with regard to the regulation of his own internal experience (through the defensive processes I discuss below), the regulation of his demands on and relationship to the caregiver, and the regulation of his exploratory behavior (which is conditioned on expectancies regarding availability of the attachment figure as a secure base and safe haven). These self-regulatory processes are how the individual fits his experience and behavior to the conditions under which the attachment figure is most likely to provide coordination and caregiving. They guide the shaping of the self in order to obtain a relationship with the other; they denote which states in the other must be elicited and which avoided in order to obtain a caregiving response.

The experiential or psychological goal is to avoid the dreaded and intensely anxious state of involuntary, unwanted aloneness; the biological or evolutionary function is to fit the individual to the conditions under which survival-enhancing coordination, responsiveness, and caregiving may be obtained. The first biological mandate for the developing infant and child is to survive, and survival for the human infant rests on coordination with and attachment to the caregiver. The difficulties attendant on particular strategies for remaining close to the caregiver come later, in environments external to the original relationship with the particular caregiver. This process does not represent malfunction; it is not pathological in and of itself. Rather, it represents a naturally selected adaptive shaping and fitting of the self to the environment. Allen was right to learn to be suspicious of his mother, and while he was with her, he was right to conceal his needs from her and to seek to satisfy those needs in relationships where he was less genuinely dependent. Internal working models are accurate as well as adaptive in the childhood situation in which they arise, where they probably provided the best that could be gotten. But in their persistence beyond those original conditions, they distort, mislead, and constrain the individual in new and different circumstances, with people other than the original attachment figures, where more could be gotten than was possible originally (Bowlby, 1973, pp. 201–209; Hinde & Stevenson-Hinde, 1991). Allen's fiancée is not his mother. But his internal working models lead the adult Allen to re-create the interpersonal and intrapsychic experience of his childhood in ways that distort and delimit present experience. That is where therapy comes in.

In his emphasis on the importance of emotional availability and responsiveness, Bowlby made it clear that he was conceiving of presence and absence of the attachment figure as a psychological experience of being-with or being-alone. It is entirely possible and not uncommon to be alone while in the presence of another; the essential task of the therapist is to become a trusted companion with precise regard to what it is most difficult for the patient to know about himself and to communicate to another. These two phenomena—knowing about the self and communicating that self-knowledge to another—are intrinsically linked. As Allen said one day during a session, "I don't really know what I think or feel about something until I begin to talk about it." The psychological experience of being-with rests on the extent to which what one is feeling and thinking is registered by one's companion and is then reflected in a responsive and helpful way in the companion's communication and behavior. It is an experience of being understood, of attunement, of a coordinated state. The crucial contribution of therapy is to seek out and to coordinate with those aspects of the self that have been lost to defensive exclusion.

What We Are Not Allowed to Know and to Feel

Bowlby's conception of defensive exclusion is based on an information-processing model, and it emphasizes the exclusion of information at the levels of perception, cognition, emotion, memory, and communication. Defensively excluded information is excluded from further processing with the result that relevant behavioral options become unavailable to the individual, constraining her or his options in the real world. Bowlby believed that defensive exclusion was the central component in the full array of defenses identified by theorists and clinicians. Bowlby (1980) wrote,

> The basic concept in the theory of defense proposed is that of the exclusion from further processing of information of certain specific types for relatively long periods or even permanently. Some of this information is already stored in long-term memory, in which case defensive exclusion results in some type of amnesia. Other information is arriving via sense organs, in which case defensive exclusion results in some degree of perceptual blocking. . . . The many other phenomena described by clinicians as defensive, notably certain types of belief and certain patterns either of activity or inactivity together with their associated feeling, can be understood within this framework as being the profound consequences of certain significant information having been excluded. (pp. 45–46)

Bowlby (1980) thought that psychotherapy should be understood "as procedures aimed at enabling a person to accept for processing information that hitherto he has been excluding, in the hope that the consequences of his doing so will be . . . profound" (p. 46). The information that has been excluded is that which was systematically excluded from coordination with the attachment figure.

Defensive exclusion takes the form of shaping our attentional processes, and this shaping includes both underattending to some and overattending to other specific types of information. Bowlby's description of defensive exclusion thus includes the idea of valences or weightings that produce both selective exclusion and selective emphasis in the processing of information from internal sources (e.g., feelings) and external sources (e.g., messages from others).

Often, what is underattended to is some important aspect of our internal self-experience, for example, our own feelings or desires or goals. Stern (1985) gave an example of a child who was attuned with only in the moments after her enthusiasm ended but not in the enthusiasm itself; such a child is likely to direct attention away from and to lose awareness of her own experiences of enthusiasm. Similarly, another child may suppress and underattend to his own desire for comfort, if the desire for comfort elicits irritation in the attachment figure, or that for self-assertion and autonomous accomplishment, if the communication of those states causes the attachment figure anxiety. Sometimes, what is overattended to is some aspect of the other's internal state or communications (e.g., when Allen is especially vigilant about signs that indicate the possibility of the other's rejection, or when the child of an alcoholic parent becomes vigilant about the parent's mental state).

These two processes are often intertwined and reciprocal: As the individual overattends to some types of interactional information, other information is ignored. The patterns created by these processes may be complex and may require a detailed clinical understanding of the individual. The child who suppresses and underattends to his own desire for comfort may overattend to an externally focused activity, like playing with his toys or watching television. Allen, by overattending to the possibility of rejection, also overattends to flaws in himself for which he might be rejected and underattends to experiences of being loved.

Jude Cassidy (1994) discussed the avoidant and the ambivalent forms of insecure attachment in terms of the minimizing and suppression of emotions or their heightening via processes of emotion regulation. The process of emotional self-regulation is interwoven with the suppression or heightening of affective communications to others. In terms of excluded states, the distortion of experience, and the coherence of behavior, both avoidant and ambivalent individuals exclude information that would be available to them if the emotional distortions were not necessary in order to maintain coordination with the mother. In the case of the avoidantly attached, the infant or child would have more information about his or her own internal state (e.g., his distress and desire for comfort). In the case of the ambivalently attached, the individual would have more information related to his or her own interest in and exploration of the environment and would be less preoccupied with maintaining anxiety-driven vigilance and contact with the other.

The avoidantly attached exclude information about attachment longings and distress because fully processing it would lead to a painful experience of longing for but being rejected by a dismissing mother. The ambivalently attached exclude information about their own interests and about the environment because processing it would risk losing the involvement of an inconsistently attentive and self-preoccupied mother. "This accurate perception of the mother is thought to necessitate a distorted perception of the environment" (Cassidy, 1994, p. 242). In both cases, the pain derives from the loss of coordination with a particular type of mother and is avoided by exclusionary forms of processing. In both cases, the process is effected by the child's pattern of affective communications and by internal emotion regulation in relation to these communications and to the communicative responses of the mother.

The notion of defensive exclusion necessarily entails a conception of the possibility, in health, of relatively free and open access to information and communication about self-experience and the environment. This is the situation of secure attachment, which is characterized by the most open patterns of communication between the partners (Bretherton, 1990a, 1990b; Cassidy, 1994, 2001). Communication that is open and relatively unconstrained, in which neither partner rigidly censors what he or she is permitted to bring within the orbit of the interaction, is characteristic of secure dyads precisely because it permits the creation of coordination around the widest range of important self-experiences. The openness of the communication and the receptiveness of the other render the other as a trusted companion. Conversely, within an insecure attachment, communication must be constrained and important self-experiences excluded in order to maintain a more limited and insecure attachment and coordination with the other.

"Where defensive exclusion differs from the usual forms of [perceptual] exclusion the difference lies not in the mechanisms responsible for it but in the nature of the information that is excluded" (Bowlby, 1980, p. 69). In the case of defensive exclusion, Bowlby (1980) argued, information is excluded because it "is of a kind that, when accepted for processing in the past, has led the person to suffer more or less severely" (p. 69). It is the nature of the particular type of information that is excluded that gives the self its particular form of misshaping and creates the specific set of constraints on adaptive behavior that limits the individual's relationships and general functioning.

There is an important difference between information that when processed allows us to avoid a danger, thereby reducing suffering, and information that when processed produces a danger; between information that when further processed allows us to avoid suffering and information that in itself, when further processed, leads to suffering. We become hypervigilant and heighten our sensitivity about information that when processed allows us to avoid suffering; we suppress and become insensitive to information that when processed leads to suffering. The patterns in what we are over- or undersensitive to in our affective self-experience and communications with others give shape to our self.

For example, one would not exclude information about an attachment figure's anger if processing information about the caregiver's anger has in the past enabled one to reduce one's suffering; one would exclude information about one's own anger at the caregiver if in the past the full processing of one's anger has led one to get "burned" because of the way in which one's anger is responded to by the attachment figure (e.g., by retaliation or withdrawal). In the latter case, important information about one's own internal state has been defensively excluded from further processing.

The key to the problematics of defensive exclusion and defensive communication is that information from the environment or from within the organism that is personally relevant and that would normally be incorporated in further processing leading toward consciousness, aware feeling, and behavior is nonetheless excluded. We are thereby deprived of important information about what is happening to us and of important affective and motivational states for responding to what is happening. As a necessary consequence, our behavior becomes less coherent, less accurate, less purposive, and less adaptive.

In the case of defensive exclusion, then, information about the self and the environment is selectively excluded precisely because it is personally relevant, but part of its relevance is that it is dangerous to process—to know and to feel. Defensive exclusion is concerned with what we cannot let ourselves know and feel. It is also concerned with what we cannot let ourselves *do*. The key, for Bowlby, is incorporating what has previously been excluded. Describing his own view of psychotherapy, Bowlby (1985) wrote, "Our role is in sanctioning the patient to think thoughts that his parents have discouraged or forbidden him to think, to experience feelings his parents have discouraged or forbidden him to experience, and to consider actions his parents have forbidden him to contemplate" (p. 198).

This brings us to a consideration of clinical issues and problems in psychotherapy.

THE FOCUS OF ATTACHMENT-BASED THERAPY

There is a practical side to attachment theory. It provides a blueprint for change in the real world of patients' lives. For example, Bowlby's foundational "case studies" were not records of a treatment within a psychotherapy setting but were rather a documentary film record of a child's separation from his mother during his stay in a hospital. The habit of looking closely at the real world has remained an important component of the attachment framework and set of concerns. It is expressed in various ways, from a prominent focus by attachment researchers and theorists on matters of social policy that affect children and their caretakers (e.g., Belsky, 2009; Rutter, 2008) to a theoretical framework that locates difficulties and opportunities for change not only within the individual but also within the individual's relationships and real-world setting. It is this latter framework, for example, that has led attachment researchers to ask what happens to a child's attachment status when his mother's means of social support improves (it gets better). Attachment theory is perhaps unique among contemporary theories in the extent to which it views problematic aspects of personal functioning as forms of adaptation to and interaction with a real environment. Attachment models of psychotherapy look for therapeutic change in the *relationships* the individual engages in (as in varying capacities for communicative coordination) and in changes in the *capacity for adaptive action* in the world.

Thus, an attachment psychotherapy is frequently focused on what actions the patient needs to take but is unable to bring to effect, with promoting and eliciting these actions and looking at how they are impeded when they fail to occur. In significant part, the focus on action is closely related to the focus on affect. Affect, remember, is the way in which the body and mind become organized in relation to the environment; it is how we become prepared—cognitively, motivationally, physiologically—and disposed to act with regard to the environment.

And, as I have explored at length elsewhere, the actions we take are closely related to our processes of affect regulation. Affects that are regulated away by becoming disowned, displaced, or suppressed are thereby made unavailable for the motivation of adaptive action or for accurately informing the individual about what is happening to him. Worse, displaced affects can create confusion and incoherence in our own mind and behavior, as when, for example, our own fear of being close to another person leads us to think that the other person does not want to be close to us. A securely attached individual who wants to be close to another simply approaches. In contrast, an avoidantly or anxiously attached individual will create cognitions and perceptions in accord with his or her own disordered affect regulation and is therefore likely to inaccurately perceive the other as unresponsive or rejecting; he or she acts nonadaptively on the basis of the inaccurate perception.

Our lives are lived as a series of moments of affect regulation and dysregulation in which we make choices, based on what the process of affect regulation makes available to us in each moment, about how to act and what to do. We may approach or avoid a particular person, pick up and deepen a thread of conversation or change the subject, pursue a project or an opportunity for a relationship, or prefer to lie fallow and inert within a shelter of avoidance and tolerable familiarity.

So, action is closely related to affect and to affect regulation in that our affects prepare us and dispose us to take actions, and the taking of action to alter a situation is itself a form of affect regulation, as is the misconstrual or avoidance of a situation (Gross, 1999a). Affect regulation is also directly related to our communications with others (Adamson, 1996; Bretherton, 1990a, 1990b; Gross, 1999a; Tronick, 1989). Thus, the capacity for open communication, the processes of affect regulation, and the capacity for adaptive action are closely interwoven and vary together. A focus on action leads directly to issues of communication and of emotional experience; taken together, action, communication, and affect regulation constitute a triadic interactive process. A focus on these three phenomena together, as part of the same therapeutic process and intervention, leads directly toward greater adaptive capacities.

An example will help illustrate how attachment-based therapy focuses on communication, action, and affect regulation.

SHELLY

Shelly is a 38-year-old, Australian-born, import–export broker who has lived in the United States for a decade. Her presenting complaint has been that her relationships with men are prone to bickering and fights and never seem to move beyond a superficial level. She has no one special in her life. She is reporting happily about a recent visit home to visit her parents, which had gone well, and during which she found herself fighting much less with her mother and feeling much better understood by her father. "My mother even came over and gave me a hug while I was eating a piece of toast!" (said happily and with some surprise). As Shelly remembers this moment and becomes more immersed in the memory, she stiffens slightly and says, with bristled annoyance, "God, what a time to give someone a hug, while they're eating." In the next moment, a microexpression of sadness moves across Shelly's face. Then she slumps slightly and shrugs her shoulders to indicate she is done thinking about it.

In terms of affect and affect regulation, action, and communication, this is what has just happened: Shelly began to have an experience of being loved and of experiencing closeness with her mother. But Shelly's mother, historically, has been so inconsistent that Shelly has learned not to try to coordinate with her mother around such states, or if she does do so, to be prepared for an abrupt withdrawal by her mother. Experiences of closeness make her anxious, which is the source of her difficulty in establishing a close relationship with a man. Shelly regulates the feelings of closeness and consequent anxiety by displacing her emotional responses into anger at the other, as she does when she becomes irritated at her mother for hugging her while she was eating the toast. She succeeds in displacing the anxiety about closeness, but in the next moment she becomes sad about the loss of that very closeness.

This is exactly the sequence that takes place between Shelly and men. When they start to get emotionally close, she gets anxious. She then finds something to criticize or become angry about. She bickers and distances herself from the man. And she then becomes sad about the loss of the wished-for but anxiety-provoking closeness. So, she becomes close, anxious, angry, and sad in a regular and repeated cycle. Sometimes, she becomes depressed about her inability to find a way to be with someone. This is what Shelly knows how to do in order to deal with the relationships and feelings that are problematic and dangerous to her. These are actions she takes with respect to herself and others.

She does the same with her therapist in the sessions. At the moment in the above sequence when the microexpression of sadness appeared, her therapist intervened by saying, "What's the sadness on your face?" Caught in the moment, Shelly's face melted as the therapist's coordination with the

it more deeply and with more focused
ss it more completely). This made her
the next moment she became angry
; her mother's closeness. She snaps, "I
Vhy are you asking about this?" When
"I think it makes you feel uncomfort-
maintaining a coordination with the
ointing to the avoidant and defensive
len, her face softens, and she in fact
sense of closeness with her therapist.
tern of experiences of closeness fol-
lf, but with less anxiety and anger in
sense of closeness at the close of each
cycle. Snelly is learning how to do something different in a relationship. By
knowing about and directly experiencing her anxiety about closeness, in a
safe and secure context where she feels she will not be hurt, Shelly is led to
not engage her avoidant defenses (her anger) so quickly; she thus experiences
the closeness more directly, and she likes this enormously. In more theoretical
terms, Shelly is taking different actions in regard to her own affect regulation
and her communication with the other. As a result of the therapy, Shelly's
relationships, with men and with others, begin to deepen. Her life, in her own
report, begins to change.

IMPLICIT RELATIONAL KNOWING
AND PROCEDURAL KNOWLEDGE

The actions that Shelly is learning to do differently, both in the sessions with her therapist and in the relationships she has in her life, constitute
implicit relational knowing (Lyons-Ruth, 1998b). These actions are the things
that we know how to do in the formation and conduct of our relationships.
They include actions we take with regard to ourselves while we are in a relationship and the actions we take toward others as part of establishing communication with them. For example, Shelly "knows" how to go to anger within
herself when she begins to experience a closeness that makes her anxious,
and she is adept at communicating this anger to others. Implicit relational
knowing is a type of procedural knowledge (knowledge of how to do something that is expressed by the action of actually doing the thing rather than
by talking about or describing it) that includes how we communicate with
others and how we regulate affect in ourself.

This procedural knowledge begins with our relational experience with
others and shapes its subsequent evolution (e.g., as Shelly's way of handling

the anxiety about an unreliable closeness with her mother has shaped her intimate relationships with men). The contours of the affective communication and self-experience that were created in the child's earlier coordinations with his mother—including the defenses against excluded feelings and thoughts—influence, shape, and delimit these interactions. In terms of both the fluent internal experience of affect and its communication to others, the child is able to do some things and not do others; those affective experiences that the child cannot "do" well are attended by defensive maneuvers and distortions. The child's behavior with others in relationships is shaped by the contours of affective experiencing, expression, and defenses, and so these contours also shape his relational world.

A child who cannot become angry and assertive without feeling self-critical and depressed might well become an affable "politician" in his interpersonal relationships in order to get some of what he wants and still avoid the depressing experience of anger; a child whose enthusiasm led to discoordination by her mother (Stern, 1985) may find it difficult to be happy and excited in the presence of others and so find herself in relationships, personal and professional, where being happy and excited is not necessary. And a child like Shelly, whose experiences of closeness so often led to a feeling of abandonment, may become angry when she begins to depend on another person.

The affective-relational configurations that are and are not available to a patient constitute a major patterning of his or her life. For Shelly, this has meant that close relationships with men are unavailable to her. The relational constraints are structured by defensive exclusions of affects, cognitions, and behaviors. By facilitating the emergence of what has been excluded, psychotherapy expands the range of the relational configurations that are possible for an individual. It does this both by eliminating the necessity for defensive relational patterns, such as those that avoid anger or excitement, and by making more affectively open relationships directly available. It does this through a focus on affective and communicative actions, at both a micro and a macro level.

The prerepresentational procedural learnings that occur early in development are communicative and affect-regulating *actions*, more akin to learning to ride a bicycle or to swing a tennis racket than they are to forms of intellectual or representational understanding. Communication and affect regulation, taken together, may be seen as encoding relational experience, at the prerepresentational level of implicit, procedural knowledge—as actions that we know how take and things that we know how to do both to ourself and to others—in order to establish communicative coordination and to regulate our emotional experience. At the fine-grained, micro level, they influence the component processes of communication and affect regulation, such as which expressions we are best at recognizing and making and how we soothe ourselves when we are anxious. At the macro level, they influence the course of our life in the world—which situations we enter and which we avoid; how we approach relationships; how we focus our attention or maintain inattention; what cognitions and meanings we create to interpret what is happening; what we see to change and to maintain (Gross, 1999). They characterize and shape our experience in the world.

In this sense, the situation of a psychotherapy patient with respect to affective communication and defensive exclusions is akin to the situation of someone trying to learn to perform a complex physical action, like skiing or swinging a golf club, that requires the integration of feedback from within the body with information from the external environment; worse, it is the situation of someone who has learned how to perform the action the wrong way and is now trying to change. This is what our patients are struggling with as they try to learn new forms of affect regulation and new ways to create communicative coordinations with others. Just as one cannot change one's golf or tennis swing simply by altering one's cognitive knowledge of how the club or racket should be swung, so also one cannot alter one's affective and relational communication simply by altering one's conscious representations. Implicit procedural processes operate in a different way, using different brain regions that are not responsive to conscious control (LeDoux, 1996, 1998, pp. 200–203). They require implicit procedural experience for their alteration—both experience with the therapist and experience with new forms of actions in the world outside of the therapy sessions.

A focus on experience concentrates directly on the processes of communicative coordination and affect regulation in relation to adaptive capacities. What this means practically in the conduct of therapy is that

- the therapist is focused on concrete instances of what the patient *does*, in relationships with others and in action toward the environment generally; the therapist looks for and inquires about these concrete actions with special focus on the fluctuations of affect that attend these actions and the ways in which the patient communicates or avoids communicating about aspects of them.
- the therapist is very attentive to actions the patient takes with respect to the therapist, both in and around the sessions; there is a focus on how the patient's coordinations and affect regulations with the therapist are similar to those with others outside the sessions. The therapist talks very directly to the patient about the interpersonal process between them, again with special attention to fluctuations and microexpressions of affect and to what is and what is not communicated about easily. The

immediacy of this process often requires bravery on the part of both the patient and the therapist.

- the therapist supports, explores, and sometimes prescribes the taking of new adaptive actions by the patient. It is in the taking of new and previously avoided actions that the issues of constrained coordination and affect regulation are encountered most directly. The taking of new action directly confronts the misshaping of the self. It directly raises the issue of adaptive capacity. The difference between talking about emotions and relationships and directly experiencing them is vast. It is in the course of action that a patient's anxieties and avoidances are most heightened and may therefore be redressed, when his or her distortions can be most directly challenged (Cain, 2004; Cain, Blouin, & Barad, 2003; Fosha, 2000; L. Greenberg, 2008; Stampfl & Levis, 1967; Watson, McMullen, Prosser, & Bedard, 2011). Indeed, the new procedural learning that is essential to changes in coordinative capacity and emotional self-regulation can only be accomplished through actions that embody them. The patient has been unable to take these steps on his or her own. The therapist's task is to identify, encourage, and foster them.

For these reasons, an attachment-based psychotherapy is an action-oriented, experiential therapy. It emphasizes what the patient feels and does—what she (or he) experiences, both in and out of sessions—as well as what she knows and thinks. What the patient knows will also change, and a consciously held template can be a powerful tool for shaping and promoting and practicing change. But the most crucial and enduring changes will take place at the level of procedural processes—what the patient knows how to do, within herself and with others, as a result of her corrective experiences with the therapist and as a result of the new actions she takes—and the new experiences she therefore has outside the sessions.

8

ANXIETY, DEPRESSION, AND MALADAPTIVE ANGER

This chapter provides an attachment-based perspective on anxiety, depression, and inappropriate or nonadaptive anger—three common, distressing experiences for patients that cause trouble and suffering in their lives. Given the ubiquity of these phenomena, one important aspect of any clinical theory is how they are conceptualized. Each appears on its face to be a quite different type of experience, but the frequency of their appearance in psychopathology, the high comorbidity of anxiety and depression (Fava et al., 2010), and proposed links between depression and anger (Busch, 2009; Tao et al., 2011) make their systematic explanation and interrelationship from a theoretical point of view especially interesting and significant.

http://dx.doi.org/10.1037/14185-008
Attachment-Based Psychotherapy: Helping Patients Develop Adaptive Capacities, by Peter C. Costello

ANXIETY AND THE MISSHAPING OF THE SELF

Anxiety plays a central role in the development of pathology. It is itself the principal pathogenic agent and impetus for defensive exclusions and impairments of affective communication and self-states.

The Two Types of Attachment Anxiety

Anxiety was a term that Bowlby (1973) wished to reserve exclusively for fears related to the availability of the attachment figure. He described anxiety about attachment as coming in two varieties, and these correspond to the strategies of suppression and of heightening, first noted in Chapter 5 of this volume. The first type of anxiety occurs when we, in a moment of fear or distress, are actively seeking an attachment figure but are unsuccessful in securing one; the second is a more chronic anxiety, occurring even when we are not acutely distressed, that our attachment figure will not be available if we were to want her. The distinction between these types of attachment anxiety is subtle but important. We manage and regulate the first type of anxiety through the strategy of the suppression of feeling. We begin by suppressing any feelings or self-states that are likely to make our attachment figure unresponsive; eventually, we may also suppress the very feeling of wanting our attachment figure at all. We manage and regulate the second type of anxiety through the strategy of the heightening of feelings and signals that do elicit responses from our attachment figure (Cassidy, 1994). This second type of anxiety occurs in the absence of fear and even while in contact with the attachment figure. It engages a strategy of hypervigilance about the attachment figure and the heightening of self-experiences that summon or maintain the involvement of the attachment figure while indirectly excluding other self-experiences, such as exploration and autonomy, that are thereby neglected.

Suppression Versus Heightening

Anxiety misshapes the self. This misshaping occurs as part of the process of reaching a coordinated state with the caregiver within which what each communicates is more or less matched to the other. It is described as *misshaping* because particular rigidities in the caregiver do not allow certain optimal and adaptively useful affective communications and self-states in the attachment seeker. These useful and naturally occurring capacities are then diminished or lost—defensively excluded—and are replaced by defensive processes. The individual is constrained, even deformed, in a pattern that is determined by the rigidities of the attachment figure.

This process is driven by anxiety about the loss of a coordinated state, and it is effected through processes of suppression of some affective communications and self-states and the heightening of others. The strategy of suppression is directed primarily inward, toward the self, toward the suppression of affective communications and self-states. The strategy of heightening, on the other hand, is directed primarily outward, toward the other, toward the heightening of those affective communications and self-states that actively engage coordination with the caregiver. Each strategy results in implicit procedural learnings about how to reach communicative coordination with others, and each leaves out and misshapes important aspects of the self. Both strategies misshape the self, with very different consequences, and are central to what is addressed in clinical work.

Derek exemplifies the suppressive style. He is a 42-year-old television producer who works very hard and has become quite successful. He is married and has two children. In most ways, his life seems in very good order. But he has come to treatment because he is depressed and angry and because he and his wife have stopped having sex, though he says that he finds her attractive and loves her. Indeed, she is a very important person for him, virtually the only person with whom he has other than a working relationship. Derek frequently drinks to excess on weekends. Despite the therapist's several attempts, Derek will refuse a referral for antidepressant medication, saying, "It's bad enough that I come here. I don't want to think of myself as someone who needs drugs."

When Derek enters the therapist's office, he is tense and makes only the slightest degree of eye contact, slipping sideways past the therapist as the door is opened. His lips are pressed together, his eyes averted, and when he sits down he keeps his body still and self-contained. But there is also a great deal of tension in his body. There is no sense of relaxation or openness. His entire aspect is of someone who is screwed down tight and who also is bursting at the seams.

Derek's experience of his own distress is that it is something that he must handle on his own. When he was 12 years old, a 17-year-old girl next door half-seduced and half-bullied him into a sexual relationship that continued for 5 years, until Derek left for college. He was frightened of the girl, who was physically larger than he and much more expressive emotionally. She threatened him when he sought to withdraw from the relationship, telling him she had friends at school who would beat him up if she requested it. On several occasions, she did in fact physically attack him.

Throughout the years of this relationship, Derek concealed it from everyone. Derek experienced his mother as withdrawn from close involvement with him and as preoccupied with housework and cooking; she seemed always on the periphery of whatever was happening at home. Derek's father "talked all the time" but only about himself. He would become angry if interrupted or disagreed with. "When I was with them in the living room," Derek said, "I would act like everything was all right, but I wouldn't feel anything. When I would be alone in my room later, I felt like all of these problems were suddenly weighing on my head and I didn't know what to do about them. Then I just felt terrible."

In the terms of the attachment perspective being discussed, Derek could not find an attachment figure to coordinate with around his considerable fear and distress over what was happening to him. The long-standing family communication pattern was one that offered very few opportunities for coordination around Derek's experiences or concerns. His mother was routinely withdrawn and distant; his father was preoccupied with his own experiences and concerns, around which he demanded that others coordinate.

Derek learned that the only way he could manage what was happening to him was by suppressing both his affect and his communications about what was going on internally. He became adept at not talking and at distracting himself from feeling. When he sidles so avoidantly into the therapist's office, he is anxious and avoidant because he is doing something that is enormously difficult for him: He is going into a room where the primary task is to reveal what he is feeling by talking about it to another person. Derek experiences the therapy sessions with a combination of dread and relief. He reports, "I always hate coming here the night before, but I always start to feel better during the sessions." Derek is learning a new way of establishing coordination with another person, one that does not require suppression but rather focuses on communication and awareness of what he is feeling and thinking.

The therapist's role in this is to find ways to spot and to establish contact with the suppressed aspects of Derek's experience and to facilitate Derek's communicative elaboration of what is happening to him, both with the therapist and in his relationships in the world. This requires a close reading of Derek's nonverbal communication, a gradual enlargement of the coordination between them about what has not been expressed, a clear and repeated cognitively oriented statement for Derek of what the problem and the process of change are, and some behaviorally oriented homework to take the work of the sessions into the outside world.

For example, in one meeting, as Derek sits down warily and tensely says that he has nothing to talk about, the therapist observes mildly that it looks like it is very uncomfortable for Derek to come into the sessions. Derek looks a bit startled, even frightened, as though he had been found out, as though a secret had been unexpectedly revealed. But he then begins to relax and to talk about how difficult in fact it is for him to come. He says that starting to talk about himself feels like he is going to have to jump off a high cliff into the water below, and that he can't do that. He needs, he says, to walk slowly down the cliff until he can stand on the beach and walk slowly into the water. As he says this, his body relaxes, and he gets a big and very soft smile on his face. The therapist participates with Derek in the coordination around these feelings. He helps Derek to elaborate them. Derek's anxiety rises and falls repeatedly in the session; each time a suppression is brought into coordination, Derek feels some anxiety and then relaxation and a sense of expansiveness.

The therapist also provides Derek with a cognitive framework to relate the difficulty he has in talking within the sessions to his experiences of never being able to reveal his distress as a boy at home. And the therapist inquires about how this might affect Derek's relationships with other people. Derek then begins to talk about how difficult it is to say anything to his wife if he disagrees with her or is upset. This leads to some homework for Derek to do before the next session—talking to his wife about some minor disagreements—in order to take the work of the session into the outside world.

Derek's affective communication was based in a suppressive style. Patients who use affective heightening look different. Jennifer, a 28-year-old woman, comes to sessions in gorgeous clothes so striking that they have a touch of costume about them. They are hard not to notice. She brings coffee for her therapist so that he has some to drink while she drinks her own. Rather than avoiding eye contact, as does Derek, she begins talking to the therapist as she comes through the door, and she sits facing him directly. Her tone of voice is affectively rich. There is an immediate sense of emotional intensity, presence, and reactivity. Jennifer attracts attention, even commands it, but she often complains about not being noticed or seen by other people.

In fact, Jennifer's mother seems to have been unusually inconsistent in her relationship with Jennifer, sometimes (especially around Jennifer's appearance) very involved and attentive but at other times suddenly preoccupied with her own concerns and uninterested in what was happening with her daughter. Jennifer has learned to work hard to establish coordination with an other who—in Jennifer's childhood experience and thus in her internal working model—is fundamentally unreliable and prone to withdraw. Even when leaving a message on voice mail, Jennifer often worries that the machine has stopped recording. She sometimes calls back to repeat a message, just in case.

In her adult relationships, Jennifer heightens those aspects of herself and her affect that were most likely to maintain coordination with her mother. But this is an often exhausting process that requires a heightened focus on the state of the other and a constant readiness to act in order to maintain the other's involvement. In her relationships with men and other women, Jennifer always does a lot to please the other. For example, her friends often describe her as one of the funniest people they know. She works hard to be funny. But she finds social contacts exhausting and draining and can't wait to be alone at the end of an evening. Intimate relationships inflame her need to please and her anxiety about the other's withdrawal even more strongly, so they are extraordinarily difficult for her to enter into and maintain. While with an intimate other, she often feels like she loses contact with herself.

It is very hard for Jennifer to believe that the other will be there for her when needed, so she acts proactively to retain a sense of connection. This assuages her anxiety about connection and availability in the short term, and this reduction in anxiety then soothes her and reinforces her strategy of hyperactive involvement with the needed other. But the difficulty is that the heightening strategy distracts her from her own purposes and goals and is also often unrelated to the actual needs and behaviors of the other person. So, the real needs and purposes of herself and the other are ignored while the drama of threatened and regained connection is enacted. Within such a relationship, the partners may neglect important life issues while they struggle over frequent anxiety-driven disruptions of their relationship.

This pattern is both compelling and exhausting for the participants within it. It is often compelling because the heightening of affective involvement is passionate and often rewarding in itself; it is exhausting because it has a compulsive quality that is driven by anxiety that cannot be fully soothed, and that occurs with diminished reference to other needs and circumstances.

For Jennifer, therapy requires an experience of consistent response, a deepening and more aware experience of the persistent fears of unavailability that drive her interpersonal behaviors, and a focus on her own purposes and goals and the real needs of the others with whom she is involved. The experience of consistent response may require the therapist to be especially accommodating and responsive to her demands and needs until she begins to feel safe and cared for within the relationship. It also requires that the intimate other in her life be someone who in fact is responsive and trustworthy, and individuals such as Jennifer may often become involved with others who in fact are not consistently trustworthy. Finally, within the context of a good-enough relationship with an other and as her attachment anxiety diminishes, Jennifer needs to be helped to see her own purposes and needs and the legitimate needs of her partner and to begin to focus on these.

Fear of Feeling and Fear of Absence

We might call the two varieties of anxiety identified by Bowlby, with their associated defensive strategies of suppression and heightening (as seen in Derek and Jennifer, respectively), the *fear of feeling* and the *fear of absence*. The first is fear directed at an internal state. The second is fear directed externally toward the other. Both are versions of the overarching fear of aloneness and of the loss of coordination with the other. In fear of feeling, anxiety is resolved by damping the self; in fear of absence, anxiety is managed by focusing on the other. But in keeping with the dyadic, self-with-other doubleness of attachment processes, fear of feeling and fear of absence each simultaneously alter both affective communication toward the other and internal self-experience in characteristic ways. This is done in the interest of managing self-with-other and of modulating the fear of aloneness. Each type of anxiety constrains adaptive action and misshapes the self. Each type of anxiety limits the relational configurations that are available to an individual.

From within the attachment perspective, fear of feeling and fear of absence are the two fundamental types of anxiety that are met with in the clinical situation; each of these anxieties also appears as anxiety about particular affects and relational configurations that are important in the individual's developmental experiences of fear of feeling and fear of absence. They bear a relationship to the Strange Situation classifications of avoidant and resistant attachment (see Cassidy, 1994). But it is more clinically useful to approach these phenomena in terms of the processes of suppression or heightening of feelings and of signals, rather than in terms of classification or categories of being. Depending on their developmental histories, individuals may present with a preponderance of one or the other type of anxiety or, sometimes, with a mixture of the types.

The two types of anxiety may manifest themselves in very different ways. Where the suppression of self-states has been relatively successful, fear of feeling will become visible as overt anxiety primarily when relational configurations or events—either in external circumstances or within the therapeutic setting—provoke an inchoate experience of the suppressed feeling; otherwise, the individual's fear of feeling may lead him or her to focus everywhere except on these feelings and to be relatively comfortable while doing so. The clinical marker of this situation is likely to be a degree of flatness or deadness in the interpersonal exchange. The clinician may feel that something is missing in the interaction, and indeed he would be right.

Fear of absence is more likely to be directly visible as overt anxiety. The clinician may feel swept up in the patient's distress but notably may also feel controlled by it as the patient heightens affective communications and self-states that create engagement and ensure against absence. With heighteners, the clinician may also feel that there is somewhere a rigidity and coercive quality in the interaction that ignores other aspects of the patient's experience and of what is going on in the interaction, and indeed there is.

But it is important not to conceive of these types of anxieties and associated defensive strategies only as possible global types. Each type of anxiety occurs in relation to some affects, self-states, and relational configurations but not to others. Indeed, even the most globally avoidant patient may have a pet, never discussed with the therapist, or even an inanimate object, such as a computer or a photograph, with which excluded affect states inchoately emerge. Few individuals who come for therapy are either globally avoidant or globally anxious. Rather, they fear feeling or fear absence in very particular ways, based on complex histories, that have become established as implicit procedural communicative processes that encode self and other and that have been elaborated as cognitive, representational models of self and other.

The key issue is what particular affective communications, self-states, and relational configurations are being suppressed or heightened and excluded (remember that when some states are heightened, others are necessarily disregarded), what in particular these exclusions are related to in the other, and how the patient's life has been constrained by the primary and preemptive excluded states (discussed in Chapter 5). This is a matter of detailed focus on what the patient can and cannot affectively communicate and feel under particular circumstances and how these inabilities and defensive overemphases have structured and misshapen his or her life, thoughts, and relationships.

In an attachment-based therapy, anxiety is an indication that something has been or is about to be excluded and that this "something" is needed by the individual. It is also an indication that in the individual's past, this "something" led to the loss of coordination with the caregiver; something in the self is potential but excluded because it previously led to the loss of attachment and of a felt sense of security. In this sense, anxiety is not itself the primary problem to be solved but rather a nettlesome symptom, a pathogenic agent. Even more important, it is a marker that something important and needed is being excluded and distorted. The clinician's task is to help the patient undo the exclusion by finding and facilitating the affective communication, the self-state, and the relational configurations that have been left out (and had to be left out of the communication with the primary caregiver but do not have to be in the therapeutic relationship).

DEPRESSION AND THE MISSHAPING OF THE SELF

A central principle of the conceptual understanding of emotions that is presented in Chapter 6 is the proposition that "each affect has a fundamentally adaptive purpose that serves to facilitate commerce with the environment" (Malatesta & Wilson, 1988, p. 100). Sadness and depression are close kin, although they are not identical. They are considered here together, in terms both of their commonalities and of their differences. What are the adaptive purposes of sadness, and how is sadness related to depression?

The Adaptive Purposes of Sadness

Sadness is the emotional state that occurs in order to facilitate and dispose one toward a reduction in activity and withdrawal from a situation in which going forward or maintaining a high level of active involvement can produce no good or satisfactory result. This is how it is allied to experiences of helplessness or loss and the way it is opposite to anger, which disposes us toward very high levels of activity in order to produce change in an unsatisfactory situation. Sadness is a response to situations in which we are unable to produce change.

Sadness occurs when we are in a situation in which the adaptive response is to discontinue doing what we have been doing and to withdraw. Sadness slows our cognitive and motor systems. The situation we are in may be of various actual kinds; the key is that the emotional states that would accompany going forward or continuing past activity are no longer useful, whether those emotional states are interest, joy, or anger. The communications and actions for which these states dispose us are apprehended as not possible, and therefore the experience of those states in relationship to the current situation becomes maladaptive.

This common thread may be seen in a variety of very different situations. It is present when someone we love has died and all of the activities and emotions and communications (including negative emotions) that constituted our relationship with the living person are no longer possible, at least not in anything like the same way, because the person is irredeemably not there. The sadness of mourning is an aspect of the process of the giving up of the actions and affective communications that were involved in our going forward with the lost loved one. In a very different context, the same pattern is visible in a study of the effect of mothers' expressions of sadness on the activity levels of their 9-month-old infants (Termine & Izard, 1988): The mothers' expressions of sadness increased sadness expressions in their infants and led to a reduction in the activity level of the exploratory play in which the infants had been engaging. Sadness disposes us to lower our activity levels and to withdraw from a situation in which going forward in the way that was once pleasurable and important is not possible. This is why a parent may cry at a wedding or a moviegoer may cry at a happy ending. Sadness is a prelude to a reorganization of our activities, and this is a vital adaptive function. This is the understanding of sadness that the poet Rilke (1903/2001) conveyed to a young colleague:

> So you must not be frightened . . . if a sadness rises up before you larger than any you have ever seen; if a restiveness, like light and cloud-shadows, passes over your hands and over all you do. You must think that something is happening with you, that life has not forgotten you, that it holds you in its hand; it will not let you fall. (p. 92)

The Difference Between Sadness and Depression

The qualitative difference between sadness and depression is less one of degree of negative affect than one of the absence in depression of adaptive progress toward the withdrawal and reorganization to which sadness disposes us and which we often begin to anticipate, in fleeting thoughts, even in the midst of our sadness. Depression is stuck sadness. It is extended and stuck sadness in relation to a situation from which we cannot withdraw but with which we remain in contact and try to go forward in a nonadaptive way. We get stuck either because external circumstances require us to continue going forward with actions that can produce no adaptive outcome or because for internal reasons we are unable to access the affective states that would reorganize our relational configurations and self-states and thereby permit more adaptive responses to our situation. In both situations, our body is prompting us to stop doing what we are doing and to try something else, but we are unable to do so, for internal or external reasons. We are stuck in a continuing experience of sadness without reasonable hope of a useful or desirable response. This is why a key component of depression that distinguishes it from sadness is the element of hopelessness.

Sadness begins, just barely, to look over the horizon of a loss. It includes a version of hope and a sense of progress either in the form of intended change related to what we had been doing or in the form of a withdrawal and then a going forward with other things. These possibilities are not experienced in the depressed state. Then, there is only inability and loss; there is no future. In general, sadness is not a clinical problem; depression, of course, is. How do people get stuck in their sadness?

The Origins of Depressive Hopelessness: Envirogenic and Autonomous Depression

There are two sources of depressive hopelessness. The first type, which I call *envirogenic* depression, results from external circumstances that require us to go forward in a situation with actions that can produce no adaptive outcome. It is exemplified in the classic experiments on learned helplessness conducted by Seligman and his associates (e.g., Maier & Seligman, 1976) that are understood to have illuminated the central role of hopelessness in depression.

In these experiments, an environment is manipulated so that the animal or human subjects experience a situation in which no response they make to the situation is adaptive (i.e., nothing they do produces a real change in a situation that they very much need to change). For humans, the situations have included inescapable loud noise and unsolvable word problems.

Subjects are stuck in a situation in which their attempts to cope, to go forward, produce no desirable result. Eventually, when the situation itself is finally altered so as to permit an adaptively useful response, the subjects do not attempt the adaptive actions that would in fact now produce a useful result. The subjects have "learned" that there is nothing they can usefully do in a situation which they cannot leave.

Seligman and his colleagues (e.g., Rosenhan & Seligman, 1989) considered learned helplessness to be a central component of many types of depression, and this is how it is still widely understood today (e.g., Greenwood & Fleshner, 2008; Hajszan et al., 2009; Li et al., 2011; Mallei et al., 2011; McLaughlin, Lefaivre, & Cummings, 2010; Reed et al., 2009; Rotenberg, Costa, Trueman, & Lattimore, 2012; Ryan, Vollmayr, Klyubin, Gass, & Rowan, 2010; Seligman, 2011; Winter, Vollmayr, Djodari-Irani, Klein, & Sartorius, 2011). The key element of Seligman and his colleagues' model is that depression emerges from a situation, demanding change, with which one must remain in contact but in which no adaptive action is possible.

In Seligman's classic experiments, the external world is carefully manipulated so that in reality no adaptive action is possible with regard to a highly specific and discrete aversive stimulus. Such situations do occur in the lives of individuals, for example, in cases of repeated or prolonged trauma (Herman, 1992). They constitute the occasion for the first type of depression, envirogenic depression, just described.

But there is a second type of depression—call it *autonomous* depression—in which adaptive actions are not possible and are not taken because the individual cannot access the internal affective states that would produce adaptive action and alter his or her relationship to the environment. This type of depression is also exemplified in Seligman's experiments: It is exemplified by the stage of the experiments, noted above, at which the experimental conditions are changed so that the subjects could in fact escape the noise or solve the word puzzles but do not attempt to do so.

The inability to access a possible adaptive state leaves the individual in a situation of remaining in contact with a situation in which no satisfactory response or outcome is possible—but for internal, intrinsic reasons. This inability occurs in relation to particular relational configurations and external stimuli. Thus, autonomous depression includes real problems presented by the external world, but the term describes an internal–external situation in which adaptive responses exist but are not taken because they are not personally accessible to the individual.

The difference between envirogenic and autonomous depression then is not whether there is an external stressor or stimulus. The difference is whether the constraints on an adaptive response are internal or external, on whether there is—internal constraints aside—a possible adaptive response. In the learned helplessness experiments, the learning of the helplessness marks a transition from envirogenic to autonomous depression. At the point where animal subjects that have been exposed to inescapable shock are placed in a new situation in which the shocks could be avoided, they fail to take the possible actions that would avoid the shock because these actions have become internally inaccessible to them. What begins as a realistic appraisal of possible responses to an environmental stimulus becomes eventually an internally maintained constraint on responses and an intrinsic feature of the individual.

This pattern of realistically appraised external constraints on responses that eventually become autonomous, internal, and intrinsic to the individual is the same as that proposed for the influence of developmentally experienced coordinated states on the affective communications, self-states, and relational configurations that are internally available to the individual. Affective communications and associated self-states and relational configurations that were systematically not coordinated with during development become internally inaccessible; other affective states and relational configurations—those that were coordinated with—are substituted and experienced. When the individual later encounters and remains in contact with a situation to which the excluded affective and relational states constitute part of an adaptive response, these states are unavailable. When the individual is faced with a situation that cannot be left and to which an adaptive response is impossible, his or her initial experience of sadness transforms into hopeless depression.

Autonomous depression is the more commonly encountered clinical experience. This occurs in response both to external stressors and to particular relational configurations within which the individual is unable to access adaptive affective responses that would reorganize his relationship to others and to the environment. The individual is stuck in a particular situation or relational configuration to which he cannot, for internal reasons, make the adaptive response. His sadness prompts him to stop going forward with what he is doing, but the alternative adaptive responses are not available, and so he cannot; this converts adaptive sadness to the intransigent, sustained, unremitting, hopeless sadness of depression.

The clinician's task in these circumstances is to reawaken and facilitate access to the affective self-states and affective communications that are necessary to behave adaptively in the patient's real-life situation.

Daniel, for example, grew up in a home in which what was real was not addressed. When Daniel was 10 years old, the youngest of five children, his mother died of amyotrophic lateral sclerosis. During the 3 years of his mother's dying, Daniel had known that something terrible was happening. He felt especially close to his mother and would often spend time sitting with her in her room. But what exactly was happening was never spoken of between them, nor between Daniel and his father, his brothers and sisters, his aunts and uncles, nor with anyone else. That his mother was ill was inevitably mentioned, and the requirements of her care were an everyday part of the family's routine. That a near day was coming when she would not be there was never spoken about; rather, even in her last days, it was implicitly but unconvincingly denied. Daniel's anxiety, confusion, and grief were not engaged. Thus Daniel, during an intense and frightening period of his young life, repeatedly had an experience of sitting with and feeling close to a mother he loved but with whom he could never address the thing between them that frightened and threatened him. Precisely the most important affective communication was precisely left out. It was a coordination built of deep need and disengaged and uncommunicated feeling, marked by fear and avoidance.

Although Daniel now recalls and describes the period of his mother's death as a "holocaust," at the time he spoke to no one about what he was feeling. Daniel's father was in many ways caring, but he had a distant interpersonal style and a very demanding medical career; he was overwhelmed by the death of his wife and the practical requirements of caring for his sons and daughters. When someone would ask Daniel how he was (there was a particular female teacher at school who was especially tender and solicitous), he recalls saying that he was fine but then immediately feeling a flood of bad feeling, "like a poison," spread through his face and then into his body, leaving him enervated and weak. This feeling of a poison spreading through his face—the physical locus of critical affective communication—and then his body as he fails to communicate his grief and anxiety to another is a central memory for Daniel; it captures both the experience and the consequences (the enervation and the weakness) of his essential defense against the communication of real internal experience. This defense had come to characterize and to dog Daniel's life.

The style of not talking about what was emotionally real became a hallmark of Daniel's way of being in the world. He developed a manner of interacting that featured rapid-fire conversation, puns and jokes, frequent changes of topics, and overconventionalized, overpolite mannerisms. At the same time, he developed an accurate and overriding concern that other people might not "get him," that they didn't appreciate him, like him, or understand why he did things in the way that he did. His interactional style characterized his adult life as a whole—a life in a kind of limbo, without genuine engagement. He went to college and received his degree but without interest or enthusiasm for anything he did there; he worked part-time but failed to pursue the career he really wanted; he began relationships but ended them when they began to deepen. Daniel came to treatment because he was increasingly depressed and hopeless about the direction of his life and because medication had failed to alleviate his depression. The common thread in Daniel's difficulties was a disconnection from the experience and communication of genuine affective experience. In consequence, without the orientation and sense of self-direction that arise from fully processed affect, Daniel was unmotivated and actually uninformed about his own needs, desires, and goals. He literally did not know what to do in various situations, because his emotional reactions were not informing him about what was happening to him or about what he wanted to do. This gave his daily life a vague and frittered-away quality. But he was stuck. He did not have access to the resources that would permit him to move his life from its derailed state, and he did not, on his own, know how to get those resources. He was a very bright, talented, and attractive young man, but his life had become sidetracked.

In therapy, there were two major processes at work. One was the undoing of Daniel's state of pathological mourning in regard to his mother. The other, a closely related but more general process, was addressing Daniel's way of avoiding the communication and full experience of what was affectively real to him in his daily life. This was the issue in regard to his mother's death. But it was also the larger difficulty that kept his life and relationships from moving forward into more satisfying engagement and accomplishment. Daniel's defenses created hopelessness and depression by making forward movement impossible. The task for the therapist was to find his way through the welter and vagueness of Daniel's defenses and to help him to locate, experience, and then communicate to others his more genuine affect.

As the therapy progressed, the therapist would often question Daniel gently but closely about both the loss of his mother and his covert feelings in regard to events and relationships in his present life. The two areas opened together. The process was one of elaborating experiences that he had excluded from communication and thus from full awareness. As Daniel talked more about the period of his mother's death, more details emerged about her last months and especially about the hours and weeks after her death. He recalled aspects of his own reactions and feelings and the ways in which others had responded to him. He brought in photographs of his mother, some of them with him, and once, on a computer, a film of his mother at his birthday party, with her hand resting on his shoulder. His feelings about his mother and about losing her deepened in a mature, truly sad way, and they became more available to him for expression to the therapist. Daniel was doing the work of a full and very sad mourning that had been unavailable to him years earlier. As this work progressed, Daniel also became more realistically aware of his father as a real person, with flaws and strengths, who loved him and with whom he could be closer and more open. The therapist also focused on Daniel's feelings about events and relationships in the present. Just as Daniel more fully and deeply engaged his feelings about his family, he also became better at knowing and communicating what he was feeling with other people in his day-to-day life. Many of these feelings involved displaced anger or fear of rejection. As these feelings became more accurately acknowledged, Daniel became better able to think about them and to reevaluate them and the relationships of which they were a part. His friendships and working relationships began to shift and deepen. People told him that he seemed more confident, and he felt that people looked at him differently, in a more positive way. He became involved with a new woman who clearly cared for him and with whom he gradually, despite real fear and anxiety, became closer than he had been to any other person in his adult life. His life began to move forward.

Two concepts for understanding sadness and depression are Bowlby's conception of pathological and adaptive mourning (Bowlby, 1963, 1980; Bowlby & Parkes, 1970) and Gerald Klerman's interpersonal psychotherapy for depression.

Pathological and Adaptive Mourning

Bowlby (1980) described two main variants of pathological mourning:

> In one of the two disordered variants the emotional responses to loss are unusually intense and prolonged, in many cases with anger or self-reproach dominant and persistent, and sorrow notably absent. So long as these responses continue the mourner is unable to replan his life, which commonly becomes and remains sadly disorganized. Depression is a principal symptom, often combined or alternating with anxiety, "agoraphobia," hypochondria or alcoholism. This variant can be termed chronic mourning. At first sight the other variant appears to be exactly the opposite, in that there is a more or less prolonged absence of conscious grieving and the bereaved's life continues to be organized much as before. Nevertheless, he is apt to be afflicted with a variety of psychological or physiological ills; and he may suddenly, and it seems inexplicably, become acutely depressed. (pp. 137–138)

These apparently divergent variants of disordered mourning have a central, core difficulty in common. Depression is described above as a response to a situation in which one tries or is obliged to continue going forward with affective states that can produce no useful or adaptive result—that cannot lead within that situation to the goal that the affect states dispose one to achieve. The sadness or sorrow of the individual does not successfully lead him (or her) to stop doing, affectively, what he has been doing. Nor is the individual able to withdraw from the situation; his sadness becomes "stuck" and does not lead to a reorganization. The adaptive function of sadness is about the need to say good-bye to a situation or way of going forward that can produce no adaptive result; depression occurs when the patient is unable to get to the moment of saying good-bye. This is precisely the phenomenon that Bowlby placed at the core of the variants of pathological mourning. In both types of pathological mourning, the individual continues trying to do that which can achieve no desirable or adaptive result within the situation. He is unable to get to an affective state that can produce an adaptive result. Bowlby (1980) wrote, "So long as he does not believe that his loss is irretrievable a mourner is given hope and feels impelled to action; yet that leads to all the anxiety and pain of frustrated effort" (p. 139).

Bowlby's two forms of pathological mourning are closely related to the two forms of attachment anxiety described earlier (i.e., fear of feeling and fear of absence) and are also related to the two forms in which depression commonly occurs. Prolonged absence of mourning appears to be an instance of fear of feeling; chronic mourning, with its heightened engagement with the lost beloved, appears to be a form of fear of absence. These parallel the vegetative, anergic and the irritable, agitated forms of depression that are encountered clinically. Fear of feeling and a prolonged absence of mourning may be thought of as associated with a defensive affect strategy of suppression; fear of absence and chronic mourning may be thought of as associated with a defensive affect strategy of heightening. In terms of Strange Situation classifications, these are respectively avoidant and anxious attachment.

However, our focus here is on types of anxieties and broad strategies of defense rather than on the Strange Situation classifications. Those described as avoidant in Strange Situation classifications suppress some affects and heighten others (e.g., they heighten interest in mastery of the environment); those described as anxious in Strange Situation classifications heighten some affects but suppress others (e.g., they suppress interest in exploring the environment because they are preoccupied with preventing absence). From the perspective of clinical work, the issue is what keeps a patient repeating nonadaptive affects and behaviors. Bowlby's answer is defensive processes that produce defensive exclusion, an answer that accords with the relationship of the two variants of pathological mourning to the two forms of attachment anxiety and to the development of defenses that manage that anxiety.

Bowlby argued that defenses in the case of mourning (and implicitly in other difficult situations) may be healthy if they are temporary and limited in scope. Depression is not necessarily pathological as a response to a frank emotional assault, such as the death of a loved one, if it is a temporary stage on the way to sadness. Bowlby (1980) wrote, "The criteria that most clearly distinguish healthy forms of defensive process from pathological ones are the length of time during which they persist and the extent to which they influence a part only of mental functioning or come to dominate it completely" (p. 140).

But two defensive processes, Bowlby (1980, p. 141) argued, are rarely effective as temporary palliatives and are incompatible with nonpathological mourning if they lead the patient to get stuck prior to withdrawal and reorganization. These include

- processes that redirect anger away from the person who elicited it and toward someone else; such a process is usually referred to in the psychoanalytic literature as *displacement*.
- processes whereby all the emotional responses to loss become cognitively disconnected from the situation that elicited them. Such processes may be referred to in traditional terminology as *repression*, *splitting*, or *dissociation*.

In terms of the more general account of depression, of which Bowlby's analysis of mourning is given as an instance, clinical treatment of depression may therefore be expected to focus on defenses and exclusions related to forms of attachment anxiety about coordination that prevent an individual from accessing adaptive affective states in relation to salient situations in which he finds himself. It has previously been argued that a principal source of these defenses and exclusions is that these affective states, in relation to particular relational configurations, have previously been excluded from coordination with major attachment figures; thus, they have become sources of attachment anxiety and are dyadically and internally unavailable. What, then, is needed is a therapeutic engagement around making adaptive affects and actions possible in the context of loss and difficulty. One leading instance of such an approach to depression, well documented in terms of clinical efficacy, is Gerald Klerman's interpersonal psychotherapy for depression (Klerman, Weissman, Rounsaville, & Chevron, 1984).

Klerman's Interpersonal Psychotherapy for Depression

Interpersonal psychotherapy (IPT) for depression arises from within a Sullivanian interpersonalist approach to psychotherapy. This framework is consistent with but not the same as the framework of attachment theory. IPT is a model of psychotherapy for depression that is interesting in the present context because it illustrates the efficacy of a focus on changing what the patient is able to do in terms of affect and communication in real situations.

IPT focuses on depressed patients' actual situations and interpersonal interactions. It is an active form of psychotherapy in which the therapist offers direct advice, assists the patient in making decisions, and repeatedly seeks to clarify what the patient is actually doing and feeling while with others. The consequences and implications of these behaviors and feelings are then examined. In IPT, it is assumed that current interpersonal problems likely originated in dysfunctional aspects of early relationships and that the current interpersonal situation of the patient is directly related to the patient's depression. IPT is an empirically well-validated treatment for depression that compares favorably with cognitive therapy and psychopharmacological treatment, especially with moderately depressed patients, and it may be the psychotherapy of choice with severely depressed patients when psychotherapy alone (without medication) is the treatment modality (Cuijpers et al., 2011; Cuijpers, van Straten, Andersson, & van Oppen, 2008).

Because IPT assumes that a current interpersonal situation is directly related to a patient's depression, it focuses on fostering in the patient the ability to take interpersonal actions—to communicate affects, intentions, and goals—that the patient had been unable to take before. Its major techniques are clarification of feeling states; improvement of interpersonal communication; testing of interpersonal perceptions; development of interpersonal skills; and reassurance of the patient as he or she attempts new interpersonal actions (Bleiberg & Markowitz, 2008; Law, 2011; Ursano & Silberman, 1988). The clarification, experiencing, and communication of affect are central to these techniques and are understood by Klerman as a principal context for the development of new interpersonal actions. In its work with affect, IPT emphasizes

> 1. facilitating acknowledgment and acceptance of painful affects that cannot or should not be changed; 2. helping the patient use his affective experiences in bringing about desired interpersonal changes; and 3. encouraging the development of new and unacknowledged desirable affects which, in turn, may facilitate growth and change. (Klerman et al., 1984, p. 144)

Although it arises from a distinct theoretical context, this view of the therapeutic role of affects is entirely consistent with the understanding of depression that is described above. Viewed from within the perspective elaborated in this book, IPT encourages, coaches, and teaches the patient to include within his coordinative communication with others affective states that have previously been excluded. This effectively reshapes and frees a patient's constrained and misshapen self. It makes possible new affective coordinated states and relational configurations—new and more adaptive ways of going forward in a situation. This dissolves a patient's stuck sadness and depression by effecting the discontinuation of nonadaptive approaches to a situation (which is the adaptive function of the sadness) and thereby permitting a more adaptive reorganization of affective state and behavior.

ANGER AND THE MISSHAPING OF THE SELF

Anger often figures prominently in psychopathology. Within our present terms, there are three reasons why anger appears so frequently and figures so prominently within the clinical situation.

First, as Bowlby's analysis suggests, anger is a prominent and principal response—whether in suppressed or heightened form, whether displaced or accurately attributed—to an experience of actual or threatened noncoordination and loss of connection. The patient who is insecurely attached is struggling with experiences in which his important and necessary affective communications were not coordinated with. These experiences are the origin of what he comes to therapy for. In the course of eliciting, identifying, and discussing these experiences, either in the past or in present interactions and situations, the patient's anger is a key marker and necessary component of the patient's affective response. It is an indication that the therapy is at that moment working in a region of torment and misery for the patient, where he has experienced or been threatened with the loss of the other, and around which he has had to engage in defensive processes and exclusions. This type of anger—and it may be difficult to discover in its suppressed or displaced form—is a thread for the therapist to follow.

Anger does not occur only in response to noncoordination but also appears in relation to other frustration of goals, in response to the anger of others, and as an aspect of self-assertion and appetite. A second reason why anger appears so often in clinical work is because normal anger is a difficult affect state for many caregivers to coordinate with. The expression of anger often elicits anger or withdrawal in others (Cummings, Zahn-Waxler, & Radke-Yarrow, 2006; Haviland & Lelwica, 1987; Lelwica & Haviland, 1883; Tomkins, 1963; Tronick, 1989); when this occurs between a parent and a child, the child is likely to be the loser and to be forced to give way. For this reason, many individuals—and especially those who have experienced constrained coordinated states with anxious, brittle, or depressed caregivers—are likely to have difficulty in coordinating around negative or aversive affective states such as anger. Their anger may be difficult for them to feel or express accurately and coherently; it may be displaced onto inconsequential situations or persons. In these cases, a key aspect of clinical work is finding and coordinating with the patient's anger and thereby helping to make it available to him to think and feel affirmatively and fluently about important situations and relationships.

This raises the issue of the adaptive function of anger. The third reason why anger is important in clinical work is that anger is often an agent and midwife of change and may facilitate breakthroughs to new forms of coordinated states. Anger is useful in reshaping a misshapen self. Malatesta and Wilson (1988) argued that the principal adaptive function of anger is to effect "removal of barriers or sources of frustration towards goals" (p. 99) and to communicate "warning of possible impending attack [or] aggression" (p. 99). Izard (1993) suggested that "a unique function of anger is that of mobilizing and sustaining energy at high levels" (p. 635) and that anger serves to "mobilize energy and sustain goal-directed activity" (p. 635) at a higher level than any other emotional state. Tomkins wrote that "of all the negative affects [anger] is the least likely to remain under the skin of the one who feels it" (Tomkins & Demos, 1995, p. 197); he proposed that the principal function of anger is to make bad situations worse and so to increase the level of activation both of self and of other in the interests of promoting change. Anger is often experienced as a positive emotion by the person feeling it, and the experience of anger is related to activation, approach, and a positive orientation toward engagement (Carver & Harmon-Jones, 2009; Harmon-Jones, Harmon-Jones, Abramson, & Peterson, 2009; Reifen Tagar, Federico, & Halperin, 2011). These conceptualizations all suggest that a major adaptive function of anger is to increase the probability of change and reorganization in a situation. In its function as a demand for change, anger is a precursor and catalyst for new relational configurations and new forms of affective coordination.

The expression of anger communicates a shift in state and an intention to begin doing something different that is likely to affect others. It has a threatening, "or else" quality. In this sense, anger is a call for a change in state or behavior in the other; it calls on the other to stop doing something and to begin doing something else. Earlier, sadness was described as a call for a change in state or behavior in the self, an emotion that disposes the self to stop doing or going forward with what it had been doing. It is in this sense that anger is reciprocal, or obliquely opposite, to sadness; a difference between the two is whether the state to be stopped exists in the self or the other. For this reason, anger and sadness may occur as alternatives to each other: Sadness switches off anger by focusing on changing what the self is doing wrong; anger switches off sadness by focusing on changing what the other is doing wrong. In the "stuck" form of sadness that is described above as depression, anger, when properly harnessed and expressed, may be an agent of change and serve as an antidote to depression. This phenomenon, first observed by Freud, has recently been supported by imaging studies of the coupling and uncoupling of brain circuits involving anger in depressed and nondepressed individuals (Tao et al., 2011). The so-called *hate circuit* in the brain, which involves directed anger, had been "uncoupled"—functionally disconnected—from other brain circuits in individuals struggling with first-episode or treatment-resistant severe depression. Other circuits that had become disconnected in depressed patients involved "risk and action responses, reward and emotion, [and] attention and memory processing" (Tao et al., 2011, p. 1), thus also supporting an account of depression as a form of inaction, withdrawal, and hopelessness about the possibility of change—and of accurately focused anger as a possible antidote.

Adaptive anger, in its function of removing obstacles, signaling the other of a need to change, and raising levels of energy and activation, is useful in altering existing patterns in order to create the basis for new forms of coordinated state and new relational configurations. In clinical work, this type of anger must be cultivated, clarified, integrated, and focused. When this is accomplished, the patient's anger—rather than persisting endlessly—gradually gives way to a sense of energy, possibility, and potency in taking new actions to create needed change.

However, as any clinician will have frequently observed, anger can also occur in destructive, nonadaptive forms that threaten mayhem to self and others. This is the case when anger is used defensively to avoid vulnerabilities and when it is displaced, misdirected, or cognitively disconnected from its source. Consider the case of Harry and his wife, Elissa.

Harry grew up in the British West Indies in a family filled with tension. His mother and father were both highly critical people who seemed to find comfort in discerning the flaws of others. His mother was often irritable and angry. She often drank in the evenings and on weekends. When she had consumed some alcohol, her anger became disinhibited, and she would lash out at her three sons. Harry was the youngest of the three children and was most frightened by his mother's anger.

Harry's mother worked outside the home, and from an early age he had significant chores to do around the house. These included vacuuming and laundry. Each day before his mother left for work and the three boys left for school, Harry's mother would post a set of chores to be completed before she returned home at the end of the day. For the boys, this meant that when they came home from school they needed to get housework chores done, unsupervised, before 5:30 or so, when their mother returned. Often they managed to do this, but sometimes they did not.

If the chores were not done when she returned home, their mother would sometimes scold them, but more often she would express her anger by refusing to speak to them. A long period of sullen silence would ensue, lasting until the undone chores were completed. In practice, this often meant that the silence lasted into the next evening. During this time, relationships in the house were conducted in a state of suppressed anger.

Harry was able to feel safely close to his mother only when he was compliant with her wishes. But he was often angry at his mother's demands and the way she responded when he did not meet them. His own expressions of anger or dissent were not tolerated and in fact were met with silence and withdrawal. Harry and his brothers were allowed to join with their parents in criticisms of other people, and doing so allowed them to feel allied with their parents. This became a practiced form of conversation within the family. Criticisms of the parents, however, were rejected and met with instant emotional escalation.

When the therapist first met Harry, he appeared as a polite and smiling but reserved young man in his mid-20s, with a soft but distinct British accent. He came to couples therapy at his wife's insistence because of difficulties in their relationship and because Harry was stymied and dissatisfied in his career as a graphic artist in a design firm. Harry had also begun to consume alcohol in the evenings and on weekends to a degree that worried his wife. Their marital problems revolved around unresolvable tensions over both major and minor life decisions: what color to paint their home; when to start a family; which health club to join; how to divide their holiday time with their families; which living room furniture to select; where to go out for dinner; how and when to initiate sex and how to conduct their lovemaking. In short, Harry and Elissa could disagree about almost anything, and each could maintain an opposed position without compromise for a very long time. One brief detail about Elissa is important here: She was a woman who could easily become openly angry; in her family, as she grew up, the expression of anger was a reliable way to bring her loving but very distracted mother and her rather passive father into closer coordination with her. Anger for Elissa was a prelude to obtaining connection.

The conflicts between Harry and Elissa had a characteristic form. Elissa would initiate an activity or plan, such as painting the kitchen or planning a weekend with friends, and Harry would demur. His demurral would be understated but persistent and effective. He might say nothing at first, but then over a period of days he would indirectly criticize Elissa's plan or in some way impede it. For example, if Elissa expressed sexual interest, he might take a very long shower, become involved in web surfing, or fall asleep. Predictably, given the role of anger in eliciting connection in Elissa's early family life, Elissa would become furious, and an angry and tense period would ensue. During these tense periods, Harry would withdraw except for occasional emotional grenades, in the form of brief but provocative remarks, casually thrown into the tense atmosphere. Also during these periods, Harry would criticize Elissa intensely to his friends and family.

As this pattern in the marriage unfolded and became clearer in the couples therapy sessions, it also became clear that a similar pattern operated for Harry at work. He appeared to be seen as an uncooperative and even subversive colleague who would often obstruct initiatives in indirect ways.

In short, Harry was expressing a great deal of indirect, passive aggression and anger in a way that was souring his relationships at work and with his wife. The problem for Harry was that he was very uncomfortable and unpracticed in the direct expression of anger and of the assertiveness that is its more socially acceptable form. Harry felt anger easily. It could be elicited simply by someone asking him to do something, which for Harry felt like an imposition and a demand that he was unable to resist or openly negotiate. But when he felt anger within himself, it became for him a signal to hunker down resentfully and to try to find ways to resist what the other was "demanding." The idea that he might openly negotiate with the other in an assertive way seemed to be unavailable to him. If the therapist questioned Harry directly about his passivity and nonassertiveness, Harry said that negotiating or saying that he might want to do things differently would simply lead to more of a fight and that there was no point in doing it—the other person had already made up his or her mind. So, passive resistance and covert aggression became his only means of expressing his own interests and preferences in the face of the expressed needs or desires of others—needs and desires that he experienced as demands and domination.

The solution for Harry was to learn how to let himself feel his anger more comfortably and then to assert his views in a socially acceptable way. The therapist encouraged Harry to express his disagreements with Elissa openly and at some length and questioned him to draw out his views. Initially, this often took the form of angry expressions of disagreement with Elissa. Harry asked whether the therapist really wanted him to do so much open complaining, and he seemed genuinely surprised but also pleased when he was encouraged to continue to speak his mind. The therapist was careful never to side with Harry in any of his complaints. The point was simply to have Harry more clearly and openly express his own views and preferences.

Harry was surprised by how often Elissa said she agreed with him, at least in part, and expressed a willingness to adjust or change what she was proposing. Her main interest seemed to be that Harry remain involved with her on whatever the project or plan might be rather than withdraw from her in sullen but mostly silent hostility. She, for her own reasons, often experienced his more open anger as a welcome form of involvement and interest and would often get a small smile of relief on her face as he asserted himself. It was Harry's withdrawal rather than his assertiveness that was most likely to elicit her own anger. As Harry's anger was harnessed and directed in a socially reasonable way, their relationship began to improve and there began to be much more genuine communication, contact, and engagement between them. Harry's drinking became moderated.

This was a couples therapy, so there is more to this story than has been told here. Elissa's relationship to anger also had to be reworked. But the key point here is that appropriately directed adaptive anger is a useful and even creative form of fostering change and adjustment in relationships and of preserving and advancing our own interests. Distortions and misdirections of anger curdle relationships.

The distinction between adaptive and defensive (i.e., distorted) anger—and between adaptive and defensive affect generally—is crucial. I now turn to a consideration of the differences and of how to tell them apart.

ADAPTIVE AND DEFENSIVE AFFECT

The perspective taken throughout this book has emphasized the issue of fluent access to and communication of adaptive affect states. In discussions of pathology, the concern has been with the constraints that are imposed on this access by attachment experiences involving the threatened or actual disruption of coordinated states with the caregiver because of these affects—as they pertain within particular relational configurations—and the subsequent attachment anxiety and defensive processes that thereby attach to and are stimulated by them.

However, all affects may be used defensively (i.e., as they were used during or in response to experiences of noncoordination) rather than adaptively (Averill, 1987; Basch, 1996; Fosha & Slowiaczek, 1997; Gross, 1998, McCullough-Vaillant, 1997). This may be especially apparent in the cases of anger and sadness but also applies to the other categorical emotions. In the case of anger, a patient may be furious at another person or at a situation in a way that seems inappropriate to the clinician. The anger may threaten the patient's job or disrupt and constrain his personal relationships. It may isolate him from his own interests and from relationships to which an adaptive response would lead him to become more involved. It may interfere with, rather than further, intimacy and exploration. Anger may exist as a chronic state rather than as a form of appraisal and response to particular situations, thereby perfusing an individual's experience with inappropriate emotion. Similarly, in the case of sadness and particularly in the defensively stuck form of sadness discussed above as autonomous depression, a patient may become sad about events or in situations where it seems to the clinician to be inappropriate or open to repair. The patient's inappropriate sadness may sap his energy from projects, interests, and relationships that if zestfully engaged in would offer substantial rewards. The sadness may lead the patient to withdraw from situations or from relationships that offer intimacy or achievement and to which a more adaptive response would lead him forward. In chronic form, such sadness invokes an undifferentiated appraisal and motivational stance with regard to situations and relationships that are in fact very different, creating a kind of affective blindness. And as with anger and sadness, so also with the defensive versions of the other categorical affects.

Distinguishing between adaptive and defensive forms of affect, with regard to anger as well as other emotional states, is a critical task for the clinician. It is a fundamental task upon which clinical work with affective communication and affect states is based. How may the distinction be reliably made?

McCullough-Vaillant (1997) proposed markers to distinguish between adaptive and maladaptive affect. Her distinguishing markers are as follows for adaptive and maladaptive or defensive affect:

- a flowing, surging, or resonating of physical energy in adaptive affect versus an acting out or intense rush of physical energy in defensive affect;
- the generation of an adaptive action tendency in adaptive affect versus the generation of either a heightened or an overly urgent action tendency in defensive affect; or, the constriction of energy and inhibition of action in defensive affect;
- an interpersonally adaptive reaction versus a maladaptive reaction resulting in greater conflict or problems;
- an experience of satisfying and continuing relief following adaptive affect versus momentary relief (followed by worsened problems) if the urgent action tendency is performed; increased frustration if it is not or if energy is constricted and action is inhibited. (pp. 232–234)

Among her other criteria, McCullough-Vaillant (1997) specified the adaptiveness of an affective experience as a criterion for whether or not it is defensive. What are the likely effects of the experience and expression of affect?

This requires clinicians to make a judgment about whether an affective experience and the actions to which the affect disposes the patient are adaptive in the patient's real world. This may both comfort and disquiet clinicians. It may comfort them because, even aside from the directly self-destructive behavior around which clinicians routinely intervene, most clinicians do not attempt neutrality when patients are acting in a way that is likely to cause other types of less catastrophic but nonetheless significant harm. It may disquiet clinicians because this stance more directly reveals their role and responsibility in their patients' lives, in terms of what actually happens to their patients.

9

THE SECURITY-ENGENDERING THERAPEUTIC RELATIONSHIP

This chapter describes the first component of attachment-based therapy: a security-engendering therapeutic relationship. This type of relationship is viewed not as an adjunctive aspect of therapy but as a primary factor in altering the patient's life. The similarities between the qualities and behavior of a security-engendering mother and an effective attachment-based therapist are described. Bowlby explicitly described such a mother as a model for the kind of therapist he had in mind, and the implications of this are elaborated. Research findings on the qualities of the security-engendering mother are detailed and related to the role of the therapist with the patient.

http://dx.doi.org/10.1037/14185-009
Attachment-Based Psychotherapy: Helping Patients Develop Adaptive Capacities, by Peter C. Costello

ATTACHMENT THEORY AND THE ROLE
OF THE RELATIONSHIP IN THERAPY

The crucial role of the relationship in psychotherapy has always been recognized, but it has not always been clear why the relationship was so important or even what to do about it. The very first psychotherapy—the conversations between Dr. Josef Breuer and Bertha Pappenheim, who called her treatment with Breuer "the talking cure" and whom Freud wrote about under the pseudonym "Anna O"—was based on the strength of the personal connection between patient and therapist. Freud recognized the importance of the positive personal relationship, but he could not explain why it was so important; it did not fit into or follow from any of his theoretical constructions. He called it *unobjectionable positive transference*—thereby making it a quality of the individual patient rather than of the dyadic patient–therapist pair—and put it down as a helpful and necessary precondition to therapy but not as an active agent in the therapy itself. Freud's influence on psychotherapy has been such that this view has colored understandings of the psychotherapy relationship ever since. The relationship has been seen as a general or nonspecific factor that helps specific techniques to work rather than as an active intervention that in itself potentially contains specific elements that enable a person in therapy to change in deep and clinically significant ways.

Yet, the single most consistent finding in psychotherapy outcome and process research is that the most potent curative factor in psychotherapy is a relationship that has characteristics of helpfulness, warmth, and commitment and that this relationship is itself curative and more important than any specific psychotherapeutic techniques that might be used by the therapist (for a review of related studies, see Wampold, 2001). As Wampold (2001) wrote, "The relationship accounts for dramatically more of the variability in outcomes than does the totality of specific ingredients" (p. 158).

Although recognizing the importance of the relationship has been unavoidable—Strupp (1993) found that untrained "therapists" with the right interactional characteristics were more effective in helping clients than were trained therapists without those interactional characteristics—the reasons for the importance of the relationship have been undertheorized and underdeveloped. The relationship has been treated mostly in passing by many theorists. This has diminished our focus on the ways in which the effectiveness of the relationship can be enhanced within psychotherapy.

A SPECIFIC TYPE OF RELATIONSHIP: THE SECURITY-ENGENDERING MOTHER AS A MODEL FOR PSYCHOTHERAPY

Attachment psychotherapy is fundamentally based on the agentic change capacities of a relationship that has specific characteristics and that is brought to bear on specific difficulties or incapacities in the individual. True to Bertha Pappenheim's description of psychotherapy as a talking cure, this relationship does its work through the communication between the therapist and the patient. This special type of relationship and communication is the agent of change. The key model for a change-fostering relationship between therapist and patient is the relationship between a security-engendering mother and her child, translated into an age- and context-appropriate form. The fundamental stance and behaviors of an attachment-based psychotherapist are the essential stance and behaviors of the security-engendering mother.

The reason that the security-engendering mother of attachment theory is an appropriate model for the therapist has to do with the basic and intrinsic human developmental and social process that the security-engendering mother taps into. The processes that she shapes in the child are the social and emotional processes that shape the adult's life. These processes are our basic forms of self-experience and interaction with others and with the world itself (remember that attachment processes are closely related to exploration and learning processes, to adult intimate relationships, and to the way we use our emotional and cognitive resources). These behaviors participate in profound physiological and psychological processes that are at the heart of what it is to be a human being. Although these processes operate most robustly during early development, their importance and effectiveness—and especially their capacity to shape or reshape a self—continue throughout the life span. By focusing the patient's attention on the same fundamental systems that were once influenced by the mother, the therapist can produce significant and lasting change. In some ways, the process is like learning a second language in adulthood; the process is more effortful than acquiring the mother tongue learned in infancy and childhood. But one can nonetheless become fluent and learn to live within the new language.

A mother is most effective in promoting security and optimum development when she provides the child with a sense of safety and openness while she simultaneously and actively supports the child's goals. In such circumstances, the child's innate capacities and tendencies have a chance to express themselves in constructive relationship to his environment and to other people. His strengths unfold and become reinforced through practice and application, reaching their maximum degree of unhampered extension.

Bowlby's conception of psychotherapy should feel welcoming and encouraging to therapists from many and diverse clinical perspectives. This is because Bowlby himself was remarkably diverse in the clinical approaches to treatment that he embraced. He never claimed attachment theory for psychoanalysis or for any other specific approach. He was more welcoming to different schools and approaches to psychotherapy than these different schools have usually been to each other. His own approach to clinical work was essentially flexible and nondoctrinaire. It focused principally on his understanding of clinical problems as arising within the operation of the attachment behavioral system and through the dynamics of attachment, communication, and emotion in relationships. Particularly during the last 10 years of his life, he noted and wrote about therapeutic approaches that he thought were consistent with his own understanding of what troubled patients in their lives (Bowlby, 1980, 1988, 1991). The listing of the therapies he thought could work within an attachment framework included cognitive and behavioral therapies; interpersonal and object relational psychotherapy; self-psychology; short-term, brief, and time-limited therapies; bereavement and trauma therapies; social work; and infant–parent psychotherapies. He had once been exiled from the psychotherapy establishment in Britain for his own ideas, so perhaps he was not interested in excluding others. Attachment theory offers open arms to diverse therapists.

The basic stance described by Bowlby differs markedly from that of the somewhat remote, minimally responsive, and emotionally removed therapist of classical psychotherapy. Sigmund Freud, from whose work the traditional psychotherapeutic stance principally derives, had a much-discussed central image or metaphor for how the psychoanalyst should relate to the patient. Freud advised analysts "to model themselves during psychoanalytic treatment on the surgeon, who puts aside all his feelings, even his human sympathy, and concentrates his mental forces on the single aim of performing the operation as skillfully as possible. [Analysis requires] this emotional coldness in the analyst" (S. Freud, 1912/1958, p. 115). Freud famously also disliked looking at his patients face-to-face, and so he invented the arrangement of the analyst sitting out of sight behind the patient.

The attitudes and behaviors of a security-engendering mother are in many, many ways different from those that classical psychotherapy has espoused. So, if we want to merge the security-engendering mother with Freud's surgery metaphor, the security-engendering mother might be thought of as a kind of precision neurosurgeon sculpting neurophysiology during infancy and childhood. She acts not with cool dispassion but with sensitive responsiveness and warmth. The sculpting takes place primarily in terms of how we regulate emotions, how we communicate and interact with others, and how we go about exploring and learning about the world. These key central elements of the self—emotion, communication, and exploration—are all key dimensions of attachment.

The task for the therapist is to partly redo what the security-engendering mother (or other early attachment figures) has done in terms of communication, emotion regulation, and the sense of insecurity that inhibits exploration and effective action. To do this, the therapist has to engage the patient's emotions, communications, and explorations in a way that is analogous to what a security-engendering mother would do, with the added burden that the patient is now distorted in some way in all three realms.

CHARACTERISTICS OF THE SECURITY-ENGENDERING MOTHER (AND THERAPIST)

Much more is now known about the maternal characteristics that encourage secure attachment than was known when Bowlby began to write. Ainsworth and her colleagues (Ainsworth, Bell, & Stayton, 1974; Ainsworth, Blehar, Waters, & Wall, 1978) did the groundbreaking work in this area. Ainsworth identified the fundamental dimensions of insecure attachment (*anxious*, *avoidant*, and *other* or *nonclassifiable*, which has developed into the important category of *disorganized*). She also identified the four main characteristics of mothers who engendered security in their children: sensitivity to the infant's signals and communications; the positive acceptance and regard for the baby; the mother's cooperation and facilitation of the child; and the mother's accessibility and responsiveness—her ability to shift from her own thoughts and activities to focus on the baby.

Each of them is important for us, but the central characteristic identified by Ainsworth is especially important. It lies at the heart of the psychotherapy process when that process is understood from within an attachment framework.

Sensitive and Helpful Responsiveness to Signals and Communications

The central variable that distinguished mothers who raised securely attached children from others who did not was the degree of the mother's sensitive and helpful responsiveness to the infant's signals and communications. This short phrase says a lot. When the child felt or expressed or needed something, the mother did something that was responsive and helpful.

One of the things this phrase contains is that the mothers were observant and perceptive about what their children were feeling and expressing. Each read her child well. She could notice the fleeting changes in the child's face, body, and voice that signaled something was up. This is not a small skill, for mothers or for therapists. The ability of a mother to accurately read what her child is communicating is the target of some of the most effective mother–infant intervention programs. It requires a degree of interest and openness that is maintained at a consistently high level over an extended period of time. And, very critically, it also requires the ability to respond with an action that is helpful. The child feels seen by an important other, understood, and then helped with a difficulty.

The experiences of feeling seen by someone who is powerful and important, of feeling understood even though we have not ourselves completely understood what we are feeling, and of feeling helped with a difficulty or an experience that requires the cooperation of another are extremely powerful. It is not difficult to imagine the sense of personal self-worth and goodness and of trust and closeness to another that derives from such experiences. When these experiences are consistently repeated, we take our own internal state as valid and worthy of helpful and affirming responses from another. Knowing the self and openly communicating the self to another person becomes a very safe thing to do. The social tie grows dense, intimate, and supple. We like to be close to others, and we feel safe when we are close to someone else. We expect help when we need it. These characteristics define secure attachment in both children and adults.

In the setting of therapy, part of the process of sensitive and helpful responsiveness to signals and communications is what has been called "moment-to-moment" tracking of the patient (Fosha, 2000). What this means is that the therapist is closely attentive to the signals, especially the nonverbal signals, given off by the patient. Through her attention and responses to these signals, the therapist evokes a state of close emotional attunement with what the patient is feeling. Patients' faces and voices change in a moment-to-moment way as they are talking. These changes reflect shifting internal emotional responses to what they are talking about.

This may not seem new to many therapists; of course, they closely observe the patient's nonverbal signals. But the security-engendering mother is not simply observing. She is reading the signals very actively with an interest in furthering and facilitating what the child is attempting to do. She is prone to be active, though always nonintrusive and noninterfering.

Translated into the therapy setting, this means that the therapist actively and frequently engages the patient's nonverbal signals and communications by inquiring about what is happening internally when a shift in nonverbal signals takes place. The stance is one not of passive understanding but rather of active companionship, including the lively elicitation of what the patient may be feeling only inchoately and without much awareness. Thus, the therapist makes frequent inquires about nonverbal signals in order to understand more fully, interactively, and with fuller and fuller conscious awareness what the patient is feeling. The therapist, like the security-engendering mother, is especially attentive to the circumstances involving relationships and exploration (the domains of attachment processes) that are the context and elicitors of the feelings. Edward Tronick (Tronick, 2005, 2009; Tronick et al., 1998) has described this process as the "dyadic expansion of consciousness," and he placed it at the center of what is transformative about therapy. But this process requires very intent observation and very active engagement in a continuously deepening conversation with the patient.

This type of "dyadic expansion of consciousness" requires considerable skill and judgment by the therapist because the patient is not very good at being understood in exactly the areas that trouble him. So he talks over his own feelings or talks around them by shifting the subject or concentrating on a detail that is not the real difficulty. He has been trained in his primary attachment relationship not to communicate and not to know about certain areas of his own experience. In other words, the patient has constructed defenses against feelings, thoughts, and communications that were the cause of difficulty or painful experience with the attachment figure.

The therapist's task is to find the traces of the disowned feelings that appear as fleeting nonverbal signals and to bring them forward into conversation with the therapist. To do this accurately and to not waste time in the session, the therapist needs to be guided in her inquiries and elicitations by her understanding of the patient's formative attachment experiences. The therapist needs especially to become adept at seeing how these formative experiences have resulted in processes of communication and emotional experience that are related to current difficulties in the attachment domains of relationships and in exploration of the world (or love and work, as Freud had it).

Other Characteristics of the Security-Engendering Mother and Therapist

Although the centrality of sensitive, helpful responsiveness to signals and communications is central to an attachment-based psychotherapy, there are many other characteristics of the security-engendering attachment figure that researchers have identified and that are pertinent to creating a basic stance for attachment psychotherapy. Following is a list of the key characteristics from three major studies, two of which were seminal in creating a fundamental understanding of what a security-engendering attachment figure actually does, and a third that provided a meta-analysis of 66 published studies of security-engendering characteristics. Together, with minor adjustments, these studies provide a guide for a basic stance in attachment-based therapy. Although these come from studies of mothers with their children,

I invite the reader to review them while considering what their equivalents would look and feel like in the therapy setting with adults.

The basic stance that is suggested by these characteristics may seem quite acceptable to some therapists but unusually active and involved to others.

Key security-engendering characteristics from Ainsworth (1976) and Ainsworth et al. (1978) include the following:

- Sensitive, helpful responsiveness to signals and communications.
- Sensitive and accurate perception of signals and a prompt and helpful response. When it is reasonably best not to comply with a demand or a behavior, tactfulness and the offering of an acceptable alternative are emphasized.
- A fundamental and clearly communicated positive attitude toward and acceptance of the other.
- The balance between positive and negative elements in the relationship is strongly weighted toward the positive, and any negative elements are clearly subsumed and integrated within the context of a positive relationship.
- Active facilitation of what the other is trying to do, without interference or intrusiveness. The sense is that the attachment figure is cooperating and supporting rather than directing.
- Psychological accessibility through responsiveness and the ability to shift from one's own thoughts and activities in order to focus closely on the other.

Key security-engendering characteristics from Bates, Maslin, and Frankel (1985) include

- sensitivity and responsiveness to signals
  - quick responsiveness to distress with a high level of intervention.
  - quick responsiveness to social elicitations;
- high emotional involvement, especially warmth and affection;
- active teaching and organization of the environment;
- emotional and verbal responsiveness and the mother's general competence as a communicator;
- positive mutuality of the pair;
- low negative control;
- harmonious handling of the independence and autonomy of the other;
- acceptance of explorations by the other; and
- active personal involvement.

Key security-engendering characteristics from De Wolff and van IJzendoorn's (1997) meta-analysis of 66 published studies include

- sensitivity to infant and child communications (from Ainsworth et al., 1978);
- promptness and frequency of response to communications (from Ainsworth et al., 1978);
- cooperation, defined as the presence of facilitation and the absence of interference (from Ainsworth et al., 1978);
- synchrony, defined as "the extent to which interaction appeared to be reciprocal, and mutually rewarding" (p. 574, quoting Isabella et al., 1989);
- mutuality, which entails "the mother's skill at modulating the baby's arousal, her entertainment value, and her responsiveness to the infant's cues" and the infant's "expression of positive affect, nonavoidance, active maintenance of the interaction, and amount of gazing at the mother" (pp. 574–575, quoting Kiser, Bates, Maslin, & Bayles, 1986);
- supportive emotional presence, defined as "the extent to which the mothers appeared attentive and available to the children and supportive to their efforts . . . [by] providing a secure base by making the child feel comfortable . . . [and by] being involved as manifested by attentiveness to the child and the task" (p. 575, quoting Matas, Arend, & Sroufe, 1978);
- positive attitude, defined as "the mother's expression of positive affect to the baby" (p. 575, quoting Zaslow, Rabinovich, Suwalsky, & Klein, 1988); and
- stimulation, including encouragement, actual physical stimulation, and the general stimulus potential of the attachment figure as an interactional partner.

If we think of these characteristics not in terms of a mother and a baby but rather in terms of an attachment figure with her dependent person (the term *dependent person*, following Bowlby, is appropriate and not pejorative), a clear picture of a psychotherapy setting and basic stance begins to appear. The setting and relationship are warm, very positive, and often highly interactive, with the therapist actively engaging the patient whenever the patient gives any signal of wanting a response. The therapist answers questions rather than turning them back on the patient. Patient and therapist are together engaged in a mutual activity. The therapist is not simply listening and commenting from a distance but rather is working with the patient in an effort to wrestle with the patient's difficulties. The therapist is a warm, responsive, and actively engaged trusted companion to the patient. Therefore, the patient can talk openly to the therapist without feeling alone, judged, or shamed, because the therapist has established a clear sense of acceptance and of being an ally to the patient, on his side as he tries to change himself and his life. There is a great deal of communication in the session and a great deal of focus on feelings, but the therapist does not interfere or intrude when the patient needs time to withdraw or to think. The therapist is skilled at knowing when her active help is needed and when the patient wants to do something or go somewhere on his own. The session deepens continuously, with the therapist continuously, through her communications, uncovering and bringing forward what the patient is feeling and trying to do. The therapist is continuously responsive to the patient's needs. The patient has a strong sense of being at the center of everything that happens in the room. This room is his, and the attention and activities of the therapist focus entirely on his needs and purposes. The therapist likes the patient, understands him, and thinks highly of him. The patient experiences a gradually growing feeling of warmth and safety as he works on intractable difficulties.

With regard to these difficulties and in accordance with her role as a proto-attachment figure, the therapist is also bringing to the session the skills and knowledge of someone who is stronger and wiser and therefore can offer safety and a secure base from which to attempt new explorations both in the session and afterward in the world. As part of her skills and knowledge, the therapist offers to the patient questions, comments, and suggestions. Through her part of the conversation and always in a way that is responsive to the patient in the moment, she structures the conversation in accordance with her understanding of the attachment issues that are troublesome to the patient. She offers her understanding openly—there is no reason to hide what she thinks about this—and thereby begins to provide the patient with a new way of thinking and talking about both his past and his present. This conversation leads naturally toward the patient's increased awareness and understanding of his own feelings and ways of being with others.

As well, this new understanding and the increased acceptance and expression of avoided feelings lead naturally toward new ideas about actions the patient might take in the world. Although the patient's life outside the session is an area in which the patient's own autonomy must be paramount, the therapist does explore and suggest possible ways of acting in the world and explicitly discusses the feelings and thoughts that these possible behaviors arouse in the patient. The very process of communicating these troubling feelings and thoughts to a strongly accepting and strong companion initiates a process of interindividual emotional regulation and soothing that makes the patient's feelings more manageable.

The therapist's warmth and positive regard must be palpable and, of course, genuine. A child raised by a mother who does not love him, no matter how competent the details of daily care, will live with a deep and unfillable abyss within himself. A therapy devoid of genuine warmth and positive feeling will always be at some level dry and technical, unable to touch the core of vulnerability and difficult emotion that lies at the center of our most painful difficulties. If a therapist cannot find this genuine positive warmth for a patient within herself, she should not treat the patient. This is not a matter of sentiment. The experience of warmth and genuine positive feeling from our attachment figures and trusted companions is a fundamental condition of safety. It is crucial to what makes possible a real transformation of a dysfunctional internal working model of the self in relation to an other. As suggested by the research on security-engendering mothers, this positive regard need not be present at every moment or for every behavior of the patient. Moments of negative feeling are necessary to the texture of a genuine relationship and to the experience of the therapist's authentic response. Nevertheless, as Ainsworth suggested, the negative moments in the relationship must be subsumed and integrated within a genuinely positive relationship.

The general point about all of these characteristics is that they delineate the interpersonal conditions under which an individual can experience a sense of security and safety. Bowlby always said that the principal obligation for a therapist is to provide a secure base for her patient and that the appropriate model for this is the behavior and attitudes of the security-engendering mother. These characteristics elicit a secure-base state in the patient and make it possible to explore the self and the world with a new degree of intrepid openness and trust in one's ultimate safety. Several decades of research on exactly what these characteristics are provides a guide to the basic stance we need to find with our patients.

JEREMY

Jeremy's mother was a very fragile and vulnerable woman who was often afraid of and disparaging about interactions with people outside of the family. When Jeremy began to play with friends outside the home, his mother often responded to his interest in other children with tension, anxiety, and criticism of Jeremy and his playmates. She often told him that his friends were "not like us" and that he had to be careful about them. In subtle ways, she would imply that his friends were not really good friends and that they were doing things that were unfair to Jeremy. This was very much the way she viewed her own relationship to the world. The view was defensive and brittle, and there was little that she could tolerate in challenge to what she needed to believe.

His mother's worried brittleness was a constant feature of his interactions with her. He remembers sitting at the kitchen table and listening to her talk about other people in a threatened and hostile way. Although he could not articulate it to himself as a child, he had a sense of his mother as delicately balanced and in need of careful handling. He became her caretaker and source of security more than she became his.

For Jeremy, the only way to stay close to such a fragile caretaker was to carefully control how he stimulated her. He became very attuned to the nuances of how she was feeling and became expert at reading her moods. He found that if he varied himself too much from what made her comfortable, she would become more intense and hostile and more critical of him.

Under these circumstances, what Jeremy could allow himself to communicate was very limited, and therefore what he allowed himself to know and feel became quite limited also. His emotional realm was small and restricted. His relational expertise was in monitoring the state of the other and in taking care of her. In attachment terms, this relationship has many of the characteristics of a disorganized attachment: Jeremy's mother was a frightened and sometimes frightening attachment figure, and Jeremy's response was to become a controlling and sometimes dissociated caretaker.

Jeremy felt a need to respond to his mother's anxiety because it threatened him and made him feel unsafe rather than leaving him free to focus on his own goals. It became unsafe to let his mother know what he wanted, and the source of the danger was his own desire for connection. Thus, his own feelings were a source of danger. As he was unable to communicate his desires, his own goals and feelings became less distinct and compelling to him. As he less often communicated a desire for social contact, his friendships and social contacts became more and more limited, and his skills at social contact became more constrained.

Some of Jeremy's problematic feelings based on attachment experiences had to do with anxiety about losing control of the mood of the other person. His basic internal working model told him that if he lost control of how the other was feeling, the other would become more hostile and rejecting toward him. So he would try to be both very caretaking and very controlling with other people. When he was experiencing a situation in which he was losing some control over the other's mood, he would feel anxious but would talk about the details of the situation in which he was maneuvering to obtain control. But the situational details he talked about were a distraction from the fundamental experience of anxiety about loss of control and caretaking leading, in his internal working model, to rejection and hostility toward him.

At work, Jeremy was always doing much more than he needed to do (in other words, he was being a caretaker), and he was often taking responsibility for other people's tasks (being controlling). Therefore, he was also always finding himself relegated to the role of assistant or second or third fiddle, and he grew frustrated by this. Nevertheless, he kept acting in a way that elicited the role of assistant.

The problem for Jeremy was not his competence but rather the anxiety he felt about the possibility of becoming something other than an assistant. Being the caretaking assistant was the role prescribed for him by his experiences with his mother, and it was now encoded in his internal working model. Not to be an assistant, in Jeremy's internal working model, would inevitably bring hostility and rejection.

In closely attuning to Jeremy's emotional signals, the therapist picked up the thread of anxiety. The issue, however, is complicated because Jeremy did not have an easy way of knowing what caused his anxiety. He couldn't directly tell the therapist much about it. In fact, he didn't want to think about it; he wanted to talk about something else.

It is at this point that a formulation and history of the patient in attachment terms become indispensable. Part of the therapist's attunement to the patient is to hear emotional communications in the context of the patient's attachment history and issues and in terms of the patient's frustration in meeting adaptive goals in living. This represents the first part of Ainsworth's description of the security-engendering mother: sensitivity to signals and communications. The questions are these:

- How do attachment concerns derived from the attachment history of the patient create the emotional nuance that appears in his signaling?
- Are the attachment concerns distorting or displacing an emotion that is necessary for meeting adaptive goals in relationships or in exploration?

In therapeutic practices, problems in relationships and problems in meeting the adaptive goals of a full life are exactly the difficulties that bring patients to therapy. The attachment therapist understands these issues in terms of the intertwined processes of attachment history, internal working models, emotional self-experience, and communicative interaction with others.

In Jeremy's case, the therapist had an attachment understanding in mind. The therapist had listened to many stories about Jeremy and his mother and about Jeremy's difficulties in finding a comfortable and self-assertive place in the social world, about his constant fear of impending rejection by others, and about how he constrained himself and substituted being helpful to others for his own goals. These elements were highlighted in her understanding of Jeremy in terms of the controlling/caretaking style of disorganized attachment—that his sense of the other was that she was so fragile that she had to be very carefully managed and helped. This took Jeremy's attention and capacities away from meeting other adaptive goals, like his own interests and success in his career.

This is where the second part of Ainsworth's description of the security-engendering mother is important: response to signals and communications. The security-engendering mother gives a helpful response. If the therapist feels in her bones that part of her professional task is to be actively helpful, she will intervene to address the anxiety that is forcing Jeremy into an assistant role (when his talent and his professional gifts support a more powerful role). She will go beyond the details of Jeremy's account of a situation at work and notice the emotional signals that are left out or underattended to in his account. She will understand these in terms of his attachment history. She will actively move to address it. Exactly how she addresses it has to do with the processes of deconstructing aloneness and restoring lost adaptive capabilities, which I discuss in the next chapter. For now, the point is the close reading of Jeremy's signals and communications and the readiness to provide a helpful response.

One last point about this, which I think would be dear to Bowlby's heart and mind. Although the importance of understanding the patient's formative attachment experiences may seem to suggest a historical and psychodynamic way of working, the attachment history is for the purpose of understanding the patient and sketching a formulation or diagnosis in terms of attachment processes so that present difficulties can be understood. The focus of the work is not the past but the present. It is useful, as discussed in the chapter on deconstructing aloneness, for the patient to learn to talk about the past in a new way. However, the attachment therapist wants to help the patient in the present—just as a security-engendering mother deals with her child's presently felt difficulties. Nor do the interventions used by the therapist to address current difficulties have to be psychodynamically based (though they may be). Behavioral, cognitive, experiential, and other ways of working can all be extremely powerful and, I think, necessary in the context of an attachment-based understanding of what to do with a patient. The common thread and key is that interventions are directed at attachment-related difficulties. In Jeremy's case, for example, an understanding of his present patterns in terms of his past was combined with behavioral prescriptions—like making a list of weekly work goals—and cognitive challenges to his beliefs that others didn't like him or were about to reject him. The same general pattern of diverse and integrative interventions was used in other areas, such as his relationships with his wife and daughters. But the selection of where to intervene was done in accordance with the psychopathology of attachment, communication, and affect.

10

DECONSTRUCTING ALONENESS: HELPING THE PATIENT ACCESS AND COMMUNICATE EXCLUDED THOUGHTS, FEELINGS, AND BEHAVIORS

Involuntary aloneness with respect to specific issues, experiences, and feelings is central to attachment theory's conception of psychopathology. From this perspective, therapy is the process of disassembling forms of aloneness that were constructed in formative relationships. This chapter explains how to elicit the important elements of a patient's attachment style in early and current relationships and also in terms of personal characteristics—a series of evocative questions drawn from attachment research. The chapter then suggests how to communicatively coordinate with the patient as he or she accesses more adaptive feelings, thoughts, and behaviors.

http://dx.doi.org/10.1037/14185-010
Attachment-Based Psychotherapy: Helping Patients Develop Adaptive Capacities, by Peter C. Costello

COMMUNICATION AND THE DOUBLENESS
OF ATTACHMENT PATHOLOGY

A central process in attachment theory is the transformation of a dyadic experience into an individual characteristic and the subsequent retransformation of this individual characteristic into dyadic experience (Rutter, 1997). This dyadic-individual dynamic is associated with the characteristic doubleness of attachment pathology. Attachment processes face inward and outward simultaneously. In pathology, they simultaneously impair both internal experience and interaction in the outer world. In terms of the outer world, they exclude affective communications and situations or relationships that require communications or behavior that, it is felt and believed, will lead to the loss of the other; and they overemphasize affective communications and associated situations and relationships that are felt and believed to be necessary to preventing the loss of the other. In terms of internal experience, there is an isomorphic pattern that excludes some affective experiences and overattends to others; this prevents the individual from accurately knowing and feeling what is happening and leads to defensive and incoherent self-experience. In attachment pathology, the individual avoids outer and inner experience in the same patterned ways.

In Bowlby's (1991) view, what cannot be communicated to another cannot be fully known or processed by the individual. There is a close relationship between the patterns that operate within an individual's own mind and the

> patterns of communication that obtain between him and those whom he feels he can trust. The more complete the information that a person is able to communicate to someone he trusts the more he himself becomes able to dwell on it, to understand it and to see its implications. A child who has experienced open and coherent communication with his mother develops a pattern of communication within his own mind that is equally open and coherent, and the same holds for faulty patterns. (Bowlby, 1991, pp. 293–296)

INVOLUNTARY ALONENESS

Susan grew up in a suburban neighborhood near Chicago. She came from a large and intact family, with both older and younger brothers and sisters, all of whom were less than 2 years apart. Her parents have remained married to this day, and though she and her siblings have mostly moved to California or New York, they still gather twice or more a year for family holidays or other reasons, mostly in order to see each other. Susan and her siblings are talented and hardworking. Each is a professionally accomplished adult, though none are married.

Some of Susan's earliest memories—from the age of 4 or 5—are of her parents fighting with each other. The arguments were never physical, but they were angry and often extended, with an air of tension persisting for hours or days afterward. The anger usually reached a peak of intensity in the evening, when the day's work was done. Susan and her sisters would sometimes stand quietly and listen, down the hall from the living room, where the arguments took place. Her parents usually did not shout but spoke to each other with an angry and bitter intensity that felt as though it might flare at any moment. The atmosphere was tense and sullen. After a while, the girls would sneak back into their rooms to sleep. They never talked about what they had heard or about what was going on in the living room. They would look at each other and experience it together, but there was never any actual talking to each other about what had happened and what went on regularly in the home.

One spring day when Susan was 7, a much older boy who lived next door asked her to come with him into his family's garage. He closed and locked the door, pulled her onto his lap, and partly undressed her while talking about other things. His sexual contact with her lasted about 10 minutes. While this was taking place, he whispered endearments. Susan felt pain and disgust and strangeness.

Afterward, Susan said nothing to anyone. Over the next several years, the scene in the garage with the older boy next door was repeated on a regular basis, as were the angry, smoldering fights between her parents in the living room. Susan's life went on. She was involved in school, where she did well. She had friends. She played with her sisters. When her neighbor would call her to the garage, usually during the day when her father was not at home, she felt as though her ordinary life was being interrupted by something unpleasant and strange that had to be gotten over with. She submitted to the unpleasantness and then went back to what she felt to be her other life. For Susan, these two experiences—the tension of her parents' continuous sullen anger that might flare at any moment and the disgust and strangeness of the times in the locked garage workshop with her neighbor—were the poles and centers of emotional gravity of her childhood, memories and feelings that were with her still.

Neither of these experiences were ever discussed by Susan or shared with anyone else. As an adult, Susan was not surprised that she had not said anything about her neighbor, but she was saddened by her memory of an inability to ever talk about anything that was happening at home—how it felt to have her parents so locked in their own tension that it pervaded the home and dimmed any sense of happiness, safety, or exuberance. There was a sense of silence that she was obligated to maintain. When Susan talked about the silence, she did so with a choked voice and in tears. "There was never any *outlet*. No one ever *said* anything," she said.

Susan felt alone in the sense that Bowlby understood aloneness to become pathogenic. She had no attachment relationship that was brought to bear on the specific difficulties created by her parents' fighting and the abuse by her neighbor. She was alone with these difficulties.

Henry David Thoreau wrote that most men lead lives of quiet desperation. The resonance with readers that has made this line so often quoted comes, I think, from the idea of *quiet* desperation. It is the word *quiet* that makes the sentence moving rather than despairing, because though we cannot avoid the difficulty of living, we can sometimes remedy the silence and loneliness of our struggles. The word *quiet* carries some implication of hope, because it suggests that the quiet might be breached. It is this possibility of being understood and seen that gives Thoreau's quote its poignancy. To suffer or struggle alone is very different than to struggle in the company of another.

There is a similar theme in a painting by the Flemish Renaissance artist Pieter Brueghel the Elder. The painting is entitled *The Fall of Icarus*. It depicts a sun-soaked pastoral scene overlooking an ocean vista. A plowman works the earth, a shepherd guards his sheep, a fisherman gathers his nets, a deckhand climbs the rigging of a stately ship. In the distance a golden city glitters, preoccupied with itself. But all are turned away from the splash in the water, the flickering trail of falling feathers, and the legs of Icarus still living and visible at the very moment he plunges headfirst into the sea to drown. No one sees his fall, his need, or his fate.

This ignoring of suffering and need is the antithesis of the responsiveness that engenders secure attachment and that we have described in the previous chapter as central to an attachment-based psychotherapy. It is this dynamic of aloneness wishing for responsiveness to which an attachment psychotherapy applies its greatest force.

Attachment theory is intensely concerned with the difference between what it is like to be alone with our experiences and thoughts and what it is like to be in connection about them with another person. It is a theory of aloneness and of witness, of whether our *I* has a *thou*, in relationship to specific goals and difficulties. This sensitivity to aloneness arose from Bowlby's own experience, in his childhood, of his "country mother" and his "town mother." During summer vacations in the country, his mother was available and attentive, warm and responsive. During the London social season, his care was given over to a nanny while his mother became distracted and remote, often absent and often encrusted by the makeup, hairstyling, clothing, and social preparations for formal company (Holmes, 1993). She became someone wanted but seen from an emotional distance across a room rather than someone whose presence and availability he sensed nearby.

Attachment theory, as I have noted, is based on a conception of the human as intrinsically social, of our "socialness" being so deeply woven into our ways of feeling, thinking, and being that we are barely aware of how deeply our interactions and experiences with others are a part of who we are. This centering on the dyadic qualities of our psyches and our experiences focuses attachment theory on the nuances of when we feel that we are alone and when we feel that we are together with someone else. Attachment theory is a theory of the difference between being alone and of having a trusted companion who knows what is happening with us and whom we count on to respond to us helpfully. This is the task of the attachment psychotherapist—to join the patient in the places he or she has been so alone. Susan's experience while growing up and while in therapy exemplifies this dynamic and the difference between experiencing aloneness and having an ally or companion in specific relationship to the difficulties that we are facing.

DECONSTRUCTING ALONENESS

Deconstructing aloneness is the process of helping the patient access and communicate what has been defensively excluded, including thoughts, feelings, and behaviors. In many ways, this is the essential theme of an attachment psychotherapy. It is the aspect of human experience addressed above by Brueghel, and it is the aspect of therapy and of psychopathology to which Bowlby was most attentive, the problem to which the security-engendering psychotherapist is the solution. Deconstructing aloneness requires seeing and hearing the patient in ways that they have not been seen or heard before and then helping the patient to see and hear himself in ways he has not previously been able to do.

Remember that a child learns the forms of integration and engagement with another that have been permitted or required by the attachment figure. This can require that some kinds of emotional experiences—for example, anger at the attachment figure or the need for reassurance about the security of the self—not be expressed. If they are, the attachment figure withdraws or otherwise communicates in a way that makes the child feel worse. So the child first learns what the attachment figure needs and then works to provide it.

E. M. Forster (1927/1985) wrote, "How can I tell what I think till I see what I say" (p. 99). Our patients come to us with large areas of silence in their lives about which they have been unable to communicate and therefore about which they have been unable to think clearly and feel coherently. But, in most cases, they do not know that these areas of silence and aloneness even exist. They just know that something is not working right in their lives, that things are not going as they should, that their relationships are not working, or that they are not doing as well in school and career as they should be able to do. Or, they feel anxious or depressed or unreasonably and ineffectively angry. These are the same problems that insecurely attached or disorganized children have in their lives, but they are now writ in the larger world and with the more inexorable and dangerous consequences of adult life.

That which we are unable to communicate because of fear and anxiety gradually becomes obscured and inaccessible, unknown even to ourself. The therapeutic task is to deconstruct this aloneness by finding what experiences, feelings, and thoughts the patient has been unable to express and gradually leading these into the light and into alliance with the therapist. In doing this, the therapist is facilitating a natural, developmental unfolding. Once the patient both knows what he or she is feeling and experiencing and feels safe with these experiences, he or she will know how to proceed. The inherent adaptiveness of fluent, nondefensive responding will lead in the right direction.

Susan exemplified all of these characteristics when she came to therapy. She was poised and polished, but there was a formality and neutrality to her voice and her face that made the therapist feel a bit formal also. The therapist found herself being overly polite and overly conventional in her interactions with Susan. When the therapist asked her, as homework, to write about her memories of her childhood, Susan demurred, saying that wasn't something she wanted to do. Susan had learned to keep her own counsel.

But if the therapist listened closely and watched Susan's face—in the mode of moment-to-moment tracking—there were times when a fleeting expression of sadness or sometimes a sigh would appear. When the therapist inquired about what had just happened, Susan was at first unaware that anything had happened. When the therapist said that she had looked sad for just a moment, Susan at first shook her head to indicate that nothing had happened. When the therapist repeated the question a few minutes later, after another moment of sadness, Susan became quiet, lips pressed together. A struggle appeared on her face as she fought to maintain neutrality and composure. She sat quietly, with extreme stillness. Slowly, her face reddened and tears began to run down her cheeks, but she was still unable to speak. She sat and shook her head, her face wet with tears. When at last she could speak, Susan said that she did not know what she was feeling but that she felt overcome by emotion:

> This happens to me. Why does this happen to me? I just get overwhelmed with these feelings, and I don't have anything to say about them. I start to cry. I can't talk. I don't even know what the feelings are or what it is I am feeling.

MEASURING COHERENT COMMUNICATION WITH THE ADULT ATTACHMENT INTERVIEW

From an attachment perspective, the essential conditions that create security are helpful responsiveness, emotional availability, and open communication. Attachment security does not require that we have had a life in which nothing bad has ever happened to us. But it does require that when something bad does happen to us we be able to communicate our experience to someone we trust and who will answer us in a way that is specifically responsive to what we are communicating and actively helpful in regulating our feelings. Under these conditions, we will learn to expect that communication will lead to a helpful response from others, and it becomes worthwhile to tell others what is happening with us. We assume that our feelings are important and can be shared. The very process of elaborately communicating our feelings to a trusted other helps us to know more fully and clearly what our feelings are. We develop a habit of emotional and communicative openness, with others and with ourselves. This open communication to others and our emotional availability to ourselves make it possible for us to more deeply know ourselves and our own experience. This is the opposite of the process of defensive exclusion.

However, if we do not have the opportunity to communicate our experiences—especially our difficult experiences—to a responsive and helpful other, our internal situation is very different. When a difficult experience occurs and we are not able to communicate it to someone who will help us, we are forced to struggle with and to find a way to regulate the feelings on our own. This is an extremely difficult thing to do. When we are alone with a major difficulty, we may withdraw inside ourselves or we may distract ourselves with something else (e.g., displaced hyperemotionality, obsessive thoughts, compulsive actions, cigarette smoking, drugs, sex, self-cutting, aggression, violence) that is intense enough to take our internal attention away from the difficult things we are feeling. These two responses represent the basic defensive processes of emotional suppression and emotional heightening that are discussed in Chapter 6.

Susan took the path of emotional suppression. In the absence of someone to communicate her difficult experiences to, Susan withdrew into herself. After each episode of abuse in the toolshed, Susan would withdraw to her room and close the door. She would sit still and try to calm her body. She wished she were like her mother or her much older sister, both of whom were big and strong and who had angry tempers that would surely blast away the neighbor boy were he to try anything with them. In this way, Susan construed what had happened as her own fault, a result of her weakness, and at the same time experienced a wish for closeness and support—attachment—to her mother or older sister, whom she understood as powerful enough to save and protect her. If only they knew. If only they were close enough.

However, they didn't know, and they weren't close enough. Susan learned how not to show what she was feeling, even when those feelings were very intense. She learned how to manage and suppress her most upsetting feelings by pressing them down within herself and by not letting a glimmer of them appear on her face. She could make her face become entirely neutral. This was an exercise in self-control and deliberate avoidance of communication. The suppression and noncommunication turned Susan's resources away from her own most personal experience. She became unfamiliar with key aspects of her own feelings, expert at avoiding, not showing, not knowing—at least not in any fully conscious and actively engaged way—what was happening in the intimate parts of her own life. Susan did not have a sensitive and responsive relationship to her own feelings and internal experiences because no one else had given her such responsiveness as her emotional and interactive patterns were being formed. She lived many of her interactions, even very intimate interactions, including her adult sexual relationships, as though they were stage events. She lived them in terms of the appearance of normality rather than from within her own feelings.

This defensively created incoherence and lack of clarity about internal experience is exactly what is measured by the Adult Attachment Interview (AAI), which has for many years been one of the principal means of measuring degrees and types of attachment security, insecurity and disorganization (Steele & Steele, 2008). Its measurement of these characteristics is the basis of much of the fundamental research on attachment. The AAI is an extended interview designed to have interviewees remember and think and talk about their early attachment experiences (Hesse, 2008). But the AAI does not measure how good or bad these experiences were. Instead, it measures how well an individual is able to communicate about these experiences now, in the present.

The measurement of attachment characteristics that is made by the scoring of an AAI for a particular individual is based on the quality of the individual's communications about his or her attachment experiences (Crittenden & Landini, 2011; Main, Hesse, & Goldwyn, 2008). The scoring is based on Grice's maxims, which are the specific qualities of good and cooperative conversational discourse that were proposed by the philosopher of language Paul Grice (Grice, 1989). Grice was on the faculty at the University of California at Berkeley during the years that Mary Main was there developing the AAI. Grice (1975, 1989) thought of the following "maxims" as the qualities of good and coherent communication:

> *Quality or truth.* What is said is true, and there is actual evidence
> for the statement.

Quantity. One provides an appropriate amount of information—neither too little nor too much—for the purposes of the communication.

Relation. What one says is directly relevant to the topic under discussion. Questions are answered. Diversions are not taken.

Manner. What one says is clear and easily understood. It is not obscure or confusing. There is not an overwhelming amount of detail or unpredictable changes of direction that are difficult to follow. The person doesn't lose track of what he is saying or become confused or hesitate excessively. He doesn't go into a fog. Things are said in an orderly and comprehensible way.

Grice's idea was that when these qualities are present, the quality of the conversation will be high. When they are not present, communication is impaired.

Main adopted these maxims for the AAI (Hesse, 2008). The question was whether someone could communicate well about his attachment experiences, not whether his attachment experiences had been good or bad. It was a brilliant idea and one that came from deep within an understanding of what an attachment to another person was for—to obtain communicative and emotional contact in a real way when it was needed. Could the individual who was being interviewed do this? Could he communicate well about his attachment experiences? Or was he trapped in an aloneness with his deepest and most important experiences in a way that had become involuntary and that operated even when he was being asked about those specific experiences by a sympathetic and interested interviewer?

Those who were insecure or disorganized had trouble communicating about their attachment experiences. They could not convey these experiences with the conversational qualities that Grice thought marked good discourse. But they differed in the kind of difficulties that they had.

For example, one question on the AAI asks interviewees to list five adjectives that describe their relationship with their most important early attachment figure. On this question, individuals with avoidant attachments often have difficulties with the maxims of truth and quantity. This is not to say that the individuals are intentionally lying but rather that their statements, which the individuals appear to believe, don't seem to fit the facts or that the individuals cannot provide support for the statements. These individuals often describe their attachment relationships in fairly rosy terms but cannot provide specific examples that fit their descriptions. They might say that their relationship with their mother had been "happy," but when asked for an example they may offer an incident when they had played out in the yard alone while their mother was at work—not exactly a moment of happy relatedness. In terms of quantity, avoidant individuals sometimes have difficulty providing any examples for the adjectives describing their attachment relationship or have difficulty coming up with five adjectives to begin with. It is as if they have never paid close attention or encoded in memory what was going on in their closest relationship to another human being. AAI interviews with avoidant individuals tended to be relatively brief.

Anxious individuals have a different pattern of difficulties in meeting Grice's maxims while taking about their attachment experiences. Rather than failing the criterion of quantity by having too little to say, they talk extensively about their attachment relationship—much more than is called for by the question—providing a great deal of detail as though the thoughts about attachment immersed them in an overwhelming experience that they cannot stop talking about. Interviews with anxious individuals often take much longer than average because the individuals have difficulty putting a question aside even after it has been answered.

Disorganized individuals might have difficulties with the criteria of relation and manner. They get lost in their accounts of attachment relationships. They themselves show signs of confusion while remembering and speaking. They might drift off into a daze, become frightened and confused in the present moment, lose track of what they are saying, or speak in the present tense as if events were happening now rather than having taken place years in the past.

The point is that insecurity and disorganization make it very difficult for individuals to communicate their experience. The experience is inaccessible, overwhelming, or very confusing. It could not in the present be brought into a meaningful relationship with another person. Insecure individuals are trapped in an aloneness with a difficult set of experiences, just as they had been when they were in the original attachment relationship.

It is the situation of the child who lives on in the adult that must be undone. The lesson of the AAI is that being able to communicate openly and accurately about difficult experiences marks a transition to security and strength. This is what the therapist has to accomplish. And a major part of the difficulty is that patients usually do not really know what they are not able to say.

ADDITIONAL QUESTIONS FOR ASSESSING ATTACHMENT

Evocative questions about attachment experiences and styles can also be found in the three versions of the Experiences in Close Relationships Questionnaire (Fraley, Heffernan, Vicary, & Brumbaugh, 2011; Fraley, Waller, & Brennan, 2000) and the Relationship Scales Questionnaire (Griffin & Bartholomew, 1994). These and many other instruments (Crowell, Fraley, & Shaver, 2008; Ravitz et al., 2010) were designed to elicit, measure, and differentiate an individual's attachment history and characteristics. Although they are most often used for research purposes, the questions they contain, when used by a clinician, can be extremely useful in thinking about a patient's attachment history and style and in eliciting emotion-based responses from the patient that will help to understand him and to target interventions. Many of the questions below are derived from these instruments or expand on their themes.

The following questions can create a detailed understanding of an attachment history. These questions can be asked about any developmental period that is of interest.

- Who was regularly at home while the patient was growing up? Mother, father, sisters, brothers, parent's boyfriend or girlfriend, grandparents, stepparents, uncles, aunts, nannies, babysitters, other paid caretakers or housekeepers, neighbors?
- To whom did he feel closest?
- To whom did the patient turn when he was upset?
- How often was the patient alone?
- How did the patient soothe himself when he was upset?
- What happened on occasions when he was sick or injured? Who took care of him, and what was their caregiving like? What does he remember about being helped?
- Does he remember occasions when he wanted help and couldn't get it? What made it difficult to get help?
- What positive memories can the patient generate about his main attachment figure? What negative memories? What are the emotions and the situations that these memories reflect?
- What was the feeling in the home like? Did things change over time, or was there a great deal of continuity?

It is extremely important to keep in mind that patients are likely to have multiple attachment relationships in their past and present life, and they will therefore also have multiple internal working models. One attachment relationship may be primary, but the others also influence the patient's sense of self and other and of what relationships with other people can be like. For example, a patient may have a very different sense of self and feel very different when he is with one parent, either actually or representationally, than when he is with the other. Each internal working model expresses a potential in the patient, and more positive, open, flexible, and accurate internal working models can be heightened and reinforced and used to alter those that are more constraining and limiting. In the context of a rejecting and depressed mother, a warmer and more welcoming grandmother who served as a subsidiary attachment figure might be heightened, elaborated, and used as a model and a target for new or evolving relationships in the patient's life. Different attachment figures may also be important in different domains of the patient's life: A mother may be primary for security and comfort in the face of fear and feelings of closeness and warmth, and a father may be primary for exploration and activity in the world (Grossmann, Grossmann, Fremmer-Bombik, Kindler, & Scheuerer-Englisch, 2002; Lamb, 1977a). Looking for the relevant attachment figure and experiences in the arena within which the patient is having current problems can provide therapeutic focus:

- What are the multiple attachment relationships in the patient's life, both in the past and the present? Who was/is primary, who were/are secondary or subsidiary?
- What are the domains of activity and feeling in which each attachment figure is most important? How have these specific relationships shaped those particular domains and emotions in the patient's life?

The primary purpose of asking about the past is to understand and more precisely focus on the present. We are looking for ways that the present is a repetition of the past, for ways in which present relationships re-create childhood circumstances. So, the same five-adjective question and request for specific examples can also be asked about current attachment relationships in the patient's life. A comparison of the two sets of adjectives will often reveal a great deal about how a patient's early history is related to his current relationships and can be used to help a patient think about what is happening in his current relationships.

In view of the tendency for attachment characteristics to be transmitted from one generation to the next, one can also ask about the attachment figures' own attachment histories. What are the attachment figures' early and current relationships with their own parents (or other early attachment figures) like? What kind of relationship does each attachment figure have to her or his own adult partner? Although all of these relationships may show a great deal of variability, there are also likely to be important similarities and continuities. The attachment characteristics that a mother and a father bring to their relationship with each other are also brought to their relationship with their children.

We can ask more directly about the qualities that define different attachment styles and also ask about different attachment relationships with particular different people in the patient's life. As I describe in Chapter 4, the attachment characteristics of anxiety and avoidance can be thought of primarily as dimensions that can exist at varying levels of intensity: Someone may be high in avoidance but low in anxiety, low in avoidance but high in anxiety, low in both (secure), or high in both and sometimes fluctuating from one to another (disorganized). These dimensions can exist in different degrees in different types of situations and with different people in the patient's life. It is useful to ask attachment-related questions both in general and about particular people—not only early attachment figures like parents but also about specific people in the patient's adult life, like present and former romantic partners and close friends (Fraley et al., 2011).

The following questions can directly probe the dimensions of attachment anxiety and avoidance, either in general or with slight rephrasing about particular people:

- Do you think that talking about things helps? (Or, about a particular person: Do you think talking about things with _____ helps?)
- Is it usually easy for you to ask other people for help?
- When you are sick, do you prefer to be mostly alone or to have someone really take care of you?
- Do you think you can really count on other people?
- How important is it to you to be independent and self-sufficient?
- Do you find that you often want to be closer to others than they want to be to you?
- Do you think anyone really knows you deeply and truly?
- Do you expect to be rejected a lot?
- Is it easy for you to say how you feel?
- Would you say that you are generally a secure person?
- Do you think it is a good idea to ask other people for help on something important?
- Can you ask your partner for help easily?
- Do you like to keep your distance from other people or to get very close to them?
- Do you often worry about whether you will be accepted or valued by other people?
- Do you worry that your partner might leave you?
- Do you worry about being good enough for other people to want to be with you?
- Do you think you can count on other people loving you and staying with you?
- Do people often change their mind about how they feel about you?
- Do you ever push people away by trying to be too close?
- Do you fall out of touch with other people easily?
- Does your partner usually know how you are feeling?
- Do you tell your partner everything important that is happening with you?

- Does your partner know what you think about?
- Does your partner know when you are upset and anxious? How does your partner react?
- Is your partner aware of why you are coming to therapy? How much does your partner know about the issues we are talking about?

RESOLVING SUSAN'S CASE

In Susan's case, she had learned how to ward off the experiences with her neighbor and her parents. It was this very process of learning how to ward off an immediate experience of what she needed help with that was creating difficulties in her personal and intimate life as an adult. She told her therapist about two of her most important adult relationships. One had been with Mark, with whom she lived for several years. Susan worked and was successful. Mark was not working much—he was sometimes in a training program and sometimes in school, but he never provided a real share of the income by which they lived. He lived with Susan, but he also acted and felt as though they were roommates rather than partners. He had a life very much apart from hers. Despite this distance in their relationship, Susan felt very attached to him. He was her person in the world. They just weren't in much contact. Gradually, Mark seemed to lose all interest in Susan, and their relationship sank toward an end. It was only after he was gone that Susan realized that Mark had been cheating on her for years, really since the early days of their relationship. In his absence, she suddenly fully grasped what she said she had at some level known all along. But she had also denied this knowledge to herself. She had never questioned him or challenged him. She had never directly experienced sadness or anger at his unfaithfulness and deception. She had simply gone on within the form of the relationship, going through the motions but not having any depth of feeling or enough truth to create real intimacy.

This was the way in which Susan had lived in her family—with the real experiencing avoided and distanced while the forms of ordinary life were pursued. The pattern is classic avoidant: Help won't be available; if I ask for help, it won't come, and asking will only drive the other person away; it is better not to pay too much attention to what I'm feeling and thinking and experiencing and to just go on with the business of everyday life. In Bowlby's terms, these are the thoughts and feelings that the person is not allowed to have.

Essentially the same dynamics were repeated in Susan's second major relationship, except that there was more honesty about the absence of intimacy or commitment. This relationship, which also lasted for years, was with a man whom Susan liked very much. But from the first, both Susan and Robert agreed that their relationship would not become serious, that it would not be exclusive, and that neither would make any real demands on the time or loyalty of the other. They might sleep with each other, but they would always separate before the next morning. They would have sex but would never talk about their feelings with each other. After several years, they parted as friends, but Susan found herself enormously sad for months afterward. The pattern of this relationship is also classic avoidant: The relationship doesn't count for too much and is not very important; there are so many other things to be busy with and pay attention to; feelings don't really matter.

But Susan's aloneness with her own needs and truest emotions and most important experiences was not limited to romantic relationships. The same was true in many areas of her life. She could not bring herself and her needs for others into her interactions with them. She could not occupy her own life.

One of the ways in which this was reflected was in her living arrangements. Despite her very considerable professional and financial success as someone who had started and owned her own business, Susan did not furnish or decorate her own apartment, which she had lived in for many years. In fact, she did not even take a lease on the apartment but lived in it on a month-to-month basis, in an unstated and unwritten agreement with her landlord that matched in its vagueness her inattention to Mark's infidelities. The apartment was very large, so Susan would let rooms on a short-term basis to friends of friends or business associates of friends who were coming to her city. She didn't need the money. She liked having these people around. They gave her some company. But they were never her friends, and her contact with these temporary tenants was brief and superficial. Again, this is an avoidant pattern of relationships—brief, functional, nonintimate, uncommitted, superficial.

And, just as when she was a child abused by her neighbor and frightened by her parents' fighting, Susan could not ask for help when she needed it. One day, while she was struggling to bring some large boxes up the stairs to her apartment, two of her tenants, whom she liked, saw her and offered to help. Susan felt strange in the moment as the two men stood there. She liked that they had asked, and she needed their help. More than that, she appreciated that they wanted to help. In fact, she felt very moved, almost to tears, by their offer of help. But she could not accept it. She told them no, waited until they left, and then struggled on with the boxes by herself. But she felt very sad that evening and weekend.

These details were elicited by the therapist over the first several months of therapy. Gradually, a coherent narrative of Susan's life began to emerge. In the language of the AAI, Susan was becoming able to see and remember more clearly what she felt in her childhood and what she felt in her present life. She was becoming able to talk about it and to communicate her experiences more clearly and more directly to her therapist. She began to become more aware of her own longings for contact and the way in which she inhibited herself and truncated opportunities to make more intimate contact with other people. This was the early process of the therapy and the process of beginning to deconstruct the patient's aloneness, the areas of her life where she cannot see or know what she feels and thinks.

A turning point came for Susan one weekend after she returned from a business trip combined with a vacation. She got back to her apartment with her suitcase, put it on her bed, and then sat there watching television in a sort of daze for the rest of the afternoon. The day darkened, and still she sat there watching TV, essentially in a dissociated state, her suitcase sitting on the bed untouched. Gradually, Susan became more aware of the suitcase and felt irritated that it was still sitting there unopened. But she felt unable to get up and unpack it. It marked the end of her trip; it marked being home alone and going back to her life in her borrowed apartment. Then Susan had what amounted to an epiphany. She realized what she was feeling and what she wanted: She realized that she wanted and was waiting for someone to come and help her unpack the suitcase—that she didn't want to do it alone, that she wanted to do it with someone else. She didn't want to go through another episode and set of feelings in her life while she was alone. And she felt that it was important to tell this story to her therapist.

This was a double-edged moment for Susan. Part of the reason she needed somebody else to help her unpack the suitcase was because she got frozen around her own emotional experience and need to be driven by the external motivation of what someone else wanted to do. But the emergent and vital edge of what she was feeling was that she wanted to do the unpacking with someone else. She wanted another person inside her emotions and her situation. She wanted to be less alone in a meaningful event and moment of transition when she was threatened with a bit of anxiety and sadness.

Susan later told her therapist that she realized how often she waited for someone else to start something and then simply responded to their demands or expectations. She was also very aware of wanting a partner and a helper—someone who would foster and support her in what she was going through and what she needed to do—a trusted companion, Bowlby might say. She began to think of other areas of her life where she wanted help and intimate understanding and support. She also said that she thought of the therapist as her helper in life and had been waiting for someone to come along to help her in her life.

This is what we all need. It is our nature to be dyadic. The problem is when we have learned that help is very restricted and constrained or unreliable or is available to us only under very specific and narrow circumstances. These limitations on helpful, intimate contact had been trained into Susan. She was now undoing them.

In the weeks after this conversation, Susan and her therapist began to focus on how Susan might have a real companion in her life. The focus was on men: whom she met, what she thought and felt, how she acted, what happened. Although she began by feeling that she never met anyone, she began to see that in fact she met lots of people but that she didn't converse with them in a way that led toward intimacy. There was always something that derailed the contact and threw it off in another, shallower direction. She began to look longer and more thoughtfully at the men she met. She began to date, and what happened on the dates, the way she felt and acted, the characteristics and behavior of the men, began to be the focus of her thoughtful attention. She noticed how much she tried to remain in control. She noticed how contemptuous she was of signs of weakness or dependence in the men she met. She saw her great and well-warranted fear of being taken advantage of yet again. Sometimes, single moments of interaction with another person would occupy all of a therapy session, the feelings and fears slowly getting teased out. Susan became able to see and experience and talk about her relationships and yearnings and fears in a newer, much clearer, and much more complete way.

The course of this was not always smooth and straightforward. Work would get busy or the holidays would come, and Susan could very easily fall back into her old patterns. She was more expert at avoiding real communication than she was at engaging in it, despite her longing to do so. Those old synaptic networks were still intact, and they could be easily triggered. But gradually, new networks were strengthened and new connections were made. The dentate layer of her hippocampus created new emotional memories and learnings that gave her the opportunity to say more and to grow closer to others and more knowing about herself.

PROGRESSIVELY DEEPENING COORDINATION WITH THE PATIENT THROUGH COMMUNICATIVE ELABORATION

As Susan's case illustrates, deconstructing the patient's aloneness involves not only discovering that part of the patient's self that has been defensively excluded but also helping the patient to experience and communicate that part. The therapist does this by progressively elaborating the patient's experience, tiny step by tiny step if necessary, going slowly enough, in Martin Buber's phrase, to open up what might otherwise remain unopened. Although this may sound like a self-evident or an easy process, actually doing it is a specific ability that requires curiosity, openness, and an active quality of mind. Paul Ekman has often written (e.g., 2007) that most people are not as good at reading other people as they think they are but that everyone can get better by doing two things: by trying consistently and actively to read the other person and by constantly reevaluating and revising what we think the other person is feeling.

This process of communicative elaboration occurs in different ways at different points in the course of psychotherapy. Elaboration involves an interest and curiosity about the patient's story and, once a focus has been selected within a particular session, a gentle, progressive, step-by-step inquiry that leads the patient deeper into her account of her experiences. It also involves a close focus on and continuing invitation to elaborate on the feelings that are part of the patient's experiencing. The focus on feelings, which by their nature always involve an actual physiological experience and occur in the present tense, should produce in the patient a subjective sense of living through the experience again in the present moment; the therapist's responsiveness, elaborative stance, and felt closeness to the patient should give the patient the subjective sense of going through the experience in the presence of a trusted companion with whom all aspects of the experience can be freely shared and thus fully experienced and processed. The therapist actively communicates her presence through facial, postural, and vocal signals of engagement and through questions, comments, and confirming or transitional restatements that deepen and elaborate the patient's account and her experience in the session. Further, consistent with the experiential mode of accompanying the patient in her experience, the therapist may choose to occasionally self-disclose her own affect states in response to the experiences and events described and in response to the interaction with the patient, just as in fact a trusted companion actually present within the experiences would be likely to do.

This process, in its emphasis on experiential elaboration, crystallizes the difference between communicative coordination and defensive exclusion. The therapist wants to know what the patient is feeling and thinking and welcomes its expression. The patient comes to believe this and to *feel* it as a new context for his or her self-experiencing. The process is forward leaning and progressively intimate, with the patient progressively discovering excluded aspects of his experience as he communicates these to the therapist and comes to believe more deeply in the therapist's interest in and openness to their expression.

Patients often experience the close, active interest and consistent attention of the therapist as itself a remoralizing, opening, and curative factor in therapy. Under the influence of a consistent strong interest in elaborating their experience, patients are encouraged to discover within themselves more of uncommunicated self-experience that they have excluded and not previously been able to identify clearly or to share.

CLARIFYING AND RESPONDING TO THE PATIENT'S AFFECTIVE COMMUNICATIONS

Throughout therapy, the therapist more or less continuously scans and consciously processes the affective state and communications of the patient. This especially includes attention to the patient's facial expression and vocal qualities but also includes postural and rhythmic cues, such as how the patient sits and moves. But the face and voice are particularly important and are viewed, with Tomkins (Demos, 1993; Tomkins & Demos, 1995) and Ekman (Ekman, 2007; Ekman & Rosenberg, 2005), as the seat of affect and as the primary source of affective communication. The therapist is informed and guided by what is happening on the patient's face and in his voice, much as are Tronick's (Cohn & Tronick, 1988; Tronick, 1989, 2007, 2009; Tronick & Beeghly, 2011; Tronick & Cohn, 1989) optimally coordinating mothers with their infants (Cohn & Tronick, 1988; Tronick, 1989, 2007, 2009; Tronick & Beeghly, 2011; Tronick & Cohn, 1989). The patient's affective state is viewed as a continuously present phenomenon that is monitored by the therapist throughout their interaction (see Fosha, 2000, for a good description of this process). The therapist's ability to discern and register affective communications from the patient's face and other sources is a crucial component of the sensitive responsiveness to patient signals described above.

The therapist is especially alert for two affective events: fleeting expressions of affect (which Ekman called *microexpressions*) and sudden transitions in affect. Both of these events are likely to mark defended-against affect states or emergent affects or both, and they are of special importance. Fleeting expressions of affect are intrinsically difficult to catch; a need on the patient's part to keep these affects out of communication and self-experience invokes defensive maneuvers and distracts the therapist and the patient from their occurrence. The patient may change the subject or begin to tell a long story in great detail; internally, the patient seeks to move away from what he is experiencing. The therapist has to consciously watch for momentary expressions of particular affects in order to catch them. This requires close attention and watching the patient's face carefully. The stance is not unlike that of watching a summer sky for the momentary flash of a shooting star. Because the patient is very unlikely to be aware of these momentary affects, the therapist actively inquires about them, perhaps saying, "What happened on your face a moment ago?" or "You looked sad (or annoyed, frightened, etc.) for a moment." With such prompting and permission, the patient can usually identify and begin to talk about the fleeting feeling, which the therapist can then help to elaborate. The purpose is to bring warded-off affective states and self-experiences into fuller expression and conscious experience. What the therapist is doing is to try to speak for the feelings the patient is having but excluding from communication and awareness.

Transitions in feeling state as they occur during a session are especially important in regard to whether they mark a deepening of feeling and involvement, a "shallowing" of affective experience and closeness, or a repetition and recycling of a defensive emotion. A shifted-away-from affective state is likely to mark feelings with which the patient is uncomfortable because they lead to places fenced off by anxiety or because they are not well elaborated for the patient as part of her relational configurations with others (i.e., they are unfamiliar and not fluently integrated). In such a case, the task of the therapist is to return and hold the patient on the feelings that are being transitioned from. The therapist might say, "Let's go back to what you were feeling a moment ago" or "Whenever we start talking about your annoyance, we wind up talking about something else" or "It's hard to keep talking about something that makes you so uncomfortable." In the case of an affective deepening, the therapist's task is to facilitate the deepening by elaborating and resonating to it and accepting it with all the interpersonal skill at her command. In other words, the therapist coordinates with deepened affective communications and avoids coordinating with defensive shifts.

In general, the therapist is not reluctant to directly comment on the patient's affective state as it is present in the patient's nonverbal communications, fleeting or otherwise, throughout the session, and he or she often does so. The therapist comments on the patient's feelings often enough to keep them prominent as a focus for experiencing and communication. The selection of what to comment on is guided by what is being defensively excluded and what is there to be deepened.

Direct comment by the therapist about a fleeting affective expression by the patient is usually a coordination by the therapist with an excluded affect state. It often produces a striking and very marked deepening of affect in the patient, as the disowned is suddenly included and experienced.

THERAPIST'S AFFECTIVE EXPERIENCE OF THE PATIENT

The therapist's own affective experience of the patient is a critical focus in the psychotherapy we are describing. This affective experience informs the therapist and may be explicitly disclosed to the patient.

In focusing attentively on the affective communications of the patient, especially those that are conveyed by the patient's facial expressions, the therapist allows herself to participate in the patient's processes of emotional communication that permit affective states to flow in the room. The therapist's facial muscles move in subtle, often subperceptual, reflection or imitation of the patient's expressions, and, through the process of facial feedback and mirror neurons, the therapist experiences a version of the patient's affective state within herself. The patient's affective state becomes available to the therapist as an internal experience. As the therapist closely tracks what the patient is feeling in the context of the events or situations the patient is describing, the therapist achieves an experience of the patient's inner world. She experiences a version of the patient's affect in the context of particular relational configurations. This is an important source of the therapist's felt empathy with and understanding of the patient (Bavelas, Black, Lemery, & Mullett, 1987; Bavelas & Chovil, 1997, 2006; Bavelas & Gerwing, 2007).

The therapist's emotional experience of the patient's affect not only constitutes a major source of data about the patient but, in the case of genuine adaptive affects, also becomes an essential foundation for the creation of a coordinated state between them. This disclosure of the therapist's experience occurs as both implicit and explicit communication. The therapist's communications to the patient are altered as a consequence of his own experiencing of what the patient is feeling; they in significant part reflect the patient's experiencing and this may be registered and responded to by the patient. Through the inclusion of his own affective experience of the patient's emotions, the therapist matches and synchronizes with the patient in a manner that defines the experience of coordination and that is intrinsically affirming for the patient.

In the case of difficult or excluded emotions, the expressed affective experiencing of the therapist shifts the patient from a state in which affective self-regulation must be managed on an exclusively intraindividual and defensive basis to a state in which the same difficult or excluded emotions may be self-regulated dyadically and nondefensively—through the communicative coordination with the therapist. This is the essential experience of Bowlby's trusted companion, of secure-base attachment, and of security-engendering mother–infant interaction. Within the therapy setting, the patient experiences this new interpersonal, nondefensive regulation of difficult and excluded affect states as profound relief and relaxation, as an occasion of cognitive clarity and motivational purpose, and as a source of closeness to the therapist.

The therapist's experience is of course not identical to the patient's; she experiences a version of what the patient is feeling, a version that is both attenuated and also placed in the different context of the therapist's personal history, affective and cognitive processing, and current motivational state, including the motivation of helping the patient. This partial but not exact overlapping of experiencing is similar to the midrange of tracking of an infant by her mother, which has been found to be associated with optimal attunement and secure attachment (Beebe, 2004, 2010). That is, neither too little nor too much matching is associated with security. Along similar lines, Leslie Greenberg (personal communication) has suggested that an effective therapist needs to have had at least two kinds of life experiences: one experience that has led him to attune very closely to what another is feeling and thinking and a second that permits him to separate himself from the other and reflect on his experience of attunement through his own affective and cognitive responses.

The similarities and the differences between the patient's and the therapist's experiencing provide the therapist with the necessary leverage to work with the patient's experience. This work, as discussed elsewhere in this chapter, may include accepting, tolerating, and understanding the patient's affect; describing and deepening it; relating it to previous and current relationships; exploring its role in the therapy relationship; and examining how the patient defensively avoids an excluded affect and what she does and experiences instead. It may also very usefully include the therapist's explicit self-disclosure of his own experience of the patient, undertaken nonintrusively and with relevance to the patient's goals.

The therapist's self-disclosures incorporate both the similarities and differences in their experiencing. This furthers several important processes in the therapeutic dialogue. By incorporating similarities, it strengthens the patient's sense of the intersubjective reality, validity, and importance of what he is communicating and of his own previously excluded experiencing. It also deepens the degree of coordination that exists within the dyad and may further elicit the emergence of excluded affects and cognitions. By incorporating differences, it provides an opportunity to experience, to step around, and to understand defensive processes in the living moment of the interaction. And, in disclosing the differences in the therapist's experience as these are fostering of and closely relevant to the patient, it invites the patient to coordinate with another way of experiencing himself and his situations. In Vygotsky's terms (Vygotsky, Cole, John-Steiner, & Scribner, 1978), via the sympathetically offered experience of an other, it offers the patient a proximal zone of development that leads toward another way of being.

A necessary condition of this process is that the therapist be open to the affects in relational context that the patient is experiencing. As noted previously, when our emotional communications elicit matching experiences that are intrapsychically uncomfortable to others and that they do not wish to experience, they may seek to avoid us, misunderstand us, divert the interaction in another direction, or otherwise seek to block an internal experience of the state we are communicating (Fraiberg, Adelson, & Shapiro, 1975; Main & Weston, 1981). Loewald (1960) suggested, speaking of psychoanalysis, that the therapeutic relationship between patient and analyst has the effect of raising the patient to the developmental level of the analyst. Badalamenti (1984) wrote,

If the therapist is not already actualized where the client needs to be, then he cannot give the client what he needs: an affective invitation from realized human potentials to unrealized potentials. The therapist/client relation in this sense is comparable to the first and most primitive one a person has. (p. 128).

In our present terms, if the therapist is unable to permit himself to experience internally a version of the patient's affective state—if he defends against and excludes it—coordination will have failed and a repetition of the patient's pathogenic experience with earlier attachment figures may occur. If the therapist is not herself able to experience the affects and relational configurations that are difficult for the patient, it will be difficult for her to help the patient in these regards. This is just as it is in an attachment relationship between a mother and a child.

CLARIFYING BEHAVIORS AND THEIR ACCOMPANYING AFFECTS

The therapist assumes that individuals who have fluent, nondefensive access to their own affects and cognitions are able to plan their lives and to conduct themselves adaptively; given such nondefensive access, their plans and conduct will unfold in a manner that is congruent with their own circumstances, preferences, and values without the assistance or guidance of the therapist. Maladaptive behavior is understood to result from defensive exclusions and defensively distorted affects and cognitions. Therefore, the therapist surveys the patient's life and listens to the patient's accounts of experiences while thinking in terms of the differences between the circumstances in which he or she behaves adaptively and those in which behavior is maladaptive. The therapist notes the affects that accompany each type of behavior, arriving at an understanding of which affects are difficult for this particular patient, and notes the types of relational configurations that are present when defensive affective processing occurs. This is a way of understanding both the patient's strengths and the patient's difficulties.

This affective-relational analysis has two components: what is excluded or difficult and what is substituted in place of what is difficult. What emotions are difficult for this patient to bear, and what are the alternative or defensive emotions that he experiences instead? What are the characteristics of the relational configurations that are in operation when the excluded emotions occur? To which relational configurations does the patient strive to make a defensive switch? What is the patient feeling that he is not communicating? What does he communicate instead? The delineation of excluded affective communications, defensive emotional processes, and the interpersonal events that set off and occur as part of these processes constitutes a key diagnostic assessment and form of understanding of the patient.

The therapist must therefore be able to make a provisional judgment about what may be adaptive and maladaptive for the patient. The attachment-informed therapist is no more agnostic about external reality than is the security-engendering mother of a well-attached infant. But the patient is, of course, not the therapist's child, and the purpose is not to advise the patient on what to do. The security-engendering mother, as noted above, is appropriately nonintrusive and comfortable with her child's independence. However, the therapist's survey of adaptive and maladaptive areas of the patient's functioning gives the therapist a target for inquiry and intervention with the patient. Maladaptive behavior guides the therapist to excluded affect and cognition and identifies key areas of difficult attachment experiences. The relational configurations that are present when defensive processing occurs tell the therapist what type of situations with attachment figures required defensive exclusions. The therapist's task is to focus on these areas of maladaptation in terms of the defensive exclusions and distortions, to help the patient to bring the excluded material into coordination with the therapist, and thereby to make it possible for the patient to more freely enact an adaptive course of his or her own choosing.

WHEN AND HOW TO EXPLICITLY ADDRESS DEFENSES

Working with defenses as an aspect of the therapist's fundamental disposition to be helpful to the patient means that defenses are addressed as impediments to something important and adaptive that the patient is trying to do. This dictates both when they are addressed and how they are understood with the patient. Defenses are best addressed when in fact they arise in conjunction with the patient's efforts to do something important that he (or she) wants to do. At such moments, the understanding of defenses presents itself as a helpful solution to a problem with which the patient himself is actively struggling. The problem may be various: success at work, difficulties with an intimate relationship, progress in therapy, relinquishing an addiction, a surcease of anxiety or depression.

Often, the patient will present what he wants to do in negative form by saying that he is unable to do it. By understanding with the patient at that moment how the patient's defenses impede, for example, finding intimacy in a relationship, the therapist actually helps the patient with a current problem and is felt by the patient to be helpful. The patient and therapist share a goal. The understanding of defenses becomes a way of being with the patient. There is often a great deal of give-and-take between therapist and patient.

The therapist may repeatedly (but tactfully) interrupt the patient to point to the activation of a defensive distortion, evasion, or exclusion. When this is done successfully, there will be a deepening of the patient's affect. There is a joint and companionate working on an actual difficulty in the context of deepening feelings and new ideas about what is happening. Moving beyond the defenses is a joint activity.

The stance and construction of helpfulness with regard to defenses rest on the principle that defenses distort adaptive functioning by excluding useful and necessary self-experiences from full processing. It is in these terms that defenses are understood with the patient. The patient's defenses become interesting primarily for how they lead the patient to avoid something that in fact he wants, needs, and can adaptively use to do what he wants to do. Defenses are framed as what keeps the patient from accomplishing his goal. The focus is therefore on moving as rapidly as possible behind the defenses to the excluded affects and cognitions that will motivate the patient in a new direction.

The incipient experience of previously excluded affect and cognitions is likely to provoke one or both of the forms of attachment anxiety, fear of feeling, and fear of absence. With the patient, therefore, there is an emphasis on understanding how defensive functioning, impelled by adaptive purposes in an earlier, nonoptimal setting, is related to maladaptive behavior and situations and to aversive affects such as anxiety, depression, and loneliness. There is a corresponding emphasis on exploring where the excluded affects and cognitions might lead the patient and how their inclusion might produce adaptive results.

As defenses and anxiety dissolve and exclusions emerge, the patient—and the therapist with the patient—experiences an increased degree of emotional coherence, genuineness of contact, and depth of motivation. The interaction feels more real and open, more satisfying to both participants. This authenticity, coherence, and depth of motivation characteristically give the patient a feeling of sure-footedness in regard to his communication and actions. He is more comfortable with himself and feels better in his own skin.

Sometimes defenses arise within the therapeutic relationship itself. The therapist is actively attentive to the patient's defenses against closeness and intimacy within the therapeutic relationship. These defenses may take a variety of forms that are widely recognized by therapists, such as the following:

- not having anything to talk about;
- a dismissal of the significance of warm feelings;
- attacks on the self as inadequate and unworthy;
- an insistence on the purely formal and professional aspects of the relationship;

- coming late or missing sessions;
- feeling unimportant;
- rapid, difficult-to-follow speech;
- excessive detail;
- idealization of the therapist;
- passivity; and
- grandiosity.

Although such patient experiences are widely seen as resistances by therapists, from within the present perspective they are understood and attended to as defenses against closer, more intimate affective coordination—as defenses against the secure, responsive relationship that (optimally) is being offered by the therapist. Patients surely want a secure relationship. But they have learned, at the level of implicit relational knowing (Lyons-Ruth, 1998b), that they cannot have one; they have learned especially that they cannot have one in the context of certain feelings and thoughts; and they have also learned, at the implicit, procedural level of automatic functioning, how to have a nonintimate, insecure relationship. Their defenses organize and maintain insecure attachment and avoid a more intimate and secure relationship when one is available. They are defenses against something that is longed for but implicitly believed to be impossible, at least in the context of particular affective states. The therapist's steadfastness in staying with the patient in a warm and welcoming way while simultaneously naming and narrating and asking about and then elaborating what the patient might be feeling behind the defenses gradually opens the relationship to a more direct and nondefensive communication.

RECOGNIZING NEW ADAPTIVE RESPONSES

As the patient struggles to bring excluded states into communication with the therapist, the therapist is especially attentive to the emergence of new adaptive responses. The patient is seen as struggling with different ways of being in the world, and in the course of therapy these ways of being alternate with each other. Emergent adaptive responses take an endless variety of forms: A patient whose self-expression and desire to explore the world was stunted excessively by critical parents may buy a camera and register for a photography course; a narcissistically defended patient may loan his beloved car to his daughter without anxiety or regret; a patient whose anger occasions strong anxiety may stand up for his own interests at work; or a patient who hides and denies her painful feelings may begin to speak more openly to the therapist in the session. As these emergent adaptive responses show themselves in the interaction with the therapist or in the patient's life outside of the sessions, the therapist's task is to notice them and to highlight and elaborate them with the patient and to encourage the patient's experiencing, however incipient and partial they may be. The elaboration of these experiences includes noting how they are new and different forms of behavior for the patient, discussing and reducing the anxieties that may have accompanied the new behavior, and contrasting the new behavior with the old patterns of behavior in the patient's recent and distant past. Encouraging the patient to experientially focus on these emergent responses involves attending to, coordinating with, and deepening the experience of the affects and self-experiences that motivate the new responses. Cognitive-behavioral techniques can be especially helpful in offering patients a new way to think about what they are doing.

To do this with each patient, the therapist must become an expert in that individual's ways of managing affect and relationships. The therapist must know what the patient usually excludes and avoids, what defenses are invoked to implement the exclusion, and what new behaviors constitute a divergence from these old patterns.

RESPONDING TO THE INAPPROPRIATE SUPPRESSION OR HEIGHTENING OF AFFECT

In the paradigmatic modes of avoidant and anxious attachment, attachment anxiety is regulated through the defensive suppression and heightening of affect. Therefore, in listening to and interacting with the patient, the therapist is especially alert and attentive to affects that seem weaker or stronger than one might expect in the given circumstances. Such suppressions and heightening indicate defensive operations and provide a focus for the elicitation of excluded experiences.

The therapist therefore actively inquires and intervenes when the patient is elaborating an experience with what appears to be inappropriately reduced or excessive and overly intense feeling. The therapist slows down the patient and "holds" him in regions of the communicated experience that are problematic in terms of what the patient is feeling. The therapist thinks in terms of the patient's experiencing one of the two major forms of attachment anxiety—fear of feeling and fear of absence—about an anticipated separation or loss of coordination with the other.

At such moments, the patient is understood to have entered a defensive posture that excludes key elements of adaptive self-experience in an effort to control separation from or loss of coordination with the other. In understanding what has been excluded, the therapist attends to what did not happen just before the situation or problem the patient is describing (i.e., what did the patient maneuver away from within his own self-experience just before the situation he was describing began to go wrong?).

The patient's excluded state is not obviously apparent. Patients have become expert at evading their excluded states and preventing them from reaching full processing and incorporation in behavior. The therapist notices what the patient might have felt or done and actively inquires and seeks to elaborate the precursors to the problematic situation. The focus is especially on what the patient might have done if he or she had not inappropriately suppressed or heightened an affective response.

DEEPENING THE EXPERIENCE OF ADAPTIVE AFFECT IN RELATION TO PRESENT RELATIONSHIPS, SITUATIONS, AND GOALS

As adaptive affects, cognitions, and behaviors are reached and become progressively more accessible to the patient, the therapist acts to highlight and affirm these adaptive responses. For example, a therapist may choose to respond promptly and generously to a phone call from a patient who usually deals with feelings and problems through isolation and suppression or who has been afraid of how the expression of his difficulties or need for help may affect his attachment figures. Therapists working within the framework of dialectical behavior therapy sometimes provide their patients with means for reaching them on short notice and respond promptly to these calls when patients try to reach them. Attachment-based therapists might do the same with patients who need to obtain a prompt response to their distress. An attachment-based therapist should probably spend more time returning phone calls than other therapists may do.

This example is not particularly problematic, but it is worth noting that the tendency of some psychoanalytic writers and therapists in considering instances of a therapist's positively responding to a patient's request would be to focus on and to worry about the dangers of an enactment. Although the therapist's feelings, personal responses, and motivations in regard to the patient remain of great interest within attachment-based therapy, the focus and conceptual frame have a different emphasis.

To take an actual example of the differences between a therapeutic interaction grounded in therapeutic neutrality and one informed by attachment theory: A poorly educated and isolative clinic patient once began a session with her therapist by asking who had won the presidential election the day before. There are many ways to understand such a question. The therapist's supervisor, perhaps struck by the patient's not knowing what everyone else did, suggested that the question should be interpreted to the patient as an aspect of her dependence on the therapist, a tack the therapist in fact carried out. In attachment-based therapy, the patient's question would more likely be understood as an effort by the isolative patient to establish the therapist, at the beginning of a session, as a helpful and responsive secure base and therefore as a pathway to exploring the unknown and frightening wider world. The question might therefore be directly answered in a warm, open, and friendly manner and used to foster the relationship between patient and therapist. Similarly and in general, the therapist will seek to facilitate the experience and communication of other adaptive affects within the therapy relationship, including negative affects such as anger and sadness.

The therapist conceives of her role as including the active fostering of the patient in the outside world through her communications to him. But direct advice on behavior is usually therapeutically useless because what is at therapeutic issue is the patient's access to his own adaptive responses. Behaviors considered outside the context of the patient's affective motivations are generally not of interest. Therefore, as the patient presents real problems and situations with which he is struggling, the therapist will seek—through questions, elaborations, restatements, and nonverbal responses—both to elicit and to affirm the adaptive affects and cognitions of the patient as they emerge in relationship to the situation the patient is discussing. The therapist will seek to deepen the experience of these affects by focusing on them and encouraging their elaboration in the session. The therapist will also seek to elide the defensive maneuvers and to reduce the anxieties that usually accompany their emergence.

Affects include an action tendency, a disposition to particular actions and behaviors, and therefore all of this inevitably disposes the patient to some behaviors in the real world rather than to others. By eliciting, elaborating, and encouraging the experience of selected emotions, the therapist is playing an important role in making these behaviors possible and more likely for the patient. The therapist's judgment of what emotions should be facilitated in the patient has an important influence on what the patient actually does, and the therapist may well discuss particular behaviors with the patient in terms of their affective context and meaning. What is essential is that the therapist elicit, affirm, and coordinate with what is genuine and deep in the patient's experiencing rather than what is defensive and motivated by anxiety.

The therapist inquires about the patient's experience of the emergent emotions, thoughts, and behaviors. When previously unavailable affects emerge without defenses, patients experience themselves in a new and more affirmative way. This is the case even when the emotions involved are themselves painful. Patients who are experiencing deep sadness or grief that they had previously defended against may say, as one such patient recently did, "I feel really sad but really good." Or a patient who is experiencing previously excluded anger may also find himself feeling very strong and sure-footed and calm as he resolves to seek real changes in a troubling situation. The positive aspect of these emotional experiences is a key marker that the emotions involved are genuine and adaptive.

In talking about the patient's experience of adaptive affects and cognitions, the therapist may ask the patient when else he has felt this way, making an affect bridge toward actions in the future rather than toward understanding the past.

The use of affect bridges is a good way to delineate an internal working model by activating early attachment relationships and emotions in the context of current problems. When a patient is describing a difficult experience in his present life, ask the patient to focus on, clarify, and specify exactly how he is feeling in that situation. Then ask the following questions as part of an unfolding conversation: When and where else in your life have you felt the same feelings? In your early life, going as far back as you can remember, when did you feel those feelings? In what other situations in your current life do you feel that way? Usually these or related questions will elicit both early experiences with attachment figures and similar situations that are occurring in the patient's current life. This clearly sketches an internal working model, its history, and the extent of its reach, which can then become the target for interventions.

As new adaptive emotions emerge from exclusion, patients will often have a sense of themselves as being in a new state with regard to themselves and their lives. This is an important moment for the therapist to continue to stay in close coordination with the patient and to not back away. For what the patient is doing is new—and fragile. The exploration of and mutual coordination with these feelings in the patient–therapist relationship, perhaps involving the therapist's self-disclosure and expression of feeling, can provide an emotionally deepening experience for the patient.

THE INTERHUMAN: A FINAL NOTE ON THE POWER OF NONEXCLUSIONARY COMMUNICATION

As psychotherapists, we work with our patients by communicating with them, and a central theme of this book has been the power of coordination and communication with an attentive and responsive other to shape and also to transform the self. The emphasis throughout has been on the affirmative power of this communicative coordination when it permits the emergence of authentic and nonexclusionary self-experience—affects and cognitions that are not distorted by fear and anxiety. This has been described as a natural and biologically embedded human process that is not unique to the setting of psychotherapy. In this sense, psychotherapy participates in and makes special use of a dimension of experience that is always potentially present in human relationships. It is psychotherapy's focused participation in this dimension of experience that confers its power and efficacy. We do, after all is said and done, only talk with our patients.

Martin Buber (1965) described this natural and broader process, in which psychotherapy may sometimes participate, in words that emphasize the emergence of the excluded and the power of authentic, nonexclusionary communication:

> In the great faithfulness which is the climate of genuine dialogue, what I have to say at any one time already has in me the character of something that wishes to be uttered, and I must not keep it back, keep it in myself. . . . Where the dialogical word genuinely exists, it must be given its right by keeping nothing back. . . . To speak is both nature and work, something that grows and something that is made, and where it appears dialogically, in the climate of great faithfulness, it has to fulfill ever anew the unity of the two.
>
> But where the dialogue is fulfilled in its being, between partners who have turned to one another in truth, who express themselves without reserve and are free of the desire for semblance, there is brought into being a memorable common fruitfulness which is to be found nowhere else. At such times, at each such time, the word arises in a substantial way by men who have been seized in their depths and opened out by the dynamic of an elemental togetherness. The interhuman opens out what otherwise remains unopened. (p. 86)

REFERENCES

Abbott, L. F., & Nelson, S. B. (2000). Synaptic plasticity: Taming the beast. *Nature Neuroscience, 3,* 1178–1183. doi:10.1038/81453

Ackerman, S. J., Benjamin, L. S., Beutler, L. E., Gelso, C. J., Goldfried, M. R., Hill, C., . . . Rainer, J. (2001). Empirically supported therapy relationships: Conclusions and recommendations to the Division 29 Task Force. *Psychotherapy: Theory, Research, Practice, Training, 38,* 495–497. doi:10.1037/0033-3204.38.4.495

Adamson, L. B. (1996). *Communication development during infancy.* New York, NY: Brown.

Ainsworth, M. D. (1964). Patterns of attachment behavior shown by the infant in interaction with his mother. *Merrill-Palmer Quarterly, 10,* 51–58.

Ainsworth, M. D. S. (1976). System for coding infant attachment and reciprocal maternal behaviors. In E. T. Service (Ed.), *Educational Testing Service test collection.* Princeton, NJ: Educational Testing Service.

Ainsworth, M. D. S. (1979). Infant–mother attachment. *American Psychologist, 34,* 932–937. doi:10.1037/0003-066X.34.10.932

Ainsworth, M. D. S., Bell, S. M., & Stayton, D. F. (1974). Infant–mother attachment and social development: Socialization as a product of reciprocal responsiveness to signals. In M. P. Richards (Ed.), *The integration of a child into a social world* (pp. 9–135). New York, NY: Cambridge University Press.

Ainsworth, M. D. S., Blehar, M. C., Waters, E., & Wall, S. (1978). *Patterns of attachment: A psychological study of the strange situation.* Oxford, England: Erlbaum.

Alston, J. F. (2001). Correlation between childhood bipolar I disorder and reactive attachment disorder, disinhibited type. In T. M. Levy (Ed.), *Handbook of attachment interventions* (pp. 193–242). San Diego, CA: Academic Press. doi:10.1016/B978-012445860-4/50009-5

Atkinson, L., Leung, E., Goldberg, S., Benoit, D., Poulton, L., Myhal, N., . . . Kerr, S. (2009). Attachment and selective attention: Disorganization and emotional Stroop reaction time. *Development and Psychopathology, 21,* 99–126. doi:10.1017/S0954579409000078

Averill, J. R. (1987). The role of emotion and psychological defense in self-protective behavior. In N. D. Weinstein (Ed.), *Taking care: Understanding and encouraging self-protective behavior* (pp. 54–78). New York, NY: Cambridge University Press.

Badalamenti, A. F. (1984). Successful psychotherapy. *Journal of Contemporary Psychotherapy, 14,* 120–130.

Bakermans-Kranenburg, M. J., van IJzendoorn, M. H., & Juffer, F. (2003). Less is more: Meta-analyses of sensitivity and attachment interventions in early childhood. *Psychological Bulletin, 129,* 195–215. doi:10.1037/0033-2909.129.2.195

Balbernie, R. (2001). Circuits and circumstances: The neurobiological consequences of early relationship experiences and how they shape later behaviour. *Journal of Child Psychotherapy, 27*, 237–255. doi:10.1080/00754170110087531

Baldwin, S. A., Wampold, B. E., & Imel, Z. E. (2007). Untangling the alliance–outcome correlation: Exploring the relative importance of therapist and patient variability in the alliance. *Journal of Consulting and Clinical Psychology, 75*, 842–852. doi:10.1037/0022-006X.75.6.842

Bales, K. L., Boone, E., Epperson, P., Hoffman, G., & Carter, C. S. (2011). Are behavioral effects of early experience mediated by oxytocin? *Frontiers in Psychiatry, 2*, Article 24. doi:10.3389/fpsyt.2011.00024

Bales, K. L., & Perkeybile, A. M. (2012). Developmental experiences and the oxytocin receptor system. *Hormones and Behavior, 61*, 313–319. doi:10.1016/j.yhbeh.2011.12.013

Bandura, A. (1997). *Self-efficacy: The exercise of control.* New York, NY: Worth.

Bao, A.-M., Meynen, G., & Swaab, D. F. (2008). The stress system in depression and neurodegeneration: Focus on the human hypothalamus. *Brain Research Reviews, 57*, 531–553. doi:10.1016/j.brainresrev.2007.04.005

Bartholomew, K., & Horowitz, L. M. (1991). Attachment styles among young adults: A test of a four-category model. *Journal of Personality and Social Psychology, 61*, 226–244. doi:10.1037/0022-3514.61.2.226

Bartholomew, K., & Shaver, P. R. (1998). Methods of assessing adult attachment: Do they converge? In J. A. Simpson & W. S. Rholes (Eds.), *Attachment theory and close relationships* (pp. 25–45). New York, NY: Guilford Press.

Bartrip, J., Morton, J., & de Schonen, S. (2001). Responses to mother's face in 3-week to 5-month-old infants. *British Journal of Developmental Psychology, 19*, 219–232. doi:10:1348/026151001166047

Basch, M. F. (1996). Affect and defense. In D. L. Nathanson (Ed.), *Knowing feeling: Affect, script, and psychotherapy* (pp. 257–259). New York, NY: Norton.

Bates, J. E., Maslin, C. A., & Frankel, K. A. (1985). Attachment security, mother–child interaction, and temperament as predictors of behavior-problem ratings at age three years. In I. Bretherton & E. Waters (Eds.), *Growing points in attachment theory and research* (pp. 167–193). Chicago, IL: University of Chicago Press.

Bavelas, J. B., Black, A., Lemery, C. R., & Mullett, J. (1987). Motor mimicry as primitive empathy. In N. Eisenberg & J. Strayer (Eds.), *Empathy and its development* (pp. 317–338). New York, NY: Cambridge University Press.

Bavelas, J. B., & Chovil, N. (1997). Faces in dialogue. In J. A. Russell & J. M. Fernandez-Dols (Eds.), *The psychology of facial expression* (pp. 334–346). New York, NY: Cambridge University Press. doi:10.1017/CBO9780511659911.017

Bavelas, J. B., & Chovil, N. (2006). Nonverbal and verbal communication: Hand gestures and facial displays as part of language use in face-to-face dialogue. In V. Manusov & M. L. Patterson (Eds.), *The Sage handbook of nonverbal communication* (pp. 97–115). Thousand Oaks, CA: Sage. doi:10.4135/9781412976152.n6

Bavelas, J. B., & Gerwing, J. (2007). Conversational hand gestures and facial displays in face-to-face dialogue. In K. Fiedler (Ed.), *Social communication* (pp. 283–308). New York, NY: Psychology Press.

Bechara, A. (2004). A neural view of the regulation of complex cognitive functions by emotion. In P. Philippot & R. S. Feldman (Eds.), *The regulation of emotion* (pp. 3–32). Mahwah, NJ: Erlbaum.

Beebe, B. (2004). Co-constructing mother–infant distress in face-to-face interactions: Contributions of microanalysis. *Zero to Three, 24*(5), 40–48.

Beebe, B. (2010). Mother–infant research informs mother–infant treatment. *Clinical Social Work Journal, 38*(1), 17–36. doi:10.1007/s10615-009-0256-7

Beebe, B., Jaffe, J., Markese, S., Buck, K., Chen, H., Cohen, P., . . . Feldstein, S. (2010). The origins of 12-month attachment: A microanalysis of 4-month mother–infant interaction. *Attachment & Human Development, 12,* 6–141. doi:10.1080/14616730903338985

Beebe, B., & McCrorie, E. (2010). The optimum midrange: Infant research, literature, and romantic attachment. *Attachment: New Directions in Psychotherapy and Relational Psychoanalysis, 4,* 39–58.

Behrens, K. Y., Parker, A. C., & Haltigan, J. D. (2011). Maternal sensitivity assessed during the Strange Situation Procedure predicts child's attachment quality and reunion behaviors. *Infant Behavior and Development, 34,* 378–381. doi:10.1016/j.infbeh.2011.02.007

Belsky, J. (2009). Early day care and infant–mother attachment security. *Encyclopedia on early childhood development.* Retrieved from http://www.child-encyclopedia.com/documents.belskyangxp-attachment.pdf

Belsky, J. (2010). Childhood experience and the development of reproductive strategies. *Psicothema, 22,* 28–34.

Belsky, J., Steinberg, L., & Draper, P. (1991). Childhood experience, interpersonal development, and reproductive strategy: An evolutionary theory of socialization. *Child Development, 62,* 647–670. doi:10.2307/1131166

Ben-Dat Fisher, D., Serbin, L. A., Stack, D. M., Ruttle, P. L., Ledingham, J. E., & Schwartzman, A. E. (2007). Intergenerational predictors of diurnal cortisol secretion in early childhood. *Infant and Child Development, 16,* 151–170. doi:10.1002/icd.474

Bianchi, S. M. (2000). Maternal employment and time with children: Dramatic change or surprising continuity? *Demography, 37,* 401–414. doi:10.1353/dem.2000.0001

Bjorklund, D. F. (1997). The role of immaturity in human development. *Psychological Bulletin, 122,* 153–169. doi:10.1037/0033-2909.122.2.153

Blair, C., Granger, D., Willoughby, M., Kivlighan, K., & the Family Life Project Investigators. (2006). Maternal sensitivity is related to hypothalamic–pituitary–adrenal axis stress reactivity and regulation in response to emotion challenge in 6-month-old infants. In B. M. Lester, A. S. Masten, & B. S. McEwen (Eds.), *Annals of the New York Academy of Sciences: Vol. 1094. Resilience in children,* 263–267. doi:10.1196/annals.1376.031

Blair, C., Granger, D. A., Kivlighan, K. T., Mills-Koonce, R., Willoughby, M., Greenberg, M. T., . . . Family Life Project Investigators. (2008). Maternal and child contributions to cortisol response to emotional arousal in young children from low-income, rural communities. *Developmental Psychology, 44,* 1095–1109. doi:10.1037/0012-1649.44.4.1095

Blanchette, I., & Richards, A. (2010). The influence of affect on higher level cognition: A review of research on interpretation, judgment, decision making and reasoning. *Cognition & Emotion, 24,* 561–595. doi:10.1080/02699930903132496

Bleiberg, K. L., & Markowitz, J. C. (2008). Interpersonal psychotherapy for depression. In D. H. Barlow (Ed.), *Clinical handbook for psychological disorders: A step-by-step treatment manual* (4th ed., pp. 306–327). New York, NY: Guilford Press.

Boldrini, M., Underwood, M. D., Hen, R., Rosoklija, G. B., Dwork, A. J., Mann, J. J., & Arango, V. (2009). Antidepressants increase neural progenitor cells in the human hippocampus. *Neuropsychopharmacology, 34,* 2376–2389. doi:10.1038/npp.2009.75

Bolhuis, J. J. (1999). The development of animal behavior: From Lorenz to neural nets. *Naturwissenschaften, 86*(3), 101–111. doi:10.1007/s001140050582

Bornstein, R. F. (1985). Review of *Object relations in psychoanalytic theory. Psychoanalytic Psychology, 2,* 373–379. doi:10.1037/0736-9735.2.4.373

Botella, L., Corbella, S., Belles, L., Pacheco, M., Gomez, A. M., Herrero, O., . . . Pedro, N. (2008). Predictors of therapeutic outcome and process. *Psychotherapy Research, 18,* 535–542. doi: 0.1080/10503300801982773

Bowlby, J. (1940). The influence of early environment in the development of neurosis and neurotic character. *International Journal of Psychoanalysis, 21,* 154–178.

Bowlby, J. (1944a). Forty-four juvenile thieves: Their characters and home-life. *International Journal of Psychoanalysis, 25,* 19–53.

Bowlby, J. (1944b). Forty-four juvenile thieves: Their characters and home-life (II). *International Journal of Psychoanalysis, 25,* 107–128.

Bowlby, J. (1958). The nature of the child's tie to his mother. *International Journal of Psychoanalysis, 39,* 350–373.

Bowlby, J. (1960a). Grief and mourning in infancy and early childhood. *Psychoanalytic Study of the Child, 15,* 9–52.

Bowlby, J. (1960b). Separation anxiety. *International Journal of Psychoanalysis, 41,* 89–113.

Bowlby, J. (1960c). Separation anxiety: A critical review of the literature. *Journal of Child Psychology and Psychiatry, 1,* 251–269.

Bowlby, J. (1963). Pathological mourning and childhood mourning. *Journal of the American Psychoanalytic Association, 11,* 500–541.

Bowlby, J. (1973). *Attachment and loss: Vol. 2. Separation: Anxiety and anger.* New York, NY: Basic Books.

Bowlby, J. (1980). *Attachment and loss: Vol. 3. Loss.* New York, NY: Basic Books.

Bowlby, J. (1982). *Attachment and loss: Vol. I. Attachment* (2nd ed.). New York, NY: Basic Books. (Original work published 1969)

Bowlby, J. (1985). The role of childhood experience in cognitive disturbance. In M. J. Mahoney & A. Freeman (Eds.), *Cognition and psychotherapy* (pp. 181–200). New York, NY: Plenum.

Bowlby, J. (1988). *A secure base: Parent–child attachment and healthy human development*. New York, NY: Basic Books.

Bowlby, J. (1991). Postscript. In C. M. Parkes, J. Stevenson-Hinde, & P. Marris (Eds.), *Attachment across the life cycle* (pp. 293–297). London, England: Routledge.

Bowlby, J., & Parkes, C. M. (1970). Separation and loss within the family. *The Child in His Family, 1*, 197–216.

Bowlby, J., & Robertson, J. (1956). A two-year-old goes to hospital. In K. Soddy (Ed.), *Mental health and infant development: Vol. I. Papers and discussions* (pp. 123–124). Oxford, England: Basic Books.

Bowlby, J., Robertson, J., & Rosenbluth, D. (1952). A two-year-old goes to the hospital. *Psychoanalytic Study of the Child, 7*, 82–94.

Boyd, R. (2007). Cultural adaptation and maladaptation: Of kayaks and commissars. In S. W. Gangestad & J. A. Simpson (Eds.), *The evolution of mind: Fundamental questions and controversies* (pp. 327–331). New York, NY: Guilford Press.

Brazelton, T. B. (1995). Fetal observations: Could they relate to another modality, such as touch? In E. Field (Ed.), *Touch in early development* (pp. 11–18). Hillsdale, NJ: Erlbaum.

Brazelton, T. B., Koslowski, B., & Main, M. (1974). The origins of reciprocity: The early mother–infant interaction. In M. Lewis & L. A. Rosenblum (Eds.), *The effect of the infant on its caregiver* (pp. 49–76). Oxford, England: Wiley-Interscience.

Bretherton, I. (1985). Attachment theory: Retrospect and prospect. *Monographs of the Society for Research in Child Development, 50*, 3–35. doi:10.2307/3333824

Bretherton, I. (1990a). Communication patterns, internal working models, and the intergenerational transmission of attachment relationships. *Infant Mental Health Journal, 11*, 237–252. doi:10.1002/1097-0355(199023)11:3<237::AID-IMHJ2280110306>3.0.CO;2-X

Bretherton, I. (1990b). Open communication and internal working models: Their role in the development of attachment relationships. In R. A. Thompson (Ed.), *Nebraska Symposium on Motivation: Vol. 36. Socioemotional development* (pp. 57–113). Lincoln: University of Nebraska Press.

Bretherton, I. (1992). Social referencing, intentional communication, and the interfacing of minds in infancy. In S. Feinman (Ed.), *Social referencing and the social construction of reality in infancy* (pp. 57–77). New York, NY: Plenum Press.

Bretherton, I. (2010). Fathers in attachment theory and research: A review. *Early Child Development and Care, 180*, 9–23. doi:10.1080/03004430903414661

Bretherton, I., Lambert, J., & Golby, B. (2005). Involved fathers of preschool children as seen by themselves and their wives: Accounts of attachment, socialization, and companionship. *Attachment & Human Development, 7*, 229–251. doi:10.1080/14616730500138341

Broad, K. D., Curley, J. P., & Keverne, E. B. (2006). Mother–infant bonding and the evolution of mammalian social relationships. *Philosophical Transactions of the Royal Society of London, Series B: Biological Sciences, 361*, 2199–2214. doi:10.1098/rstb.2006.1940

Brockman, R. (2007). Freud, Darwin, and the holding environment. *Journal of the American Academy of Psychoanalysis and Dynamic Psychiatry, 35*, 127–136. doi:10.1521/jaap.2007.35.1.127

Brody, A. L., Saxena, S., Stoessel, P., Gillies, L. A., Fairbanks, L. A., Alborzian, S., . . . Baxter, L. R., Jr. (2001). Regional brain metabolic changes in patients with major depression treated with either paroxetine or interpersonal therapy: Preliminary findings. *Archives of General Psychiatry, 58*, 631–640. doi:10.1001/archpsyc.58.7.631

Brumbaugh, C. C., & Fraley, R. C. (2006). The evolution of attachment in romantic relationships. In M. Mikulincer & G. S. Goodman (Eds.), *The dynamics of romantic love: Attachment, caregiving, and sex* (pp. 71–101). New York, NY: Guilford Press.

Buber, M. (1965). *The knowledge of man: A philosophy of the interhuman.* New York, NY: Harper & Row.

Busch, F. N. (2009). Anger and depression. *Advances in Psychiatric Treatment, 15*, 271–278. doi:10.1192/apt.bp.107.004937

Cacioppo, J. T., Berntson, G. G., Adolphs, R., Carter, C. S., Davidson, R. J., McClintock, M. K., . . . Taylor, S. E. (Eds.). (2002). *Foundations in social neuroscience.* Cambridge, MA: MIT Press.

Cain, C. K. (2004). Mechanisms of conditional fear extinction in mice. *Dissertation Abstracts International: Section B. Sciences and Engineering, 65*(6), 2792.

Cain, C. K., Blouin, A. M., & Barad, M. (2003). Temporally massed CS presentations generate more fear extinction than spaced presentations. *Journal of Experimental Psychology: Animal Behavior Processes, 29*, 323–333. doi:10.1037/0097-7403.29.4.323

Cain, C. K., Blouin, A. M., & Barad, M. (2004). Adrenergic transmission facilitates extinction of conditional fear in mice. *Learning & Memory, 11*, 179–187. doi:10.1101/lm.71504

Campbell, A. (2010). Oxytocin and human social behavior. *Personality and Social Psychology Review, 14*, 281–295. doi:10.1177/1088868310363594

Carlson, E. A., Sroufe, L. A., Collins, W. A., Jimerson, S., Weinfield, N., Henninghausen, K., . . . Meyer, S. E. (1999). Early environmental support and elementary school adjustment as predictors of school adjustment in middle adolescence. *Journal of Adolescent Research, 14*, 72–94. doi:10.1177/0743558499141005

Carpenter, L. L., Carvalho, J. P., Tyrka, A. R., Wier, L. M., Mello, A. F., Mello, M. F., . . . Price, L. H. (2007). Decreased adrenocorticotropic hormone and cortisol responses to stress in healthy adults reporting significant childhood maltreatment. *Biological Psychiatry, 62,* 1080–1087. doi:10.1016/j.biopsych.2007.05.002

Carroll, S. B. (2005). *Endless forms most beautiful: The new science of evo devo and the making of the animal kingdom.* New York, NY: Norton.

Carter, C. S. (2003). Developmental consequences of oxytocin. *Physiology & Behavior, 79,* 383–397. doi:10.1016/S0031-9384(03)00151-3

Carter, C. S., Grippo, A. J., Pournajafi-Nazarloo, H., Ruscio, M. G., & Porges, S. W. (2008). Oxytocin, vasopressin and sociality. *Progress in Brain Research, 170,* 331–336. doi:10.1016/S0079-6123(08)00427-5

Carver, C. S., & Harmon-Jones, E. (2009). Anger is an approach-related affect: Evidence and implications. *Psychological Bulletin, 135,* 183–204. doi:10.1037/a0013965

Caspi, A., & Moffitt, T. E. (2006). Gene–environment interactions in psychiatry: Joining forces with neuroscience. *Nature Reviews Neuroscience, 7,* 583–590. doi:10.1038/nrn1925

Cassidy, J. (1994). Emotion regulation: Influences of attachment relationships. *Monographs of the Society for Research in Child Development, 59,* 228–249. doi:10.2307/1166148

Cassidy, J. (2001). Truth, lies, and intimacy: An attachment perspective. *Attachment & Human Development, 3,* 121–155. doi:10.1080/14616730110058999

Champagne, F. A. (2008). Epigenetic mechanisms and the transgenerational effects of maternal care. *Frontiers in Neuroendocrinology, 29,* 386–397. doi:10.1016/j.yfrne.2008.03.003

Champagne, F. A., & Curley, J. P. (2005). How social experiences influence the brain. *Current Opinion in Neurobiology, 15,* 704–709. doi:10.1016/j.conb.2005.10.001

Champagne, F. A., & Curley, J. P. (2009). Epigenetic mechanisms mediating the long-term effects of maternal care on development. *Neuroscience & Biobehavioral Reviews, 33,* 593–600. doi:10.1016/j.neubiorev.2007.10.009

Chiao, J. Y., Iidaka, T., Gordon, H. L., Nogawa, J., Bar, M., Aminoff, E., . . . Ambady, N. (2008). Cultural specificity in amygdala response to fear faces. *Journal of Cognitive Neuroscience, 20,* 2167–2174. doi:10.1162/jocn.2008.20151

Chisholm, K., Carter, M. C., Ames, E. W., & Morison, S. J. (1995). Attachment security and indiscriminately friendly behavior in children adopted from Romanian orphanages. *Development and Psychopathology, 7,* 283–294. doi:10.1017/S0954579400006507

Cicchetti, D. (2007). Gene–environment interaction. *Development and Psychopathology, 19,* 957–959. doi:10.1017/S0954579407000466

Claes, S. J. (2004). CRH, stress, and major depression: A psychobiological interplay. *Vitamins and Hormones, 69,* 117–150. doi:10.1016/S0083-6729(04)69005-4

Cohn, J. F., & Tronick, E. Z. (1988). Mother–infant face-to-face interaction: Influence is bidirectional and unrelated to periodic cycles in either partner's behavior. *Developmental Psychology, 24,* 386–392. doi:10.1037/0012-1649.24.3.386

Collet, C., Vernet-Maury, E., Delhomme, G., & Dittmar, A. (1997). Autonomic nervous system response patterns specificity to basic emotions. *Journal of the Autonomic Nervous System, 62*, 45–57. doi:10.1016/S0165-1838(96)00108-7

Colvert, E., Rutter, M., Kreppner, J., Beckett, C., Castle, J., Groothues, C., . . . Sonuga-Barke, E. J. (2008). Do theory of mind and executive function deficits underlie the adverse outcomes associated with profound early deprivation? Findings from the English and Romanian adoptees study. *Journal of Abnormal Child Psychology, 36*, 1057–1068. doi:10.1007/s10802-008-9232-x

Coulton, G. G. (1906). *St. Francis to Dante*. London, England: Nutt.

Cozolino, L. J. (2002). *The neuroscience of psychotherapy: Building and rebuilding the human brain*. New York, NY: Norton.

Craig, L., & Powell, A. (2012). Dual-earner parents' work–family time: The effects of atypical work patterns and non-parental childcare. *Journal of Population Research, 29*, 229–247. doi:10.1007/s12546-012-9086-5

Crittenden, P. M. (1992). Quality of attachment in the preschool years. *Development and Psychopathology, 4*, 209–241. doi:10.1017/S0954579400000110

Crittenden, P. M. (1994). *Preschool assessment of attachment (2nd ed.)*. Unpublished manuscript, Family Relations Institute, Miami, FL.

Crittenden, P. M. (1997). Truth, error, omission, distortion, and deception: The application of attachment theory to the assessment and treatment of psychological disorder. In S. M. C. Dollinger & L. F. DiLalla (Eds.), *Assessment and intervention issues across the life span* (pp. 35–76). Mahwah, NJ: Erlbaum.

Crittenden, P. M., & Landini, A. (2011). *Assessing adult attachment: A dynamic-maturational approach to discourse analysis*. New York, NY: Norton.

Crowell, J. A., Fraley, R. C., & Shaver, P. R. (2008). Measurement of individual differences in adolescent and adult attachment. In J. Cassidy & P. R. Shaver (Eds.), *Handbook of attachment: Theory, research, and clinical applications* (2nd ed., pp. 599–634). New York, NY: Guilford Press.

Cuijpers, P., Geraedts, A. S., van Oppen, P., Andersson, G., Markowitz, J. C., & van Straten, A. (2011). Interpersonal psychotherapy for depression: A meta-analysis. *American Journal of Psychiatry, 168*, 581–592. doi:10.1176/appi.ajp.2010.10101411

Cuijpers, P., van Straten, A., Andersson, G., & van Oppen, P. (2008). Psychotherapy for depression in adults: A meta-analysis of comparative outcome studies. *Journal of Consulting and Clinical Psychology, 76*, 909–922. doi:10.1037/a0013075

Cummings, E. M., Zahn-Waxler, C., & Radke-Yarrow, M. (2006). Developmental changes in children's reactions to anger in the home. *Journal of Child Psychology and Psychiatry, 25*(1), 63–74. doi:10.1111/j.1469-7610.1984.tb01719.x

Curley, J. P. (2011). Is there a genomically imprinted social brain? *BioEssays, 33*, 662–673. doi:10.1002/bies.201100060

Curley, J. P., & Keverne, E. B. (2005). Genes, brains, and mammalian social bonds. *Trends in Ecology & Evolution, 20*, 561–567. doi:10.1016/j.tree.2005.05.018

Curtis, R., & Winarick, D. (2008). Unifying psychoanalysis and developmental psychology. A review of *Attachment and sexuality*. *PsycCRITIQUES, 53*(11). doi:10.1037/a0011014

Cushing, B. S., & Kramer, K. M. (2005). Mechanisms underlying epigenetic effects of early social experience: The role of neuropeptides and steroids. *Neuroscience & Biobehavioral Reviews, 29,* 1089–1105. doi:10.1016/j.neubiorev.2005.04.001

Dabrowska, J., Hazra, R., Ahern, T. H., Guo, J.-D., McDonald, A. J., Mascagni, F., ... Rainnie, D. G. (2011). Neuroanatomical evidence for reciprocal regulation of the corticotrophin-releasing factor and oxytocin systems in the hypothalamus and the bed nucleus of the stria terminalis of the rat: Implications for balancing stress and affect. *Psychoneuroendocrinology, 36,* 1312–1326. doi:10.1016/j.psyneuen.2011.03.003

Darwin, C. (2004). *The descent of man.* London, England: Penguin Classics. (Original work published 1871)

de Boysson-Bardies, B., Halle, P., Sagart, L., & Durand, C. (1989). A crosslinguistic investigation of vowel formants in babbling. *Journal of Child Language, 16,* 1–17. doi: 10.1017/S0305000900013404

de Boysson-Bardies, B., Sagart, L., & Durand, C. (1984). Discernible differences in the babbling of infants according to target language. *Journal of Child Language, 11,* 1–15. doi:10.1017/S0305000900005559

DeCasper, A. J., & Carstens, A. A. (1981). Contingencies of stimulation: Effects on learning and emotion in neonates. *Infant Behavior and Development, 4,* 19–35. doi:10.1016/S0163-6383(81)80004-5

DeCasper, A. J., & Fifer, W. P. (1987). Of human bonding: Newborns prefer their mothers' voices. In J. Oates & S. Sheldon (Eds.), *Cognitive development in infancy* (pp. 111–118). Hillsdale, NJ: Erlbaum.

DeCasper, A. J., Lecanuet, J.-P., Busnel, M.-C., & Granier-Deferre, C. (1994). Fetal reactions to recurrent maternal speech. *Infant Behavior and Development, 17,* 159–164. doi:10.1016/0163-6383(94)90051-5

DeCasper, A. J., & Sigafoos, A. D. (1983). The intrauterine heartbeat: A potent reinforcer for newborns. *Infant Behavior and Development, 6,* 19–25. doi:10.1016/S0163-6383(83)80004-6

Demos, E. V. (1993). Silvan Tomkins's theory of emotion. In M. E. Donnelly (Ed.), *Reinterpreting the legacy of William James* (pp. 211–219). Washington, DC: American Psychological Association.

De Waal, F. (2007). *Chimpanzee politics: Power and sex among apes.* Baltimore, MD: Johns Hopkins University Press. (Original work published 1982)

De Wolff, M. S., & van IJzendoorn, M. H. (1997). Sensitivity and attachment: A meta-analysis on parental antecedents of infant attachment. *Child Development, 68,* 571–591. doi:10.2307/1132107

Diamond, L. M., Hicks, A. M., & Otter-Henderson, K. D. (2008). Every time you go away: Changes in affect, behavior, and physiology associated with travel-related separations from romantic partners. *Journal of Personality and Social Psychology, 95,* 385–403. doi:10.1037/0022-3514.95.2.385

Diego, M. A., Dieter, J. N. I., Field, T., Lecanuet, J. P., Hernandez-Reif, M., Beutler, J., . . . Salman, F. A. (2002). Fetal activity following stimulation of the mother's abdomen, feet, and hands. *Developmental Psychobiology, 41,* 396–406. doi:10.1002/dev.10071

Ditzen, B., Bradley, B., & Heim, C. M. (2012). Oxytocin and pair bonding: On possible influences during the life course. *Biological Psychiatry, 72*(3), e3–e4. doi:10.1016/j.biopsych.2012.01.029

Ditzen, B., Schaer, M., Gabriel, B., Bodenmann, G., Ehlert, U., & Heinrichs, M. (2009). Intranasal oxytocin increases positive communication and reduces cortisol levels during couple conflict. *Biological Psychiatry, 65,* 728–731. doi:10.1016/j.biopsych.2008.10.011

Donaldson, Z. R., & Young, L. J. (2008). Oxytocin, vasopressin, and the neurogenetics of sociality. *Science, 322,* 900–904. doi:10.1126/science.1158668

Dozier, M., Peloso, E., Lewis, E., Levine, S., & Laurenceau, J.-P. (2008). Effects of an attachment-based intervention of the cortisol production of infants and toddlers in foster care. *Development and Psychopathology, 20,* 845–859. doi:10.1017/s0954579408000400

Dozier, M., & Tyrrell, C. (1998). The role of attachment in therapeutic relationships. In J. A. Simpson & W. S. Rholes (Eds.), *Attachment theory and close relationships* (pp. 221–248). New York, NY: Guilford Press.

Dudley, K. J., Li, X., Kobor, M. S., Kippin, T. E., & Bredy, T. W. (2011). Epigenetic mechanisms mediating vulnerability and resilience to psychiatric disorders. *Neuroscience & Biobehavioral Reviews, 35,* 1544–1551. doi:10.1016/j.neubiorev.2010.12.016

Duman, R. S., Nakagawa, S., & Malberg, J. (2001). Regulation of adult neurogenesis by antidepressant treatment. *Neuropsychopharmacology, 25,* 836–844. doi:10.1016/S0893-133X(01)00358-X

Dunbar, R. (2007). Evolution of the social brain. In S. W. Gangestad & J. A. Simpson (Eds.), *The evolution of mind: Fundamental questions and controversies* (pp. 280–286). New York, NY: Guilford Press.

Durand, K., Baudon, G., Freydefont, L., & Schaal, B. (2008). Odorization of a novel object can influence infant's exploratory behavior in unexpected ways. *Infant Behavior and Development, 31,* 629–636. doi:10.1016/j.infbeh.2008.07.002

Dykas, M. J., & Cassidy, J. (2011). Attachment and the processing of social information across the life span: Theory and evidence. *Psychological Bulletin, 137,* 19–46. doi:10.1037/a0021367

Edelman, G. M. (1987). *Neural Darwinism: The theory of neuronal group selection.* New York, NY: Basic Books.

Eibl-Eibesfeldt, I. (1989). *Human ethology.* Hawthorne, NY: Aldine de Gruyter.

Ekman, P. (1999). Basic emotions. In T. Dalgleish & M. Power (Eds.), *Handbook of cognition and emotion* (pp. 45–60). Chichester, England: Wiley.

Ekman, P. (2007). *Emotions revealed: Recognizing faces and feelings to improve communication and emotional life.* New York, NY: Holt.

Ekman, P., Levenson, R. W., & Friesen, W. V. (1983). Autonomic nervous system activity distinguishes among emotions. *Science, 221,* 1208–1210. doi:10.1126/science.6612338

Ekman, P., & Rosenberg, E. L. (2005). *What the face reveals: Basic and applied studies of spontaneous expression using the Facial Action Coding System (FACS)* (2nd ed.). New York, NY: Oxford University Press.

Erdman, P., & Caffery, T. (2003). *Attachment and family systems: Conceptual, empirical, and therapeutic relatedness.* New York, NY: Brunner-Routledge.

Evans, G. W., & Wener, R. E. (2006). Rail commuting duration and passenger stress. *Health Psychology, 25,* 408–412. doi:10.1037/0278-6133.25.3.408

Evans, G. W., Wener, R. E., & Phillips, D. (2002). The morning rush hour: Predictability and commuter stress. *Environment and Behavior, 34,* 521–530. doi:10.1177/00116502034004007

Fava, M., Hwang, I., Rush, A. J., Sampson, N., Walters, E. E., & Kessler, R. C. (2010). The importance of irritability as a symptom of major depressive disorder: Results from the National Comorbidity Survey Replication. *Molecular Psychiatry, 15,* 856–867. doi:10.1038/mp.2009.20

Feldman, R. (2012). Parent–infant synchrony: A biobehavioral model of mutual influences in the formation of affiliative bonds. *Monographs of the Society for Research in Child Development, 77*(2), 42–51. doi:10.1111/j.1540-5834.2011.00660.x

Fernandez-Duque, E., Valeggia, C. R., & Mendoza, S. P. (2009). The biology of paternal care in human and nonhuman primates. *Annual Review of Anthropology, 38,* 115–130. doi:10.1146/annurev-anthro-091908-164334

Field, T. (1994). The effects of mother's physical and emotional unavailability on emotion regulation. *Monographs of the Society for Research in Child Development, 59*(2-3), 250–283. doi:10.1111/j.1540-5834.1994.tb01286.x

Field, T. (2001a). Massage therapy facilitates weight gain in preterm infants. *Current Directions in Psychological Science, 10,* 51–54. doi:10.1111/1467-8721.00113

Field, T. (2001b). *Touch.* Cambridge, MA: MIT Press.

Field, T. (2002). Infants' need for touch. *Human Development, 45,* 100–103. doi:10.1159/000048156

Field, T. (2010). Postpartum depression effects on early interactions, parenting, and safety practices: A review. *Infant Behavior and Development, 33,* 1–6. doi:10.1016/j.infbeh.2009.10.005

Field, T., Diego, M., & Hernandez-Reif, M. (2009). Depressed mothers' infants are less responsive to faces and voices. *Infant Behavior and Development, 32,* 239–244. doi:10.1016/j.infbeh.2009.03.005

Field, T., Hernandez-Reif, M., & Diego, M. (2006). Intrusive and withdrawn depressed mothers and their infants. *Developmental Review, 26,* 15–30. doi:10.1016/j. dr.2005.04.001

Fisher, H. (2004). *Why we love: The nature and chemistry of romantic love.* New York, NY: Holt.

Fisher, L., Ames, E. W., Chisholm, K., & Savoie, L. (1997). Problems reported by parents of Romanian orphans adopted to British Columbia. *International Journal of Behavioral Development, 20,* 67–82. doi:10.1080/016502597385441

Flinn, M. V. (2005). Culture and developmental plasticity: The evolution of the human brain. In K. MacDonald & R. L. Burgess (Eds.), *Evolutionary perspectives on human development* (pp. 73–98). Thousand Oaks, CA: Sage. doi:10.4135/9781452233574.n3

Flinn, M. V., & Alexander, R. (2007). Runaway social selection in human evolution. In S. W. Gangestad & J. A. Simpson (Eds.), *The evolution of mind: Fundamental questions and controversies* (pp. 249–255). New York, NY: Guilford Press.

Florian, V., & Mikulincer, M. (1998). Symbolic immortality and the management of the terror of death: The moderating role of attachment style. *Journal of Personality and Social Psychology, 74,* 725–734. doi:10.1037/0022-3514.74.3.725

Foehring, R. C., & Lorenzon, N. M. (1999). Neuromodulation, development and synaptic plasticity. *Canadian Journal of Experimental Psychology, 53,* 45–61. doi:10.1037/h0087299

Fonagy, P. (2001). *Attachment theory and psychoanalysis.* New York, NY: Other Press.

Fonagy, P., Steele, M., Steele, H., Moran, G. S., & Higgitt, A. C. (1991). The capacity for understanding mental states: The reflective self in parent and child and its significance for security of attachment. *Infant Mental Health Journal, 12,* 201–218. doi:10.1002/1097-0355(199123)12:3<201::AID-IMHJ2280120307>3.0.CO;2-7

Ford, T., Goodman, R., & Meltzer, H. (2004). The relative importance of child, family, school and neighbourhood correlates of childhood psychiatric disorder. *Social Psychiatry and Psychiatric Epidemiology, 39,* 487–496. doi:10.1007/s00127-004-0782-0

Forster, E. M. (1985). *Aspects of the novel.* New York, NY: Mariner Books. (Original work published 1927)

Fosha, D. (2000). *The transforming power of affect: A model for accelerated change.* New York, NY: Basic Books.

Fosha, D. (2001). The dyadic regulation of affect. *Journal of Clinical Psychology, 57,* 227–242. doi:10.1002/1097-4679(200102)57:2<227::AID-JCLP8>3.0.CO;2-1

Fosha, D., Paivio, S. C., Gleiser, K., & Ford, J. D. (2009). Experiential and emotion-focused therapy. In C. A. Courtois & J. D. Ford (Eds.), *Treating complex traumatic stress disorders: An evidence-based guide* (pp. 286–311). New York, NY: Guilford Press.

Fosha, D., & Slowiaczek, M. L. (1997). Techniques to accelerate dynamic psychotherapy. *American Journal of Psychotherapy, 51,* 229–251.

Fraiberg, S., Adelson, E., & Shapiro, V. (1975). Ghosts in the nursery: A psychoanalytic approach to the problems of impaired infant–mother relationships. *Journal of the American Academy of Child Psychiatry, 14*, 387–421. doi:10.1016/S0002-7138(09)61442-4

Fraley, R. C., Brumbaugh, C. C., & Marks, M. J. (2005). The evolution and function of adult attachment: A comparative and phylogenetic analysis. *Journal of Personality and Social Psychology, 89*, 731–746. doi:10.1037/0022-3514.89.5.751

Fraley, R. C., Davis, K. E., & Shaver, P. R. (1998). Dismissing-avoidance and the defensive organization of emotion, cognition, and behavior. In J. A. Simpson & W. S. Rholes (Eds.), *Attachment theory and close relationships* (pp. 249–279). New York, NY: Guilford Press.

Fraley, R. C., Heffernan, M. E., Vicary, A. M., & Brumbaugh, C. C. (2011). The Experiences in Close Relationships—Relationship Structures Questionnaire: A method for assessing attachment orientations across relationships. *Psychological Assessment, 23*, 615–625. doi:10.1037/a0022898

Fraley, R. C., & Shaver, P. R. (1998). Airport separations: A naturalistic study of adult attachment dynamics in separating couples. *Journal of Personality and Social Psychology, 75*, 1198–1212. doi:10.1037/0022-3514.75.5.1198

Fraley, R. C., & Spieker, S. J. (2003). Are infant attachment patterns continuously or categorically distributed? A taxometric analysis of Strange Situation behavior. *Developmental Psychology, 39*, 387–404. doi:10.1037/0012-1649.39.3.387

Fraley, R. C., Waller, N. G., & Brennan, K. A. (2000). An item response theory analysis of self-report measures of adult attachment. *Journal of Personality and Social Psychology, 78*, 350–365. doi:10.1037/0022-3514.78.2.350

Franklin, T. B., Russig, H., Weiss, I. C., Gräff, J., Linder, N., Michalon, A., . . . Mansuy, I. M. (2010). Epigenetic transmission of the impact of early stress across generations. *Biological Psychiatry, 68*, 408–415. doi:10.1016/j.biopsych.2010.05.036

Freed, P. J., & Mann, J. J. (2007). Sadness and loss: Toward a neurobiopsychosocial model. *American Journal of Psychiatry, 164*, 28–34. doi:10.1176/appi.ajp.164.1.28

Freud, A., & Burlingham, D. (1942). *Young children in war-time: A year's work in a residential war nursery.* London, England: Allen & Unwin.

Freud, S. (1958). Recommendations to physicians practising psycho-analysis. In J. Strachey (Ed.), *Standard edition of the complete psychological works of Sigmund Freud: Vol. 12 (1911–1913): The case of Schreber, papers on technique and other works* (pp. 109–120). London, England: Hogarth Press. (Original work published 1912)

Friedman, B. H. (2010). Feelings and the body: The Jamesian perspective on autonomic specificity of emotion. *Biological Psychology, 84*, 383–393. doi:10.1016/j.biopsycho.2009.10.006

Fries, A. B. W., Ziegler, T. E., Kurian, J. R., Jacoris, S., & Pollak, S. D. (2005). Early experience in humans is associated with changes in neuropeptides critical for regulating social behavior. *Proceedings of the National Academy of Sciences, USA, 102*, 17237–17240. doi:10.1073/pnas.0504767102

Galbally, M., Lewis, A. J., IJzendoorn, M. H., & Permezel, M. (2011). The role of oxytocin in mother–infant relations: A systematic review of human studies. *Harvard Review of Psychiatry, 19*, 1–14. doi:10.3109/10673229.2011.549771

Gandelman, R. (1992). *Psychobiology of behavioral development.* New York, NY: Oxford University Press.

Gleiser, K., Ford, J. D., & Fosha, D. (2008). Contrasting exposure and experiential therapies for complex posttraumatic stress disorder. *Psychotherapy: Theory, Research, Practice, Training, 45*, 340–360. doi:10.1037/a0013323

Goodman, G. S. (2006). Attachment to attachment theory: A personal perspective on an attachment researcher. In M. Mikulincer & G. S. Goodman (Eds.), *Dynamics of romantic love: Attachment, caregiving, and sex* (pp. 3–22). New York, NY: Guilford Press.

Gopnik, A., Meltzoff, A. N., & Kuhl, P. K. (2000). *The scientist in the crib: What early learning tells us about the mind.* New York, NY: HarperCollins.

Gordon, I., Zagoory-Sharon, O., Leckman, J. F., & Feldman, R. (2010a). Oxytocin, cortisol, and triadic family interactions. *Physiology & Behavior, 101*, 679–684. doi:10.1016/j.physbeh.2010.08.008

Gordon, I., Zagoory-Sharon, O., Leckman, J. F., & Feldman, R. (2010b). Prolactin, oxytocin, and the development of paternal behavior across the first six months of fatherhood. *Hormones and Behavior, 58*, 513–518. doi: 10.1016/j.yhbeh.2010.04.007

Gordon, I., Zagoory-Sharon, O., Schneiderman, I., Leckman, J. F., Weller, A., & Feldman, R. (2008). Oxytocin and cortisol in romantically unattached young adults: Associations with bonding and psychological distress. *Psychophysiology, 45*, 349–352. doi:10.1111/j.1469-8986.2008.00649.x

Greenberg, J., & Mitchell, S. A. (1983). *Object relations in psychoanalytic theory.* Cambridge, MA: Harvard University Press.

Greenberg, L. (2008). Emotion and cognition in psychotherapy: The transforming power of affect. *Canadian Psychology/Psychologie canadienne, 49*, 49–59. doi:10.1037/0708-5591.49.1.49

Greenwood, B. N., & Fleshner, M. (2008). Exercise, learned helplessness, and the stress-resistant brain. *NeuroMolecular Medicine, 10*, 81–98. doi:10.1007/s12017-008-8029-y

Grice, H. P. (1975). Logic and conversation. In P. Cole & J. L. Morgan (Eds.), *Syntax and semantics: Vol. 3. Speech acts* (pp. 41–58). New York, NY: Academic Press.

Grice, P. (1989). *Studies in the way of words.* Cambridge, MA: Harvard University Press.

Griffin, D. W., & Bartholomew, K. (1994). Models of the self and other: Fundamental dimensions underlying measures of adult attachment. *Journal of Personality and Social Psychology, 67*, 430–445. doi:10.1037/0022-3514.67.3.430

Gross, J. J. (1998). The emerging field of emotion regulation: An integrative review. *Review of General Psychology, 2*, 271–299. doi:10.1037/1089-2680.2.3.271

Gross, J. J. (1999a). Emotion and emotion regulation. In L. A. Pervin & O. P. John (Eds.), *Handbook of personality: Theory and research* (2nd ed., pp. 525–552). New York, NY: Guilford Press.

Gross, J. J. (1999b). Emotion regulation: Past, present, future. *Cognition & Emotion, 13*, 551–573.

Grossmann, K., Grossmann, K. E., Fremmer-Bombik, E., Kindler, H., Scheuerer-Englisch, H., & Zimmermann, P. (2002). The uniqueness of the child–father attachment relationship: Fathers' sensitive and challenging play as a pivotal variable in a 16-year longitudinal study. *Social Development, 11*, 301–337. doi:10.1111/1467-9507.00202

Grossmann, K., Grossmann, K. E., Kindler, H., & Zimmermann, P. (2008). A wider view of attachment and exploration: The influence of mothers and fathers on the development of psychological security from infancy to young adulthood. In J. Cassidy & P. R. Shaver (Eds.), *Handbook of attachment: Theory, research, and clinical applications* (2nd ed., pp. 857–879). New York, NY: Guilford Press.

Grossmann, K. E. (1995). The evolution and history of attachment research and theory. In S. Goldberg, R. Muir, & J. Kerr (Eds.), *Attachment theory: Social, developmental and clinical perspectives* (pp. 85–102). Hillsdale, NY: Analytic Press.

Guisinger, S., & Blatt, S. J. (1994). Individuality and relatedness: Evolution of a fundamental dialectic. *American Psychologist, 49*, 104–111. doi:10.1037/0003-066X.49.2.104

Haft, W. L. (1990). Affect attunement and maternal attachment: An observational study of the intergenerational transmission of mothers' internal representations of attachment. *Dissertation Abstracts International: Section B. Sciences and Engineering, 50*(8), 3696.

Haft, W. L., & Slade, A. (1989). Affect attunement and maternal attachment: A pilot study. *Infant Mental Health Journal, 10*, 157–172. doi:10.1002/1097-0355(198923)10:3<157::AID-IMHJ2280100304>3.0.CO;2-3

Hajszan, T., Dow, A., Warner-Schmidt, J. L., Szigeti-Buck, K., Sallam, N. L., Parducz, A., . . . Duman, R. S. (2009). Remodeling of hippocampal spine synapses in the rat learned helplessness model of depression. *Biological Psychiatry, 65*, 392–400. doi:10.1016/j.biopsych.2008.09.031

Haley, D. W., Weinberg, J., & Grunau, R. E. (2006). Cortisol, contingency learning, and memory in preterm and full-term infants. *Psychoneuroendocrinology, 31*, 108–117. doi:10.1016/j.psyneuen.2005.06.007

Harmon-Jones, E., Harmon-Jones, C., Abramson, L., & Peterson, C. K. (2009). PANAS positive activation is associated with anger. *Emotion, 9*, 183–196. doi:10.1037/a0014959

Haselton, M. G., & Buss, D. M. (2001). The affective shift hypothesis: The functions of emotional changes following sexual intercourse. *Personal Relationships, 8*, 357–369. doi:10.1111/j.1475-6811.2001.tb00045.x

Haviland, J. M., & Lelwica, M. (1987). The induced affect response: 10-week-old infants' responses to three emotion expressions. *Developmental Psychology, 23,* 97–104. doi:10.1037/0012-1649.23.1.97

Hebb, D. O. (1961). *The organization of behavior: A neurophysiological theory.* Oxford, England: Basic Books.

Heinrichs, M., von Dawans, B., & Domes, G. (2009). Oxytocin, vasopressin, and human social behavior. *Frontiers in Neuroendocrinology, 30,* 548–557. doi:10.1016/j.yfrne.2009.05.005

Herman, J. L. (1992). *Trauma and recovery: The aftermath of violence—from domestic abuse to political terror.* New York, NY: Basic Books.

Herrera, E., Reissland, N., & Shepherd, J. (2004). Maternal touch and maternal child-directed speech: Effects of depressed mood in the postnatal period. *Journal of Affective Disorders, 81,* 29–39. doi:10.1016/j.jad.2003.07.001

Herrmann, E., Call, J., Hernàndez-Lloreda, M. V., Hare, B., & Tomasello, M. (2007). Humans have evolved specialized skills of social cognition: The cultural intelligence hypothesis. *Science, 317,* 1360–1366. doi:10.1126/science.1146282

Hertenstein, M. J. (2002). Touch: Its communicative functions in infancy. *Human Development, 45,* 70–94. doi:10.1159/000048154

Hertenstein, M. J., Holmes, R., McCullough, M., & Keltner, D. (2009). The communication of emotion via touch. *Emotion, 9,* 566–573. doi:10.1037/a0016108

Hesse, E. (2008). The Adult Attachment Interview: Protocol, method of analysis, and empirical studies. In J. Cassidy & P. R. Shaver (Eds.), *Handbook of attachment: Theory, research, and clinical applications* (2nd ed., pp. 552–598). New York, NY: Guilford Press.

Heywood, C. A., & Kentridge, R. W. (2000). Affective blindsight? *Trends in Cognitive Sciences, 4,* 125–126. doi:10.1016/S1364-6613(00)01469-8

Hiller, J. (2004). Speculations on the links between feelings, emotions and sexual behaviour: Are vasopressin and oxytocin involved? *Sexual and Relationship Therapy, 19,* 393–412. doi:10.1080/14681990412331297974

Hiller, J. (2005). Gender differences in sexual motivation. *Journal of Men's Health & Gender, 2,* 339–345. doi:10.1016/j.jmhg.2005.05.003

Hinde, R. A., & Stevenson-Hinde, J. (1991). Perspectives on attachment. In C. M. Parkes, J. Stevenson-Hinde, & P. Marris (Eds.), *Attachment across the life cycle* (pp. 52–65). New York, NY: Taylor & Francis.

Hinkelmann, K., Moritz, S., Botzenhardt, J., Riedesel, K., Wiedemann, K., Kellner, M., & Otte, C. (2009). Cognitive impairment in major depression: Association with salivary cortisol. *Biological Psychiatry, 66,* 879–885. doi:10.1016/j.biopsych.2009.06.023

Hofer, M. A. (1987). Early social relationships: A psychobiologist's view. *Child Development, 58,* 633–647. doi:10.2307/1130203

Hofer, M. A. (1994). Hidden regulators in attachment, separation, and loss. *Monographs of the Society for Research in Child Development, 59*, 192–207. doi:10.111/j.1540-5834.1994.tb01285.x

Hofer, M. A. (1995). Hidden regulators: Implications for a new understanding of attachment, separation, and loss. In S. Goldberg, R. Muir, & J. Kerr (Eds.), *Attachment theory: Social, developmental, and clinical perspectives* (pp. 203–230). Hillsdale, NJ: Analytic Press.

Hofer, M. A. (2004). Developmental psychobiology of early attachment. In B. J. Casey (Ed.), *Developmental psychobiology* (pp. 1–28). Arlington, VA: American Psychiatric Publishing.

Hofer, M. A. (2006). Psychobiological roots of early attachment. *Current Directions in Psychological Science, 15*, 84–88. doi:10.1111/j.0963-7214.2006.00412.x

Hofer, M. A. (2008). Early relationships as regulators of infant physiology and behavior. *Acta Paediatrica, 83*(Suppl. S397), 9–18. doi:10.1111/j.1651-2227.1994.tb13260.x

Hofer, M. A., & Sullivan, R. M. (2008). Toward a neurobiology of attachment. In C. A. Nelson & M. Luciana (Eds.), *Handbook of developmental cognitive neuroscience* (2nd ed., pp. 787–805): Cambridge, MA: MIT Press.

Hoksbergen, R., ter Laak, J., Rijk, K., van Dijkum, C., & Stoutjesdijk, F. (2005). Post-institutional autistic syndrome in Romanian adoptees. *Journal of Autism and Developmental Disorders, 35*, 615–623. doi:10.1007/s10803-005-0005-x

Hoksbergen, R., ter Laak, J., van Dijkum, C., Rijk, S., Rijk, K., & Stoutjesdijk, F. (2003). Posttraumatic stress disorder in adopted children from Romania. *American Journal of Orthopsychiatry, 73*, 255–265. doi:10.1037/0002-9432.73.3.255

Holmes, J. (1993). *John Bowlby and attachment theory.* New York, NY: Routledge.

Holmes, M., & Newman, M. G. (2006). Generalized anxiety disorder. In F. Andrasik (Ed.), *Comprehensive handbook of personality and psychopathology: Vol. 2. Adult psychopathology* (pp. 101–20). Hoboken, NJ: Wiley.

Howes, C., & Spieker, S. (2008). Attachment relationships in the context of multiple caregivers. In J. Cassidy & P. R. Shaver (Eds.), *Handbook of attachment: Theory, research, and clinical applications* (2nd ed., pp. 317–332). New York, NY: Guilford Press.

Hrdy, S. B. (2005a). Evolutionary context of human development: The cooperative breeding model. In C. S. Carter et al. (Eds.), *Attachment and bonding: A new synthesis* (pp. 9–32). Cambridge, MA: MIT Press. doi:10.1093/acprof:oso/9780195320510.003.0003

Hrdy, S. B. (2005b). On why it takes a village: Cooperative breeders, infant needs, and the future. In R. L. Burgess & K. MacDonald (Eds.), *Evolutionary perspectives on human development* (2nd ed., pp. 167–188). Thousand Oaks, CA: Sage. doi:10.4135/9781452233574.n6

Hsiao, F. H., Jow, G. M., Lai, Y. M., Chen, Y. T., Wang, K. C., Ng, S. M., . . . Yang, T. T. (2011). The long-term effects of psychotherapy added to pharmacotherapy on morning to evening diurnal cortisol patterns in outpatients with major depression. *Psychotherapy and Psychosomatics, 80,* 166–172. doi:10.1159/000321558

Hulbert, A. (2003). *Raising America: Experts, parents, and a century of advice about children.* New York, NY: Knopf.

Insel, T. R., & Young, L. J. (2001). The neurobiology of attachment. *Nature Reviews Neuroscience, 2,* 129–136. doi:10.1038/35053579

Isabella, R. A., Belsky, J., & von Eye, A. (1989). Origins of infant–mother attachment: An examination of interactional synchrony during the infant's first year. *Developmental Psychology, 25,* 12–21. doi:10.1037/0012-1649.25.1.12

Izard, C. E. (1993). Organizational and motivational functions of discrete emotions. In M. Lewis & J. M. Haviland (Eds.), *Handbook of emotions* (pp. 631–642). New York, NY: Guilford Press.

Jablonka, E. (2007). The developmental construction of heredity. *Developmental Psychobiology, 49,* 808–817. doi:10.1002/dev.20260

Jaffee, S. R., Moffitt, T. E., Caspi, A., & Taylor, A. (2003). Life with (or without) father: The benefits of living with two biological parents depend on the father's antisocial behavior. *Child Development, 74,* 109–126. doi:10.1111/1467-8624.t01-1-00524

Jänig, W., & Häbler, H.-J. (2000). Specificity in the organization of the autonomic nervous system: A basis for precise neural regulation of homeostatic and protective body functions. *Progress in Brain Research, 122,* 351–367. doi:10.1016/S0079-6123(08)62150-0

Jones, E. G. (2000). Cortical and subcortical contributions to activity-dependent plasticity in primate somatosensory cortex. *Annual Review of Neuroscience, 23,* 1–37. doi:10.1146/annurev.neuro.23.1.1

Kandel, E. R., Schwartz, J. H., & Jessell, T. M. (2000). *Principles of neural science* (4th ed.). New York, NY: McGraw-Hill.

Kappeler, P. M., & Pereira, M. E. (Eds.). (2003). *Primate life histories and socioecology.* Chicago, IL: University of Chicago Press.

Karpova, N. N., Pickenhagen, A., Lindholm, J., Tiraboschi, E., Kulesskaya, N., Ágústsdóttir, A., . . . Castrén, E. (2011). Fear erasure in mice requires synergy between antidepressant drugs and extinction training. *Science, 334,* 1731–1734. doi:10.1126/science.1214592

Kärtner, J., Keller, H., & Yovsi, R. D. (2010). Mother–infant interaction during the first 3 months: The emergence of culture specific contingency patterns. *Child Development, 81,* 540–554. doi:10.1111/j.1467-8624.2009.01414.x

Kaufman, J., Plotsky, P. M., Nemeroff, C. B., & Charney, D. S. (2000). Effects of early adverse experiences on brain structure and function: Clinical implications. *Biological Psychiatry, 48,* 778–790. doi: 10.1016/s0006-3223(00)00998-7

Kelly, K., Slade, A., & Grienenberger, J. F. (2005). Maternal reflective functioning, mother–infant affective communication, and infant attachment: Exploring the link between mental states and observed caregiving behavior in the intergenerational transmission of attachment. *Attachment & Human Development*, 7, 299–311. doi:10.1080/14616730500245963

Kempermann, G., Wiskott, L., & Gage, F. H. (2004). Functional significance of adult neurogenesis. *Current Opinion in Neurobiology*, 14, 186–191. doi:10.1016/j.conb.2004.03.001

Kidd, T., Hamer, M., & Steptoe, A. (2011). Examining the association between adult attachment style and cortisol responses to acute stress. *Psychoneuroendocrinology*, 36, 771–779. doi:10.1016/j.psyneuen.2010.10.014

Kiser, L. J., Bates, J. E., Maslin, C. A., & Bayles, K. (1986). Mother–infant play at six months as a predictor of attachment security at thirteen months. *Journal of the American Academy of Child Psychiatry*, 25, 68–75.

Klerman, G. L., Weissman, M. M., Rounsaville, B. J., & Chevron, E. S. (1984). *Interpersonal psychotherapy of depression*. New York, NY: Basic Books.

Kobak, R. (1999). The emotional dynamics of disruptions in attachment relationships: Implications for theory, research, and clinical intervention. In J. Cassidy & P. R. Shaver (Eds.), *Handbook of attachment: Theory, research, and clinical applications* (pp. 21–43). New York, NY: Guilford Press.

Kobak, R., & Madsen, S. (2008). Disruptions in attachment bonds: Implications for theory, research, and clinical intervention. In J. Cassidy & P. R. Shaver (Eds.), *Handbook of attachment: Theory, research, and clinical applications* (2nd ed., pp. 23–47). New York, NY: Guilford Press.

Kochanska, G. (2001). Emotional development in children with different attachment histories: The first three years. *Child Development*, 72, 474–490. doi:10.1111/1467-8624.00291

Kosfeld, M., Heinrichs, M., Zak, P. J., Fischbacher, U., & Fehr, E. (2005). Oxytocin increases trust in humans. *Nature*, 435, 673–676. doi:10.1038/nature03701

Kreibig, S. D. (2010). Autonomic nervous system activity in emotion: A review. *Biological Psychology*, 84, 394–421. doi:10.1016/j.biopsycho.2010.03.010

Krishnan, V., & Nestler, E. J. (2008). The molecular neurobiology of depression. *Nature*, 455, 894–902. doi:10.1038/nature07455

Krueger, C., Holditch-Davis, D., Quint, S., & DeCasper, A. (2004). Recurring auditory experience in the 28- to 34-week-old fetus. *Infant Behavior and Development*, 27, 537–543. doi:10.1016/j.infbeh.2004.03.001

Kukolja, J., Schläpfer, T. E., Keysers, C., Klingmüller, D., Maier, W., Fink, G. R., & Hurlemann, R. (2008). Modeling a negative response bias in the human amygdala by noradrenergic–glucocorticoid interactions. *Journal of Neuroscience*, 28, 12868–12876. doi:10.1523/JNEUROSCI.3592-08.2008

Labonte, B., Yerko, V., Gross, J., Mechawar, N., Meaney, M. J., Szyf, M., & Turecki, G. (2012). Differential glucocorticoid receptor exon 1(B), 1(C), and 1(H) expression and methylation in suicide completers with a history of childhood abuse. *Biological Psychiatry*, 72, 41–48. doi:10.1016/j.biopsych.2012.01.034

Lamb, M. E. (1976). Twelve-month-olds and their parents: Interaction in a laboratory playroom. *Developmental Psychology, 12,* 237–244. doi:10.1037/0012-1649.12.3.237

Lamb, M. E. (1977a). The development of mother–infant and father–infant attachments in the second year of life. *Developmental Psychology, 13,* 637–648. doi:10.1037/0012-1649.13.6.637

Lamb, M. E. (1977b). Father–infant and mother–infant interaction in the first year of life. *Child Development, 48,* 167–181. doi:10.2307/1128896

Lambert, M. J., & Barley, D. E. (2002). Research summary on the therapeutic relationship and psychotherapy outcome. In J. C. Norcross (Ed.), *Psychotherapy relationships that work: Therapist contributions and responsiveness to patients* (pp. 17–32). New York, NY: Oxford University Press.

Lamm, E., & Jablonka, E. (2008). The nurture of nature: Hereditary plasticity in evolution. *Philosophical Psychology, 21,* 305–319. doi:10.1080/09515080802170093

Lasch, C. (1976). The family as a haven in a heartless world. *Salmagundi, 35,* 42–55.

Launay, J. M., Mouillet-Richard, S., Baudry, A., Pietri, M., & Kellermann, O. (2011). Raphe-mediated signals control the hippocampal response to SRI antidepressants via miR-16. *Translational Psychiatry, 1*(11), e56. doi:10.1038/tp.2011.54

Law, R. (2011). Interpersonal psychotherapy for depression. *Advances in Psychiatric Treatment, 17,* 23–31. doi:10.1192/apt.bp.109.007641

Lecanuet, J.-P., Granier-Deferre, C., & DeCasper, A. (2005). Are we expecting too much from prenatal sensory experiences? In B. Hopkins & S. P. Johnson (Eds.), *Prenatal development of postnatal functions* (pp. 31–49). Westport, CT: Praeger.

Lecanuet, J.-P., Graniere-Deferre, C., Jacquet, A.-Y., & DeCasper, A. J. (2000). Fetal discrimination of low-pitched musical notes. *Developmental Psychobiology, 36,* 29–39. doi:10.1002/(SICI)1098-2302(200001)36:1<29::AID-DEV4>3.0.CO;2-J

Lecanuet, J.-P., & Jacquet, A.-Y. (2002). Fetal responsiveness to maternal passive swinging in low heart rate variability state: Effects of stimulation direction and duration. *Developmental Psychobiology, 40,* 57–67. doi:10.1002/dev.10013

Leckman, J. F., Carter, C. S., Hennessy, M. B., Keverne, E. B., Klann-Delius, G., Schradin, C., . . . Van Holst, D. (2005). Group report: Biobehavioral processes in attachment and bonding. In C. S. Carter et al. (Eds.), *Attachment and bonding: A new synthesis* (pp. 301–348). Cambridge, MA: MIT Press.

Leckman, J. F., & March, J. S. (2011). Editorial: Developmental neuroscience comes of age. *Journal of Child Psychology and Psychiatry, 52,* 333–338. doi:10.1111/j.1469-7610.2011.02378.x

LeDoux, J. (1996). Emotional networks and motor control: A fearful view. *Progress in Brain Research, 107,* 437–446.

LeDoux, J. (1998). *The emotional brain: The mysterious underpinnings of emotional life.* New York, NY: Simon & Schuster.

LeDoux, J. E. (1994). Emotional experience is an output of, not a cause of, emotional processing. In P. Ekman & R. Davidson (Eds.), *The nature of emotion* (pp. 394–395). New York, NY: Oxford University Press.

LeDoux, J. E. (2009). Emotion circuits in the brain. *Focus, 7*(2), 274.

Lee, H. J., Macbeth, A. H., & Pagani, J. H. (2009). Oxytocin: The great facilitator of life. *Progress in Neurobiology, 88,* 127–151. doi:10.1016/j.pneurobio.2009.04.001

Lee, K.-U., Khang, H. S., Kim, K.-T., Kim, Y.-J., Kweon, Y.-S., Shin, Y.-W., . . . Liberzon, I. (2008). Distinct processing of facial emotion of own-race versus other-race. *NeuroReport, 19,* 1021–1025. doi:10.1097/WNR.0b013e3283052df2

Lelwica, M., & Haviland, J. (1983, April). *Response or imitation: Ten-week-old infants' reactions to three emotion expressions.* Paper presented at the biennial meeting of the Society for Research in Child Development, Detroit, MI.

Lemche, E., Giampietro, V. P., Surguladze, S. A., Amaro, E. J., Andrew, C. M., Williams, S. C. R., . . . Phillips, M. L. (2006). Human attachment security is mediated by the amygdala: Evidence from combined fMRI and psycho-physiological measures. *Human Brain Mapping, 27,* 623–635. doi:10.1002/hbm.20206

Lench, H. C., Flores, S. A., & Bench, S. W. (2011). Discrete emotions predict changes in cognition, judgment, experience, behavior, and physiology: A meta-analysis of experimental emotion elicitations. *Psychological Bulletin, 137,* 834–855. doi:10.1037/a0024244

Leppanen, J. M., & Nelson, C. A. (2009). Tuning the developing brain to social signals of emotions. *Nature Reviews Neuroscience, 10,* 37–47. doi:10.1038/nrn2554

Lerner, J. S., & Tiedens, L. Z. (2006). Portrait of the angry decision maker: How appraisal tendencies shape anger's influence on cognition. *Journal of Behavioral Decision Making, 19,* 115–137. doi:10.1002/bdm.515

Li, B., Piriz, J., Mirrione, M., Chung, C. H., Proulx, C. D., Schulz, D., . . . Malinow, R. (2011). Synaptic potentiation onto habenula neurons in the learned helplessness model of depression. *Nature, 470,* 535–539. doi:10.1038/nature09742

Li, S.-C. (2003). Biocultural orchestration of developmental plasticity across levels: The interplay of biology and culture in shaping the mind and behavior across the life span. *Psychological Bulletin, 129,* 171–194. doi:10.1037/0033-2909.129.2.171

Liszkowski, U., & Tomasello, M. (2011). Individual differences in social, cognitive, and morphological aspects of infant pointing. *Cognitive Development, 26,* 16–29. doi:10.1016/j.cogdev.2010.10.001

Loewald, H. W. (1960). On the therapeutic action of psycho-analysis. *International Journal of Psychoanalysis, 41,* 16–33.

Luborsky, L., German, R. E., Diguer, L., Berman, J. S., Kirk, D., Barrett, M. S., & Luborsky, E. (2004). Is psychotherapy good for your health? *American Journal of Psychotherapy, 58,* 386–405.

Luborsky, L., Rosenthal, R., Diguer, L., Andrusyna, T. P., Berman, J. S., Levitt, J. T., . . . Krause, E. D. (2002). The dodo bird verdict is alive and well—mostly. *Clinical Psychology: Science and Practice, 9,* 2–12. doi:10.1093/clipsy/9.1.2

Lupien, S. J., Parent, S., Evans, A. C., Tremblay, R. E., Zelazo, P. D., Corbo, V., . . . Séguin, J. R. (2011). Larger amygdala but no change in hippocampal volume in 10-year-old children exposed to maternal depressive symptomatology since birth. *Proceedings of the National Academy of Sciences, USA, 108*, 14324–14329. doi:10.1073/pnas.1105371108

Luyten, P., Blatt, S. J., & Corveleyn, J. (2005). Epilogue: Towards integration in the theory and treatment of depression? The time is now. In J. Corveleyn, P. Luyten & S. J. Blatt (Eds.), *The theory and treatment of depression: Towards a dynamic interactionism model* (pp. 253–284). Mahwah, NJ: Erlbaum.

Lyons-Ruth, K. (1998a). Attachment and psychopathology. *Infant Mental Health Journal, 19*, 451–453. doi:10.1002/(SICI)1097-0355(199824)19:4<451::AID-IMHJ8>3.0.CO;2-D

Lyons-Ruth, K. (1998b). Implicit relational knowing: Its role in development and psychoanalytic treatment. *Infant Mental Health Journal, 19*, 282–289. doi:10.1002/(SICI)1097-0355(199823)19:3<282::AID-IMHJ3>3.0.CO;2-O

Lyons-Ruth, K. (2006). The interface between attachment and intersubjectivity: Perspective from the longitudinal study of disorganized attachment. *Psychoanalytic Inquiry, 26*, 595–616. doi:10.1080/07351690701310656

MacDonald, G., & Leary, M. R. (2005). Why does social exclusion hurt? The relationship between social and physical pain. *Psychological Bulletin, 131*, 202–223. doi:10.1037/0033-2909.131.2.202

Maguire, E. A., Spiers, H. J., Good, C. D., Hartley, T., Frackowiak, R. S. J., & Burgess, N. (2003). Navigation expertise and the human hippocampus: A structural brain imaging analysis. *Hippocampus, 13*, 250–259. doi:10.1002/hipo.10087

Maier, S. F., & Seligman, M. E. (1976). Learned helplessness: Theory and evidence. *Journal of Experimental Psychology: General, 105*, 3–46. doi:10.1037/0096-3445-105.1.3

Main, M., Hesse, E., & Goldwyn, R. (2008). Studying differences in language usage in recounting attachment history: An introduction to the AAI. In H. Steele & M. Steele (Eds.), *Clinical applications of the Adult Attachment Interview* (pp. 31–68). New York, NY: Guilford Press.

Main, M., & Weston, D. R. (1981). The quality of the toddler's relationship to mother and to father: Related to conflict behavior and the readiness to establish new relationships. *Child Development, 52*, 932–940. doi:10.2307/1129097

Malatesta, C. Z., Culver, C., Tesman, J. R., & Shepard, B. (1989). The development of emotion expression during the first two years of life. *Monographs of the Society for Research in Child Development, 54*, 1–104.

Malatesta, C. Z., & Wilson, A. (1988). Emotion cognition interaction in personality development: A discrete emotions, functionalist analysis. *British Journal of Social Psychology, 27*, 91–112. doi:10.1111/j.2044-8309.1988.tb00807.x

Mallei, A., Giambelli, R., Gass, P., Racagni, G., Mathé, A. A., Vollmayr, B., & Popoli, M. (2011). Synaptoproteomics of learned helpless rats involve energy metabolism and cellular remodeling pathways in depressive-like behavior and antidepressant response. *Neuropharmacology, 60,* 1243–1253. doi:10.1016/j.neuropharm.2010.12.012

Malloch, S., & Trevarthen, C. (Eds.). (2009a). *Communicative musicality: Exploring the basis of human companionship.* New York, NY: Oxford University Press.

Malloch, S., & Trevarthen, C. (2009b). Musicality: Communicating the vitality and interests of life. In S. Malloch & C. Trevarthen (Eds.), *Communicative musicality: Exploring the basis of human companionship* (pp. 1–11). New York, NY: Oxford University Press.

Malphurs, J. E., Raag, T., Field, T., Pickens, J., & Pelaez-Nogueras, M. (1996). Touch by intrusive and withdrawn mothers with depressive symptoms. *Early Development and Parenting, 5,* 111–115. doi:10.1002/(SICI)1099-0917(199606)5:2<111::AID-EDP122>3.0.CO;2-#

Marazziti, D. (2005). The neurobiology of love. *Current Psychiatry Reviews, 1,* 331–335. doi:10.2174/157340005774575037

Marazziti, D., Del Debbio, A., Roncaglia, I., Bianchi, C., Piccinni, A., & Dell'Osso, L. (2008). Neurotrophins and attachment. *Clinical Neuropsychiatry: Journal of Treatment Evaluation, 5,* 100–106.

Marin, M.-F., Lord, C., Andrews, J., Juster, R.-P., Sindi, S., Arsenault-Lapierre, G., . . . Lupien, S. J. (2011). Chronic stress, cognitive functioning and mental health. *Neurobiology of Learning and Memory, 96,* 583–595. doi:10.1016/j.nlm.2011.02.016

Marlier, L., Schaal, B., & Soussignan, R. (1998a). Bottle-fed neonates prefer an odor experienced in utero to an odor experienced postnatally in the feeding context. *Developmental Psychobiology, 33,* 133–145. doi:10.1002/(SICI)1098-2302(199809)33:2<133::AID-DEV4>3.0.CO;2-K

Marlier, L., Schaal, B., & Soussignan, R. (1998b). Neonatal responsiveness to the odor of amniotic and lacteal fluids: A test of perinatal chemosensory continuity. *Child Development, 69,* 611–623. doi:10.1111/j.1467-8624.1998.tb06232.x

Marvin, R. S. (2003). Implications of attachment research for the field of family therapy. In P. Erdman & T. Caffery (Eds.), *Attachment and family systems: Conceptual, empirical, and therapeutic relatedness* (pp. 3–27). New York, NY: Brunner-Routledge.

Masterpasqua, F. (2009). Psychology and epigenetics. *Review of General Psychology, 13,* 194–201. doi:10.1037/a0016301

Mastropieri, D., & Turkewitz, G. (1999). Prenatal experience and neonatal responsiveness to vocal expressions of emotion. *Developmental Psychobiology, 35,* 204–214. doi:10.1002/(SICI)1098-2302(199911)35:3<204::AID-DEV5>3.0.CO;2-V

Matas, L., Arend, R. A., & Sroufe, L. A. (1978). Continuity of adaptation in the second year: The relationship between quality of attachment and later competence. *Child Development, 49,* 547–556.

Matthiesen, A.-S., Ransjö-Arvidson, A. B., Nissen, E., & Uvnäs-Moberg, K. (2001). Postpartum maternal oxytocin release by newborns: Effects of infant hand massage and sucking. *Birth, 28,* 13–19. doi:10.1046/j.1523-536x.2001.00013.x

McCullough, L., Kuhn, N., Andrews, S., Kaplan, A., Wolf, J., & Hurley, C. L. (2003). *Treating affect phobia: A manual for short-term dynamic psychotherapy.* New York, NY: Guilford Press.

McCullough-Vaillant, L. (1997). *Changing character: Short-term anxiety-regulating psychotherapy for restructuring defenses, affects, and attachment.* New York, NY: Basic Books.

McGowan, P. O., Meaney, M. J., & Szyf, M. (2008). Diet and the epigenetic (re)programming of phenotypic differences in behavior. *Brain Research, 1237,* 12–24. doi:10.1016/j.brainres.2008.07.074

McGowan, P. O., Sasaki, A., D'Alessio, A. C., Dymov, S., Labonté, B., Szyf, M., . . . Meaney, M. J. (2009). Epigenetic regulation of the glucocorticoid receptor in human brain associates with childhood abuse. *Nature Neuroscience, 12,* 342–348. doi:10.1038/nn.2270

McGowan, P. O., & Szyf, M. (2010). The epigenetics of social adversity in early life: Implications for mental health outcomes. *Neurobiology of Disease, 39,* 66–72. doi:10.1016/j.nbd.2009.12.026

McLaughlin, E., Lefaivre, M., & Cummings, E. (2010). Experimentally-induced learned helplessness in adolescents with Type 1 diabetes. *Journal of Pediatric Psychology, 35,* 405–414. doi:10.1093/jpepsy/jsp061

Mehler, J., Jusczyk, P., Lambertz, G., Halsted, N., Bertoncini, J., & Amiel-Tison, C. (1988). A precursor of language acquisition in young infants. *Cognition, 29,* 143–178. doi:10.1016/0010-0277(88)900035-2

Messer, S. B., & Wampold, B. E. (2002). Let's face facts: Common factors are more potent than specific therapy ingredients. *Clinical Psychology: Science and Practice, 9,* 21–25. doi:10.1093/clipsy.9.1.21

Meston, C. M., & Buss, D. M. (2007). Why humans have sex. *Archives of Sexual Behavior, 36,* 477–507. doi:10.1007/s10508-007-9175-2

Mikulincer, M. (1997). Adult attachment style and information processing: Individual differences in curiosity and cognitive closure. *Journal of Personality and Social Psychology, 72,* 1217–1230. doi:10.1037/0022-3514.72.5.1217

Mikulincer, M., & Shaver, P. R. (2007). *Attachment in adulthood: Structure, dynamics, and change.* New York, NY: Guilford Press.

Mikulincer, M., Shaver, P. R., Cassidy, J., & Berant, E. (2009). Attachment-related defensive processes. In J. H. Obegi & E. Berant (Eds.), *Attachment theory and research in clinical work with adults* (pp. 293–327). New York, NY: Guilford Press.

Mikulincer, M., Shaver, P. R., & Pereg, D. (2003). Attachment theory and affect regulation: The dynamics, development, and cognitive consequences of attachment-related strategies. *Motivation and Emotion, 27,* 77–102. doi:10.1023/A:1024515519160

Miller, G. (2007). Brain evolution. In S. W. Gangestad & J. A. Simpson (Eds.), *The evolution of mind: Fundamental questions and controversies* (pp. 287–293). New York, NY: Guilford Press.

Minagawa-Kawai, Y., Matsuoka, S., Dan, I., Naoi, N., Nakamura, K., & Kojima, S. (2009). Prefrontal activation associated with social attachment: Facial-emotion recognition in mothers and infants. *Cerebral Cortex, 19,* 284–292. doi:10.1093/cercor/bhn081

Mitchell, S. A. (1998). Attachment theory and the psychoanalytic tradition: Reflections on human relationality. *British Journal of Psychotherapy, 15,* 177–193. doi:10.1111/j.1752-0118.1998.tb00441.x

Mitchell, S. A., & Aron, L. (Eds.). (1999). *Relational psychoanalysis: The emergence of a tradition.* Hillsdale, NJ: Analytic Press.

Moore, E. A. (1997). Effects of serotonin-specific reuptake inhibitors on intimacy. *Dissertation Abstracts International: Section B. Sciences and Engineering, 58,* 2744.

Morison, S. J., Ames, E. W., & Chisholm, K. (1995). The development of children adopted from Romanian orphanages. *Merrill-Palmer Quarterly, 41,* 411–430.

Moss, E., Dubois-Comtois, K., Cyr, C., Tarabulsy, G. M., St.-Laurent, D., & Bernier, A. (2011). Efficacy of a home-visiting intervention aimed at improving maternal sensitivity, child attachment, and behavioral outcomes for maltreated children: A randomized control trial. *Development and Psychopathology, 23,* 195–210. doi:10.1017/S0954579410000738

Mouillet-Richard, S., Baudry, A., Launay, J. M., & Kellermann, O. (2011). MicroRNAs and depression. *Neurobiology of Disease, 46,* 272–278. doi:10.1016/j.nbd.2011.12.035

Munck, A. (2000). Corticosteroids and stress. In G. Finck (Ed.), *Encyclopedia of stress* (Vol. 1, pp. 570–577). New York, NY: Academic Press.

Murray, L., & Trevarthen, C. (1986). The infant's role in mother–infant communications. *Journal of Child Language, 13,* 15–29. doi:10.1017/S0305000900000271

Nakagawa, S. (2010). [Involvement of neurogenesis in the action of psychotropic drugs]. *Nihon Shinkei Seishin Yakurigaku Zasshi, 30,* 109–113.

National Institute of Child Health and Human Development in Early Child Care Research Network. (2004). Fathers' and mothers' parenting behavior and beliefs as predictors of children's social adjustment in the transition to school. *Journal of Family Psychology, 18,* 628–638. doi:10.1037/0893-3200.18.4.628

Neigh, G. N., Gillespie, C. F., & Nemeroff, C. B. (2009). The neurobiological toll of child abuse and neglect. *Trauma, Violence, & Abuse, 10,* 389–410. doi:10.1177/1524838009339758

Nesse, R. M., & Ellsworth, P. C. (2009). Evolution, emotions, and emotional disorders. *American Psychologist, 64,* 129–139. doi:10.1037/a0013503

Neumann, I. D. (2008). Brain oxytocin: A key regulator of emotional and social behaviours in both females and males. *Journal of Neuroendocrinology, 20,* 858–865. doi:10.1111/j.1365-2826.2008.01726.x

Ng, K.-M., & Smith, S. D. (2006). The relationships between attachment theory and intergenerational family systems theory. *Family Journal, 14,* 430–440. doi:10.1177/1066480706290976

Nievar, M., & Becker, B. J. (2008). Sensitivity as a privileged predictor of attachment: A second perspective on De Wolff and Van IJzendoorn's meta-analysis. *Social Development, 17,* 102–114. doi:10.1111/j.1467-9507.2007.00417.x

Norcross, J. C. (2002a). Empirically supported therapy relationships. In J. C. Norcross (Ed.), *Psychotherapy relationships that work: Therapist contributions and responsiveness to patients* (pp. 3–16). New York, NY: Oxford University Press.

Norcross, J. C. (2002b). *Psychotherapy relationships that work: Therapist contributions and responsiveness to patients*. New York, NY: Oxford University Press.

Olff, M., De Vries, G. J., Güzelcan, Y., Assies, J., & Gersons, B. P. R. (2007). Changes in cortisol and DHEA plasma levels after psychotherapy for PTSD. *Psychoneuroendocrinology, 32,* 619–626. doi:10.1016/j.psyneuen.2007.04.001

Onaka, T., Takayanagi, Y., & Yoshida, M. (2012). Roles of oxytocin neurones in the control of stress, energy metabolisms, and social behaviour. *Journal of Neuroendocrinology, 24,* 587–598. doi:10.1111/j.1365-2826.2012.02300.x

Opacka-Juffry, J., & Mohiyeddini, C. (2012). Experience of stress in childhood negatively correlates with plasma oxytocin concentration in adult men. *Stress, 15,* 1–10.

Orlinsky, D. E., Grawe, K., & Parks, B. K. (1994). Process and outcome in psychotherapy—Noch einmal. In A. E. Bergin & S. L. Garfield (Eds.), *Handbook of psychotherapy and behavior change* (4th ed., pp. 270–376). Oxford, England: Wiley.

Padilla, Y. C., & Reichman, N. E. (2001). Low birthweight: Do unwed fathers help? *Children and Youth Services Review, 23,* 427–452. doi:10.1016/S0190-7409(01)00136-0

Panneton, R. K. (1987). *Prenatal auditory experience with melodies: Effects on postnatal auditory preferences in human newborns* (Doctoral dissertation). Available from ProQuest Dissertations and Theses database.

Pascalis, O., de Schonen, S., Morton, J., Deruelle, C., & Fabre-Grenet, M. (1995). Mother's face recognition by neonates: A replication and an extension. *Infant Behavior and Development, 18,* 79–85. doi:10.1016/0163-6383(95)90009-8

Pascalis, O., Scott, L. S., Kelly, D. J., Shannon, R. W., Nicholson, E., Coleman, M., & Nelson, C. A. (2005). Plasticity of face processing in infancy. *Proceedings of the National Academy of Sciences of the United States of America, 102,* 5297–5300. doi:10.1073/pnas.0406627102

Pauli-Pott, U., & Mertesacker, B. (2009). Affect expression in mother–infant interaction and subsequent attachment development. *Infant Behavior and Development, 32,* 208–215. doi:10.1016/j.infbeh.2008.12.010

Pedersen, C. A., & Boccia, M. L. (2002). Oxytocin links mothering received, mothering bestowed and adult stress responses. *Stress, 5,* 259–267. doi:10.1080/1025389021000037586

Pederson, D. R., & Moran, G. (1999). The relationship imperative: Arguments for a broad definition of attachment. *Journal of Family Psychology, 13,* 496–500. doi:10.1037/0893-3200.13.4.496

Perry, B. D., Pollard, R. A., Blakley, T. L., Baker, W. L., & Vigilante, D. (1995). Childhood trauma, the neurobiology of adaptation, and "use-dependent" development of the brain: How "states" become "traits." *Infant Mental Health Journal, 16*, 271–291. doi: 10.1002/1097-0355(199524)16:4<271::AID-IMHJ2280160404>3.0.CO;2-B

Peterson, C., & Park, N. (2007a). Attachment security and its benefits in context. *Psychological Inquiry, 18*, 172–176. doi:10.1080/10478400701512752

Peterson, C., & Park, N. (2007b). Explanatory style and emotion regulation. In J. J. Gross (Ed.), *Handbook of emotion regulation* (pp. 159–179). New York, NY: Guilford Press.

Pierrehumbert, B., Torrisi, R., Glatz, N., Dimitrova, N., Heinrichs, M., & Halfon, O. (2009). The influence of attachment on perceived stress and cortisol response to acute stress in women sexually abused in childhood or adolescence. *Psychoneuroendocrinology, 34*, 924–938. doi:10.1016/j.psyneuen.2009.01.006

Plutchik, R. (2003). *Emotions and life: Perspectives from psychology, biology, and evolution*. Washington, DC: American Psychological Association.

Polan, H. J., & Hofer, M. A. (1999). Psychobiological origins of infant attachment and separation responses. In J. Cassidy & P. R. Shaver (Eds.), *Handbook of attachment: Theory, research, and clinical applications* (pp. 162–180). New York, NY: Guilford Press.

Polan, H. J., & Hofer, M. A. (2008). Psychobiological origins of infant attachment and its role in development. In J. Cassidy & P. R. Shaver (Eds.), *Handbook of attachment: Theory, research, and clinical applications* (2nd ed., pp. 158–172). New York, NY: Guilford Press.

Porges, S. W. (2011). *The polyvagal theory: Neurophysiological foundations of emotions, attachment, communication, self-regulation*. New York, NY: Norton.

Quinn, P. C., Yahr, J., Kuhn, A., Slater, A. M., & Pascalis, O. (2002). Representation of the gender of human faces by infants: A preference for female. *Perception, 31*, 1109–1121. doi:10.1068/p3331

Quirin, M., Pruessner, J. C., & Kuhl, J. (2008). HPA system regulation and adult attachment anxiety: Individual differences in reactive and awakening cortisol. *Psychoneuroendocrinology, 33*, 581–590. doi:10.1016/j.psyneuen.2008.01.013

Rainville, P., Bechara, A., Naqvi, N., & Damasio, A. R. (2006). Basic emotions are associated with distinct patterns of cardiorespiratory activity. *International Journal of Psychophysiology, 61*, 5–18. doi:10.1016/j.ijpsycho.2005.10.024

Ramachandran, V. S., & Blakeslee, S. (1998). *Phantoms in the brain: Probing the mysteries of the human mind*. New York, NY: HarperCollins.

Ravitz, P., Maunder, R., Hunter, J., Sthankiya, B., & Lancee, W. (2010). Adult attachment measures: A 25-year review. *Journal of Psychosomatic Research, 69*, 419–432. doi:10.1016/j.jpsychores.2009.08.006

Reed, A. L., Anderson, J. C., Bylund, D. B., Petty, F., El Refaey, H., & Happe, H. K. (2009). Treatment with escitalopram but not desipramine decreases escape latency times in a learned helplessness model using juvenile rats. *Psychopharmacology, 205*, 249–259. doi:10.1007/s00213-009-1535-2

Reifen Tagar, M., Federico, C. M., & Halperin, E. (2011). The positive effect of negative emotions in protracted conflict: The case of anger. *Journal of Experimental Social Psychology, 47*, 157–164. doi:10.1016/j.jesp.2010.09.011

Rendon, M. (2008). Psychoanalysis, a bridge between attachment research and neurobiology. *American Journal of Psychoanalysis, 68*, 148–155. doi:10.1057/ajp.2008.4

Richeson, J. A., Todd, A. R., Trawalter, S., & Baird, A. A. (2008). Eye-gaze direction modulates race-related amygdala activity. *Group Processes & Intergroup Relations, 11*, 233–246. doi:10.1177/1368430207088040

Rilke, R. M. (2001). *Letters to a young poet*. New York, NY: Modern Library. (Original work published 1903)

Rilling, J. K. (2009). A potential role for oxytocin in the intergenerational transmission of secure attachment. *Neuropsychopharmacology, 34*, 2621–2622. doi:10.1038/npp.2009.136

Rimmele, U., Hediger, K., Heinrichs, M., & Klaver, P. (2009). Oxytocin makes a face in memory familiar. *Journal of Neuroscience, 29*, 38–42. doi:10.1523/JNEURO-SCI.4260-08.2009

Rinaman, L., Banihashemi, L., & Koehnle, T. J. (2011). Early life experience shapes the functional organization of stress-responsive visceral circuits. *Physiology & Behavior. 104*, 632–640. doi:10.1016/j.physbeh.2011.04.008

Robertson, J. (1953). *A two-year-old goes to the hospital*. London, England: Tavistock Child Development Research Unit.

Robinson, G. E., Fernald, R. D., & Clayton, D. F. (2008, November 7). Genes and social behavior. *Science, 322*, 896–900. doi:10.1126/science.1159277

Rosenhan, D. L., & Seligman, M. E. (1989). *Abnormal psychology* (2nd ed.). New York, NY: Norton.

Rotenberg, K. J., Costa, P., Trueman, M., & Lattimore, P. (2012). An interactional test of the reformulated helplessness theory of depression in women receiving clinical treatment for eating disorders. *Eating Behaviors, 13*, 264–266. doi:10.1016/j.eatbeh.2012.03.001

Roth, T. L., Lubin, F. D., Funk, A. J., & Sweatt, J. D. (2009). Lasting epigenetic influence of early-life adversity on the BDNF gene. *Biological Psychiatry, 65*, 760–769. doi:10.1016/j.biopsych.2008.11.028

Rutter, M. (1997). Clinical implications of attachment concepts: Retrospect and prospect. In L. Atkinson & K. J. Zucker (Eds.), *Attachment and psychopathology* (pp. 17–46). New York, NY: Guilford Press.

Rutter, M. (2008). Implications of attachment theory and research for child care policies. In J. Cassidy & P. R. Shaver (Eds.), *Handbook of attachment: Theory, research, and clinical applications* (pp. 958–974). New York, NY: Guilford Press.

Rutter, M., Andersen-Wood, L., Beckett, C., Bredenkamp, D., Castle, J., Groothues, C., . . . O'Connor, T. G. (1999). Quasi-autistic patterns following severe early global privation. *Journal of Child Psychology and Psychiatry, 40*, 537–549. doi:10.1017/S0021963099003935

Rutter, M., Beckett, C., Castle, J., Colvert, E., Kreppner, J., Mehta, M., . . . Sonuga-Barke, E. (2007). Effects of profound early institutional deprivation: An overview of findings from a UK longitudinal study of Romanian adoptees. *European Journal of Developmental Psychology, 4*, 332–350. doi:10.1080/17405620701401846

Rutter, M., Colvert, E., Kreppner, J., Beckett, C., Castle, J., Groothues, C., . . . Sonuga-Barke, E. J. S. (2007a). Early adolescent outcomes for institutionally-deprived and non-deprived adoptees. I: Disinhibited attachment. *Journal of Child Psychology and Psychiatry, 48*, 17–30. doi:10.1111/j.1469-7610.2006.01688.x

Rutter, M., Colvert, E., Kreppner, J., Beckett, C., Castle, J., Groothues, C., . . . Sonuga-Barke, E. J. (2007b). Erratum. *Journal of Child Psychology and Psychiatry, 48*, 848. doi:10.1111/j.1469-7610.2007.01797.x

Ryan, B. K., Vollmayr, B., Klyubin, I., Gass, P., & Rowan, M. J. (2010). Persistent inhibition of hippocampal long-term potentiation in vivo by learned helplessness stress. *Hippocampus, 20*, 758–767. doi:10.1002/hipo.20677

Rystedt, L. W., Cropley, M., Devereux, J. J., & Michalianou, G. (2008). The relationship between long-term job strain and morning and evening saliva cortisol secretion among white-collar workers. *Journal of Occupational Health Psychology, 13*, 105–113. doi:10.1037/1076-8998.13.2.105

Sandman, C. A., Wadhwa, P., Hetrick, W., Porto, M., & Peeke, H. V. S. (1997). Human fetal heart rate dishabituation between thirty and thirty-two weeks gestation. *Child Development, 68*, 1031–1040. doi:10.2307/1132289

Schaal, B., Doucet, S., Sagot, P., Hertling, E., & Soussignan, R. (2006). Human breast areolae as scent organs: Morphological data and possible involvement in maternal–neonatal coadaptation. *Developmental Psychobiology, 48*, 100–110. doi:10.1002/dev.20122

Schaal, B., Marlier, L., & Soussignan, R. (2000). Human foetuses learn odours from their pregnant mother's diet. *Chemical Senses, 25*, 729–737. doi:10.1093/chemse/25.6.729

Schaal, B., Soussignan, R., & Marlier, L. (2002). Olfactory cognition at the start of life: The perinatal shaping of selective odor responsiveness. In C. Rouby, B. Schaal, D. Dubois, R. Gervais, & A. Holley (Eds.), *Olfaction, taste, and cognition* (pp. 421–440). New York, NY: Cambridge University Press. doi:10.1017/CBO9780511546389.035

Scherer, K. R. (1993). Neuroscience projections to current debates in emotion psychology. *Cognition & Emotion, 7*, 1–41. doi:10.1080/02699939308409174

Schore, J. R., & Schore, A. N. (2008). Modern attachment theory: The central role of affect regulation in development and treatment. *Clinical Social Work Journal, 36*, 9–20. doi:dx.doi.org/10.1007/s10615-007-0111-7

Schwartz, J. M., Stoessel, P. W., Baxter, L. R., Martin, K. M., & Phelps, M. E. (1996). Systematic changes in cerebral glucose metabolic rate after successful behavior modification treatment of obsessive-compulsive disorder. *Archives of General Psychiatry, 53*, 109–113. doi:10.1001/archpsyc.1996.01830020023004

Seligman, M. E. (2011). *Learned optimism: How to change your mind and your life*. New York, NY: Vintage.

Shea, A., Walsh, C., Macmillan, H., & Steiner, M. (2005). Child maltreatment and HPA axis dysregulation: Relationship to major depressive disorder and post traumatic stress disorder in females. *Psychoneuroendocrinology, 30*, 162–178. doi:10.1016/j.psyneuen.2004.07.001

Siegel, D. J. (2007). *The mindful brain: Reflection and attunement in the cultivation of well-being*. New York, NY: Norton.

Simpson, J. A., & Belsky, J. (2008). Attachment theory within a modern evolutionary framework. In J. Cassidy & P. R. Shaver (Eds.), *Handbook of attachment: Theory, research, and clinical applications* (2nd ed., pp. 131–157). New York, NY: Guilford Press.

Skuse, D., Morris, J., & Lawrence, K. (2003). The amygdala and development of the social brain. In J. A. King, C. F. Ferris, & I. I. Lederhendler (Eds.), *Roots of mental illness in children* (pp. 91–101). New York, NY: New York Academy of Sciences. doi:10.1196/annals.1301.010

Smeets, T., Dziobek, I., & Wolf, O. T. (2009). Social cognition under stress: Differential effects of stress-induced cortisol elevations in healthy young men and women. *Hormones and Behavior, 55*, 507–513. doi:10.1016/j.yhbeh.2009.01.011

Smeets, T., Otgaar, H., Candel, I., & Wolf, O. T. (2008). True or false? Memory is differentially affected by stress-induced cortisol elevations and sympathetic activity at consolidation and retrieval. *Psychoneuroendocrinology, 33*, 1378–1386. doi:10.1016/j.psyneuen.2008.07.009

Snowdon, C. T., & Ziegler, T. E. (2000). Reproductive hormones. In J. T. Cacioppo, L. G. Tassinary, & G. G. Berntson (Eds.), *Handbook of psychophysiology* (2nd ed., pp. 368–396). New York, NY: Cambridge University Press.

Sonuga-Barke, E. J., & Rubia, K. (2008). Inattentive/overactive children with histories of profound institutional deprivation compared with standard ADHD cases: A brief report. *Child: Care, Health and Development, 34*, 596–602. doi:10.1111/j.1365-2214.2008.00863.x

Spira, A., Scippa, L., Berthet, C., Meuret, C., Besozzi, R., & Cramer, B. (2000). Hospitalism in the year 2000: The psychological development of children in a Romanian orphanage. *Psychiatrie de l'Enfant, 43*, 587–646.

Spitz, R. A. (1945). Hospitalism—An inquiry into the genesis of psychiatric conditions in early childhood. *Psychoanalytic Study of the Child, 1*, 53–74.

Sroufe, L. A. (1997). *Emotional development: The organization of emotional life in the early years*. New York, NY: Cambridge University Press.

Sroufe, L. A. (2005). Attachment and development: A prospective, longitudinal study from birth to adulthood. *Attachment & Human Development, 7*, 349–367. doi:10.1080/14616730500365928

Sroufe, L. A., Carlson, E. A., Levy, A. K., & Egeland, B. (1999). Implications of attachment theory for developmental psychopathology. *Development and Psychopathology, 11*, 1–13. doi:10.1017/S0954579499001923

Sroufe, L. A., Egeland, B., & Carlson, E. A. (1999). One social world: The integrated development of parent–child and peer relationships. In W. A. Collins & B. Laursen (Eds.), *Relationships as developmental contexts* (pp. 241–261). Mahwah, NJ: Erlbaum.

Sroufe, L. A., & Waters, E. (1977). Attachment as an organizational construct. *Child Development, 48,* 1184–1199. doi:10.2307/1128475

Stampfl, T. G., & Levis, D. J. (1967). Essentials of implosive therapy: A learning-theory-based psychodynamic behavioral therapy. *Journal of Abnormal Psychology, 72,* 496–503. doi:10.1037/h0025238

Stanford, C. B. (2007). What nonhuman primates can and can't teach us about the evolution of mind. In S. W. Gangestad & J. A. Simpson (Eds.), *The evolution of mind: Fundamental questions and controversies* (pp. 97–102). New York, NY: Guilford Press.

Steele, H., & Steele, M. (2008). *Clinical applications of the adult attachment interview.* New York, NY: Guilford Press.

Steen, R. G. (2007). *The evolving brain: The known and the unknown.* Amherst, NY: Prometheus Books.

Stern, D. N. (1985). *The interpersonal world of the infant: A view from psychoanalysis and developmental psychology.* New York, NY: Basic Books.

Stern, D. N., Hofer, L., Haft, W., & Dore, J. (1985). Affect attunement: The sharing of feeling states between mother and infant by means of inter-modal fluency. In T. M. Field & N. A. Fox (Eds.), *Social perception in infants* (pp. 249–268). New York, NY: Basic Books.

Stevens, S. E., Sonuga-Barke, E. J. S., Kreppner, J. M., Beckett, C., Castle, J., Colvert, E., . . . Rutter, M. (2008). Inattention/overactivity following early severe institutional deprivation: Presentation and associations in early adolescence. *Journal of Abnormal Child Psychology, 36,* 385–398. doi:10.1007/s10802-007-9185-5

Strathearn, L., Fonagy, P., Amico, J., & Montague, P. (2009). Adult attachment predicts mother's brain and peripheral oxytocin response to infant cues. *Neuropsychopharmacology, 34,* 2655–2666. doi:10.1038/npp.2009.103

Ströhle, A., & Holsboer, F. (2003). Stress responsive neurohormones in depression and anxiety. *Pharmacopsychiatry, 36*(Suppl. 3), S207–S214. doi:10.1055/s-2003-45132

Strupp, H. H. (1993). The Vanderbilt Psychotherapy Studies: Synopsis. *Journal of Consulting and Clinical Psychology, 61,* 431–433. doi:10.1037/0022-006X.61.3.431

Tao, H., Guo, S., Ge, T., Kendrick, K. M., Xue, Z., Liu, Z., & Feng, J. (2011). Depression uncouples brain hate circuit. *Molecular Psychiatry.* Advance online publication. doi:10.1038/mp.2011.127

Taverniers, J., Smeets, T., Van Ruysseveldt, J., Syroit, J., & von Grumbkow, J. (2011). The risk of being shot at: Stress, cortisol secretion, and their impact on memory and perceived learning during reality-based practice for armed officers. *International Journal of Stress Management, 18,* 113–132. doi:10.1037/a0023742

Termine, N. T., & Izard, C. E. (1988). Infants' responses to their mothers' expressions of joy and sadness. *Developmental Psychology, 24*, 223–229. doi:10.1037/0012-1649.24.2.223

Tomasello, M. (1998). Social cognition and the evolution of culture. In J. Langer & M. Killen (Eds.), *Piaget, evolution, and development* (pp. 221–245). Mahwah, NJ: Erlbaum.

Tomasello, M. (2008). *Origins of human communication.* Cambridge, MA: MIT Press.

Tomasello, M. (2009). Cultural transmission: A view from chimpanzees and human infants. In U. Schonpflug (Ed.), *Cultural transmission: Psychological, developmental, social, and methodological aspects* (pp. 33–47). New York, NY: Cambridge University Press.

Tomasello, M., Carpenter, M., Call, J., Behne, T., & Moll, H. (2005). Understanding and sharing intentions: The origins of cultural cognition. *Behavioral and Brain Sciences, 28*, 675–691. doi:10.1017/S0140525X05000129

Tomasello, M., Dweck, C. S., Silk, J. B., Skyrms, B., & Spelke, E. S. (2009). *Why we cooperate.* Cambridge, MA: MIT Press.

Tomasello, M., & Herrmann, E. (2010). Ape and human cognition: What's the difference? *Current Directions in Psychological Science, 19*, 3–8. doi:10.1177/0963721409359300

Tomasello, M., Kruger, A. C., & Ratner, H. H. (1993). Cultural learning. *Behavioral and Brain Sciences, 16*, 495–511. doi:10.1017/S0140525X0003123X

Tomasello, M., & Rakoczy, H. (2007). What makes human cognition unique? From individual to shared to collective intentionality. *Intellectica, 46–47*(2–3), 25–48.

Tomkins, S. S. (1963). *Affect, imagery, consciousness: II. The negative affects.* New York, NY: Springer.

Tomkins, S. S., & Demos, E. V. (1995). *Exploring affect: The selected writings of Silvan S. Tomkins.* New York, NY: Cambridge University Press.

Tops, M., Van Peer, J. M., Korf, J., Wijers, A. A., & Tucker, D. M. (2007). Anxiety, cortisol, and attachment predict plasma oxytocin. *Psychophysiology, 44*, 444–449. doi:10.1111/j.1469-8986.2007.00510.x

Tottenham, N. (2006). The development of face perception and facial expression processing: Childhood to young adulthood. *Dissertation Abstracts International: Section B. Sciences and Engineering, 66*(7), 3978.

Tottenham, N., Hare, T. A., & Casey, B. J. (2009). A developmental perspective on human amygdala function. In P. J. Whalen & E. A. Phelps (Eds.), *The human amygdala* (pp. 107–117). New York, NY: Guilford Press.

Tracy, R. L., Lamb, M. E., & Ainsworth, M. D. (1976). Infant approach behavior as related to attachment. *Child Development, 47*, 571–578. doi:10.2307/1128170

Trevarthen, C. (1988). Universal cooperative motives: How infants begin to know the language and culture of their parents. In G. Jahoda & I. M. Lewis (Eds.), *Acquiring culture: Cross cultural studies in child development* (pp. 37–90). London, England: Croom Helm.

Trevarthen, C. (1992). An infant's motives for speaking and thinking in the culture. In A. H. Wood (Ed.), *The dialogical alternative: Towards a theory of language and mind* (pp. 99–137). Oslo, Norway: Scandinavian University Press.

Trevarthen, C. (1993). The self born in intersubjectivity: The psychology of an infant communicating. In U. Neisser (Ed.), *The perceived self: Ecological and interpersonal sources of self-knowledge* (pp. 121–173). New York, NY: Cambridge University Press.

Trevarthen, C. (1998). The concept and foundations of infant intersubjectivity. In S. Braten (Ed.), *Intersubjective communication and emotion in early ontogeny* (pp. 15–46). New York, NY: Cambridge University Press.

Trevarthen, C. (2002). Making sense of infants making sense. *Intellectica, 34*, 161–188.

Trevarthen, C., & Aitken, K. J. (2001). Infant intersubjectivity: Research, theory, and clinical applications. *Journal of Child Psychology and Psychiatry, 42*, 3–48. doi:10.1111/1469-7610.00701

Trevarthen, C., & Logotheti, K. (1989). Child and culture: Genesis of co-operative knowing. In A. Gellatly, D. Rogers, & J. A. Sloboda (Eds.), *Cognition and social worlds* (pp. 37–56). New York, NY: Clarendon Press.

Tronick, E. (1978). The structure of face-to-face interaction and its developmental functions. *Sign Language Studies, 18*, 1–16.

Tronick, E. (2007). *The neurobehavioral and social-emotional development of infants and children.* New York, NY: Norton.

Tronick, E. (2009). Multilevel meaning making and dyadic expansion of consciousness theory: The emotional and the polymorphic polysemic flow of meaning. In D. Fosha, D. J. Siegel, & M. Solomon (Eds.), *The healing power of emotion: Affective neuroscience, development, and clinical practice* (pp. 86–110). New York, NY: Norton.

Tronick, E., & Beeghly, M. (2011). Infants' meaning-making and the development of mental health problems. *American Psychologist, 66*, 107–119. doi:10.1037/a0021631

Tronick, E., & Reck, C. (2009). Infants of depressed mothers. *Harvard Review of Psychiatry, 17*, 147–156. doi:10.1080/10673220902899714

Tronick, E. Z. (1989). Emotions and emotional communication in infants. *American Psychologist, 44*, 112–119. doi:10.1037/0003-066X.44.2.112

Tronick, E. Z. (2005). Why is connection with others so critical? The formation of dyadic states of consciousness and the expansion of individuals' states of consciousness: Coherence governed selection and the co-creation of meaning out of messy meaning making. In J. Nadel & D. Muir (Eds.), *Emotional development: Recent research advances* (pp. 293–315). New York, NY: Oxford University Press. doi:10.1093/acprof:oso/9780198528845.003.0011

Tronick, E. Z., Als, H., & Brazelton, T. B. (1977). Mutuality in mother–infant interaction. *Journal of Communication, 27*(2), 74–79.

Tronick, E. Z., Bruschweiler-Stern, N., Harrison, A. M., Lyons-Ruth, K., Morgan, A. C., Nahum, J. P., . . . Stern, D. N. (1998). Dyadically expanded states of consciousness and the process of therapeutic change. *Infant Mental Health Journal*, *19*, 290–299. doi:10.1002/(SICI)1097-0355(199823)19:3<290::AID-IMHJ4>3.0.CO;2-Q

Tronick, E. Z., & Cohn, J. F. (1989). Infant–mother face-to-face interaction: Age and gender differences in coordination and the occurrence of miscoordination. *Child Development*, *60*, 85–92.

Turner, R. A., Altemus, M., Enos, T., Cooper, B., & McGuinness, T. (1999). Preliminary research on plasma oxytocin in normal cycling women: Investigating emotion and interpersonal distress. *Psychiatry: Interpersonal and Biological Processes*, *62*, 97–113.

Ursano, R. J., & Silberman, E. K. (1988). *Individual psychotherapies: Cognitive therapy*. Washington, DC: American Psychiatric Press.

U.S. Census Bureau. (2012). *Facts for features: Father's Day: June 17, 2012*. Retrieved from http://www.census.gov/newsroom/releases/archives/facts_for_features_special_editions/cb12-ff11.html

Uvnäs-Moberg, K. (1994). Oxytocin and behaviour. *Annals of Medicine*, *26*, 315–317. doi:10.3109/07853899409148343

Van Bavel, J. J., Packer, D. J., & Cunningham, W. A. (2008). The neural substrates of in-group bias: A functional magnetic resonance imaging investigation. *Psychological Science*, *19*, 1131–1139. doi:10.1111/j.1467-9280.2008.02214.x

van IJzendoorn, M. H., & Bakermans-Kranenburg, M. J. (2004). Maternal sensitivity and infant temperament in the formation of attachment. In G. Bremner & A. Slater (Eds.), *Theories of infant development* (pp. 231–257). Malden, MA: Blackwell. doi:10.1002/9780470752180.ch9

van IJzendoorn, M. H., & De Wolff, M. S. (1997). In search of the absent father—Meta-analyses of infant–father attachment: A rejoinder to our discussants. *Child Development*, *68*, 604–609. doi:10.2307/1132112

Varendi, H., Christensson, K., Porter, R. H., & Winberg, J. (1998). Soothing effect of amniotic fluid smell in newborn infants. *Early Human Development*, *51*, 47–55. doi:10.1016/S0378-3782(97)00082-0

Varendi, H., & Porter, R. H. (2001). Breast odour as the only maternal stimulus elicits crawling towards the odour source. *Acta Paediatrica*, *90*, 372–375. doi:10.1111/j.1651-2227.2001.tb00434.x

Vedhara, K., Hyde, J., Gilchrist, I., Tytherleigh, M., & Plummer, S. (2000). Acute stress, memory, attention and cortisol. *Psychoneuroendocrinology*, *25*, 535–549. doi:10.1016/S0306-4530(00)00008-1

Veenema, A. H. (2012). Toward understanding how early-life social experiences alter oxytocin-and vasopressin-regulated social behaviors. *Hormones and Behavior*, *61*, 304–412. doi:10.1016/j.yhbeh.2011.1.002

Vetere, A., & Dallos, R. (2008). Systemic therapy and attachment narratives. *Journal of Family Therapy*, *30*, 374–385. doi:10.1111/j.1467-6427.2008.00449.x

Vrtička, P., Andersson, F., Grandjean, D., Sander, D., & Vuilleumier, P. (2008). Individual attachment style modulates human amygdala and striatum activation during social appraisal. *PLoS ONE, 3*(8), e2868. doi:10.1371/journal.pone.0002868

Vuilleumier, P., & Sander, D. (2008). Trust and valence processing in the amygdala. *Social Cognitive and Affective Neuroscience, 3*, 299–302. doi:10.1093/scan/nsn045

Vygotsky, L., Cole, M., John-Steiner, V., & Scribner, S. (1978). *Mind in society.* Cambridge, MA: Harvard University Press.

Wampold, B. E. (2001). *The great psychotherapy debate: Models, methods, and findings.* Mahwah, NJ: Erlbaum.

Wampold, B. E. (2007). Psychotherapy: The humanistic (and effective) treatment. *American Psychologist, 62*, 857–873. doi:10.1037/0003-066X.62.8.857

Wampold, B. E., & Bolt, D. M. (2007). Appropriate estimation of therapist effects: One more time. *Psychotherapy Research, 17*, 256–257. doi:10.1080/10503300701250339

Wampold, B. E., Goodheart, C. D., & Levant, R. F. (2007). Clarification and elaboration on evidence-based practice in psychology. *American Psychologist, 620*, 616–618. doi:10.1037/0003-066X62.6.616

Wampold, B. E., Ollendick, T. H., & King, N. J. (2006). Do therapies designated as empirically supported treatments for specific disorders produce outcomes superior to non-empirically supported treatment therapies? In J. C. Norcross, L. E. Beutler, & R. F. Levant (Eds.), *Evidence-based practices in mental health: Debate and dialogue on the fundamental questions* (pp. 299–328). Washington, DC: American Psychological Association. doi:10.1037/11265-007

Warren, S. L., Bost, K. K., Roisman, G. I., Silton, R. L., Spielberg, J. M., Engels, A. S., . . . Heller, W. (2010). Effects of adult attachment and emotional distractors on brain mechanisms of cognitive control. *Psychological Science, 21*, 1818–1826. doi:10.1177/0956797610388809

Waters, S. F., Virmani, E. A., Thompson, R. A., Meyer, S., Raikes, H. A., & Jochem, R. (2010). Emotion regulation and attachment: Unpacking two constructs and their association. *Journal of Psychopathology and Behavioral Assessment, 32*, 37–47. doi:10.1007/s10862-009-9163-z

Waters, T. (2004, February 9). Learning to love: From your mother's arms to your lover's arms. *The Medium, 30*, 1–4.

Watson, J. C., McMullen, E. J., Prosser, M. C., & Bedard, D. L. (2011). An examination of the relationships among clients' affect regulation, in-session emotional processing, the working alliance, and outcome. *Psychotherapy Research, 21*, 86–96. doi:10.1080/10503307.2010.518637

Weaver, I. C. G. (2009). Life at the interface between a dynamic environment and a fixed genome: Epigenetic programming of stress responses by maternal behavior. In D. Janigro (Ed.), *Mammalian brain development* (pp. 17–39). New York, NY: Humana Press.

Weaver, I. C. G. (2011). Epigenetic programming of stress responses and transgenerational inheritance through natural variations in maternal care: A role for DNA methylation in experience-dependent (re)programming of defensive responses. In J. d. Clelland (Ed.), *Genomics, proteomics, and the nervous system* (pp. 87–112). New York, NY: Springer-Verlag.

Weaver, I. C. G., Cervoni, N., Champagne, F. A., D'Alessio, A. C., Sharma, S., Seckl, J. R., . . . Meaney, M. J. (2004). Epigenetic programming by maternal behavior. *Nature Neuroscience, 7*, 847–854. doi:10.1038/nn1276

Weems, C. F., & Carrion, V. G. (2003). The treatment of separation anxiety disorder employing attachment theory and cognitive behavior therapy techniques. *Clinical Case Studies, 2*, 188–198. doi:10.1177/1534650103002003002

Weinberg, M. K., & Tronick, E. Z. (1998). The impact of maternal psychiatric illness on infant development. *Journal of Clinical Psychiatry, 59*(Suppl. 2), 53–61.

Weitoft, G. R., Hjern, A., Haglund, B., & Rosén, M. (2003). Mortality, severe morbidity, and injury in children living with single parents in Sweden: A population-based study. *The Lancet, 361*, 289–295. doi:10.1016/S0140-6736(03)12324-0

Welberg, L. (2012). Psychiatric disorders: Why two is better than one. *Nature Reviews Neuroscience, 13*, 73. doi:10,1038/nrn3181

Wilson, S. L. (2003). Post-institutionalization: The effects of early deprivation on development of Romanian adoptees. *Child and Adolescent Social Work Journal, 20*, 473–483. doi:10.1023/B:CASW.0000003139.14144.06

Winberg, J. (2005). Mother and newborn baby: Mutual regulation of physiology and behavior—A selective review. *Developmental Psychobiology, 47*, 217–229. doi:10.1002/dev.20094

Wingenfeld, K., Spitzer, C., Rullkötter, N., & Löwe, B. (2010). Borderline personality disorder: Hypothalamus pituitary adrenal axis and findings from neuroimaging studies. *Psychoneuroendocrinology, 35*, 154–170. doi:10.1016/j.psyneuen.2009.09.014

Winnicott, D. W. (1971). *Playing and reality*. London, England: Tavistock.

Winter, C., Vollmayr, B., Djodari-Irani, A., Klein, J., & Sartorius, A. (2011). Pharmacological inhibition of the lateral habenula improves depressive-like behavior in an animal model of treatment resistant depression. *Behavioural Brain Research, 216*, 463–465. doi:10.1016/j.bbr.2010.07.034

Wismer Fries, A. B., Shirtcliff, E. A., & Pollak, S. D. (2008). Neuroendocrine dysregulation following early social deprivation in children. *Developmental Psychobiology, 50*, 588–599. doi:10.1002/dev.20319

Wismer Fries, A. B., Ziegler, T. E., Kurian, J. R., Jacoris, S., & Pollak, S. D. (2005). Early experience in humans is associated with changes in neuropeptides critical for regulating social behavior. *Proceedings of the National Academy of Sciences, USA, 102*, 17237–17240. doi:10.1073/pnas.0504767102

Wisner, K. L., Chambers, C., & Sit, D. K. Y. (2006). Postpartum depression. *JAMA, 296*, 2616–2618. doi:10.1001/jama.296.21.2616

Yehuda, R., & Bierer, L. M. (2008). Transgenerational transmission of cortisol and PTSD risk. *Progress in Brain Research, 167*, 121–135. doi:10.1016/S0079-6123(07)67009-5

Zamanian, K. (2011). Attachment theory as defense: What happened to infantile sexuality? *Psychoanalytic Psychology, 28*, 33–47. doi:10.1037/a0022341

Zaslow, M. J., Rabinovich, B. A., Suwalsky, J. T., & Klein, R. P. (1988). The role of social context in the prediction of secure and insecure/avoidant infant–mother attachment. *Journal of Applied Developmental Psychology, 9*, 287–299.

Zimmerman, D. J., & Choi-Kain, L. W. (2009). The hypothalamic-pituitary-adrenal axis in borderline personality disorder: A review. *Harvard Review of Psychiatry, 17*, 167–183. doi:10.1080/10673220902996734

INDEX

Animals, *continued*
    monotropy in, 40
    oxytocin's role in, 64, 65
    proximity between mother and child
        in, 72
    regulation of physiological states in,
        93–94
Anterior paralimbic regions, 112
Antidepressants
    and brain plasticity, 46
    effectiveness of, 63
Anxiety, 150–156
    and attachment states, 83. *See also*
        Anxious attachment
    benefits of dissolving, 213
    centrality of, 75–76
    and communication, 194
    and cortisol, 62
    and depression, 163
    effects of, 116
    and fear of absence, 154–156
    and fear of feeling, 154–156
    and nondefended affect, 132
    resulting from separation distress, 77
    suppression vs. heightening with,
        150–154
    and types of attachment, 150
Anxious attachment
    affect regulation in, 142
    and amygdala, 54
    characteristics of, 198, 200–201
    classification of, 155, 179
    emotion regulation in, 140
    emotions in, 119–120
    overview, 9, 81
    and pathological mourning, 164
    suppression and heightening of
        affect in, 215
Apoptosis, 47–48
Arend, R. A., 183
Assessment, of attachment
    with Adult Attachment Interview,
        195–198
    evocative question for, 198–202
Attachment, 69–86. *See also specific*
    headings
    behavioral systems at play in,
        70–73, 76
    centrality of fear and anxiety in, 75–76

components of, 76–80
and internal working models of self
    and other in relationship. *See*
    Internal working models of
    self and other in relationship
motivational primacy of, 70–72, 74–75
multiple figures in, 83–85
types of, 9, 80–83. *See also*
    Disorganized attachment;
    Insecure attachment;
    Secure attachment
Attachment anxiety. *See* Anxious
    attachment
Attachment avoidance. *See* Avoidant
    attachment
Attachment-based psychotherapy. *See*
    Attachment-based therapy
Attachment-based therapy, 10–14,
    205–219. *See also specific headings*
    addressing defenses in, 212–214
    affective experience of patient in,
        208–211
    assessing attachment in, 193–202
    case example, 144–145
    clarifying and responding to patient's
        affective communications in,
        207–208
    clarifying behaviors and affects in,
        211–212
    communication elaboration in,
        205–206
    deepening experience of adaptive
        affect in, 216–218
    defined, 10
    focus of, 142–143
    implicit relational knowing in,
        145–148
    measuring coherent communication
        in, 195–196
    motivational primacy in, 76
    nonexclusionary communication in,
        218–219
    procedural knowledge in, 145–148
    reasons for embracing approach of,
        10–14
    recognizing adaptive responses in,
        212, 214–215
    responding to emotional suppression
        or heightening in, 215–216

De Wolff, M. S., 183
Disgust, 116
Disorganized attachment
    characteristics of, 198
    classification of, 179
    defined, 9
    overview, 82, 83
Displacement, of anger, 165
Dissociation, 165
Dyadic expansion of consciousness, 181
Dyadic-individual dynamic, 190
Dyadic regulation, 92–95
Dysregulated emotions, 9

Edelman, Gerald, 48
Ekman, Paul, 205
Embarrassment, 116
Emotion. *See* Affect
Emotional availability, 195
Emotional communication, 78, 120–122,
        135, 147, 207–208
Emotional difficulties, 51–52
Emotional involvement, 182
Emotional learning, 46, 54
Emotional profiles, 117
Emotional regulation
    in attachment-based therapy, 147
    and dysregulation, 142
    role of oxytocin in, 67
Emotion socialization, 117
Empathy, 209
Envirogenic depression, 158–163
Environmental influence, 25–26, 142
Environmental niche, 102–103
Erotic love, 116
Ethologists, 72
Evolution, 3–4. *See also* Adaptive
        function(s)
    as basis for attachment theory, 11,
        19–21
    and behavioral systems, 70, 71
    and emotions, 115–116
    and maladaptation, 52
Exclusion, defensive. *See* Defensive
        exclusion
Experiences in Close Relationships
        Questionnaire, 198
Exploratory behavioral system, 73
    autonomy in, 130
    suspension of, 76

Expressiveness, balanced, 118
Exthusiasm, 121

Facial expressions
    of anger, 111
    with experiencing emotions, 113–114
    processing in amygdala, 57
    sensitization to, 103
    of therapist, 208–209
    therapist's attentiveness to, 207
    winnowing and shaping of, 101–102
The Fall of Icarus (painting), 192
Fathers, 39–42. *See also* Paternal care
Fear
    of absence, 154
    centrality of, 75–76
    and communication, 194
    effects of, 116
    of feeling, 154, 164
Fetuses
    behaviors of, 28–31
    neurogenesis in, 47
Fisher, Helen, 66
Forster, E. M., 193
Frankel, K. A., 182
Frederick II, 34–35
Freud, Sigmund, 11, 176, 178

Gaze, mutual. *See* Mutual gaze
Geese, 22, 88
Genetics
    and attachment behavioral system, 71
    ontogenetic tuning, 99–102
    and personal experience of emotions,
        117
    role of, 25–26
Goals
    and adaptive affect, 216–218
    coordinated states as, 95–97
    effects of distorted affect on, 132
    physiological form of, 92–93
Goodman, G. S., 84
Greenberg, Leslie, 210
Grice, Paul, 196–198
Guilt, 116

Happiness, 116
Hare, B., 27–28
Hate circuit, 168
Heartbeat, 29, 111

Heightening of affect. *See* Affect
   heightening
Helplessness, learned, 159
Hernàndez-Lloreda, M. V., 27–28
Herrmann, E., 27–28
Hidden regulators, 94
Highly conserved strategy, 20
Hippocampus, 46, 57, 60, 63
Hofer, M. A., 94
Holmes, J., 22
Holt, L. Emmett, 35
Hopelessness, 158–163
Hormones. *See also specific hormones,*
   e.g.: Cortisol
   associated with anger, 111–112
   and stress, 61–62
HPA axis. *See* Hypothalamic-pituitary-
   adrenal axis
Hunter-gatherers, 71
Hypervigilance, 150
Hypochondria, 163
Hypothalamic-pituitary-adrenal (HPA)
   axis
   and cortisol, 59–61, 63, 64
   and oxytocin, 67
Hypothalamus
   and amygdala, 55
   and cortisol, 62

Implicit relational knowing, 145–148,
   214
Imprinting, 22–26, 28, 65
Inborn tendencies, 4, 71
Infants
   apoptosis in, 47
   and connection to the world, 11, 34
   facial recognition by, 101–102
   physical abilities of, 26
   preferences and behaviors of, 29–30
   recognition abilities of, 27
   voices and vocalization by, 100–101
Infectious disease, 35
Information-processing model, 138
Insecure attachment. *See also* Anxious
   attachment; Avoidant attachment
   affect regulation in, 142
   chronic stress resulting from, 63–64
   communication constraints and
      distortions in, 105–106
   defensive exclusion in, 141

defined, 9
dimensions of, 179
emotions in, 117–120
and oxytocin, 67
Interindividual affect regulation, 129
Internalization, 88
Internal working models of self and
   other in relationship
   and assessing attachment, 199
   overview, 32, 85–86
   psychodynamics of, 135–138
   role of communication in, 88
Interpersonal psychotherapy (IPT) for
   depression, 165–166
Intraindividual affect regulation, 129
Intrusive mothers, 38
Involuntary aloneness
   case example, 190–193, 202–205
   centrality of, 189
   and communication, 190
IPT (interpersonal psychotherapy) for
   depression, 165–166
Isabella, R. A., 183
Izard, C. E., 133, 167–168

Kierkegaard, Søren, 131
King Solomon's Ring (K. Lorenz), 22
Kiser, L. J., 183
Klein, R. P., 183
Klerman, G., 165–166
Kobak, R., 92

Language
   acquisition and development of,
      100–101
   early formations of, 21
   loss of abilities with, 50
   newborns' preferences for, 31
   sensitive period for development
      of, 49
Language acquisition, 46, 50
Learned helplessness, 159
Learning
   emotional, 46, 54
   procedural, 151
   synaptic connections created for, 48
Lee, H. J., 64
Loewald, H. W., 210
Lorenz, Konrad, 11, 22–25, 88
Lust, 116

Repression, 165
Reproduction, 64
Reproductive fitness, 52
Respiration, 111, 113
Responsiveness, 118, 179–182, 195
Rilke, Rainer Maria, 157
Romanian orphans, 36
Romantic relationships
    implications of attachment in, 11–12
    and neuroplasticity, 44
    separation distress in, 77

Sadness. *See also* Depression
    adaptive purposes of, 157, 217–218
    anger vs., 114–115
    defensive use of, 172
    depression vs., 158
    effects of, 116
Safe haven, 76, 78–79
Safety
    in attachment behavioral system, 71
    with coordinated communication, 97
Secondary attachment figures
    fathers as, 41–42
    influence of, 83–85
Secure attachment
    absence of attachment anxiety and
        avoidance in, 58
    affect regulation in, 142
    characteristics of, 9, 135
    defensive exclusion in, 140
    emotions associated with, 117–118,
        122
    exploratory behavioral system in, 73
    as having a trusted companion, 76
    overview, 80–81
    and oxytocin, 67
Secure base
    as attachment component, 76, 79–80
    therapist characteristics eliciting, 185
Secure-base relationship, 10
Security-engendering mothers
    characteristics of, 179–185
    coordinated communication with, 129
    facilitation of child autonomy by, 130
    as model for security-engendering
        therapeutic relationship,
        177–185
Security-engendering therapeutic
    relationship, 175–188

case study, 185–188
and characteristics of security-
    engendering mother, 179–185
importance of, 176
security-engendering mother as
    model for, 177–185
Selective attunement, 120
Selective serotonin reuptake inhibitors
    (SSRIs), 46
Self
    attachment relationship as element
        of, 25
    child's understanding of, 105
    in defensive exclusion, 142
    influence of secondary attachment
        figures on, 84
    internal working models of other
        and. *See* Internal working
        models of self and other in
        relationship
    interweaving of other and, 26
    misshaping of. *See* Misshaping of
        the self
    relational, 86
    social, 86
    in social environment, 102–103
Self-disclosure, therapist, 209, 210
Self-efficacy, 91
Seligman, M. E., 158, 159
Sensitive periods, 24
Sensitivity, 118. *See also* Maternal
    sensitivity
Separation, in baby geese, 22
Separation anxiety, 94
Separation distress
    as attachment component, 76–78
    defined, 77
September 11th terrorist attacks, 75–76
Sex
    attachment's effects on, 21
    release of oxytocin during, 65, 66
Sexual maturity, 52
Shame, 116
Shaping, 24
Shyness, 116
Signals, 180–182
    mother's sensitivity to, 90–92
    tuning and winnowing of, 99–102
Smells, 30
Social alliance, 98

ABOUT THE AUTHOR

Peter C. Costello, PhD, is a clinical psychologist practicing in New York City, working with individuals and couples, and an associate professor of communication at Adelphi University, where he teaches seminars in attachment theory, interpersonal communication, and adult romantic relationships. He previously served in multiple roles as a dean and an associate provost at Adelphi. He is a graduate of Swarthmore College and holds two doctoral degrees: one in clinical psychology from The Graduate School and University Center of the City University of New York (City College) and another in communication from New York University. His work combines both fields. Dr. Costello completed his clinical training at The New York State Psychiatric Institute and at the New York-Presbyterian/Columbia University Medical Center. In addition to attachment theory, his current interests include an integrative approach to psychotherapy, and in recent years he has co-chaired two international conferences sponsored by the Society for the Exploration of Psychotherapy Integration. He also serves on the editorial board of the newly launched journal of the Unified Psychotherapy Project.